Understand Psychology

Nicky Hayes

This book is dedicated to Professor Steven Rose, who first introduced me to levels of analysis as an alternative to reductionism.

Teach
Yourself®

Understand
Psychology

Nicky Hayes

First published in Great Britain in 1994 by Hodder & Stoughton. An Hachette UK company.

First published in US in 1994 by The McGraw-Hill Companies, Inc.

This edition published 2017 by John Murray Learning

Previously published as *Teach Yourself Understand Psychology*

Copyright © 1994, 2002, 2003, 2008, 2010, 2017 Nicky Hayes

The right of Nicky Hayes to be identified as the Author of the Work has been asserted by her in accordance with the Copyright, Designs and Patents Act 1988.

Database right Hodder & Stoughton (makers)

The *Teach Yourself* name is a registered trademark of Hachette UK.

British Library Cataloguing in Publication Data: a catalogue record for this title is available from the British Library.

Library of Congress Catalog Card Number: on file.

ISBN 978 1 44410 090 7

eISBN 978 1 44412 981 6

18

The publisher has used its best endeavours to ensure that any website addresses referred to in this book are correct and active at the time of going to press. However, the publisher and the author have no responsibility for the websites and can make no guarantee that a site will remain live or that the content will remain relevant, decent or appropriate.

The publisher has made every effort to mark as such all words which it believes to be trademarks. The publisher should also like to make it clear that the presence of a word in the book, whether marked or unmarked, in no way affects its legal status as a trademark.

Every reasonable effort has been made by the publisher to trace the copyright holders of material in this book. Any errors or omissions should be notified in writing to the publisher, who will endeavour to rectify the situation for any reprints and future editions.

Cover image © Shutterstock.com

Typeset by Cenveo® Publisher Services.

Printed and bound in Great Britain by CPI Group (UK) Ltd., Croydon, CR0 4YY.

John Murray Learning policy is to use papers that are natural, renewable and recyclable products and made from wood grown in sustainable forests. The logging and manufacturing processes are expected to conform to the environmental regulations of the country of origin.

Carmelite House
50 Victoria Embankment
London EC4Y 0DZ
www.hodder.co.uk

Also available in ebook

Contents

Welcome to
Understand Psychology!

Psychology is about people – how we think, act and make sense
of our worlds. It's a subject which concerns us all, being mainly
about ourselves, and in this book I have tried to give you a
straightforward and easy introduction to some of its main areas.
Human beings, as you have probably realized, are complicated
things, and what this book won't do is to tell you everything
you need to know about people. No book could do that,
because everybody's different. But what it will do is show you
some of the processes and influences which make us who we are
and, with luck, it will give you a little insight into your personal
life too. It's quite amazing how even small psychological
insights can help us to realize what is going on, and it doesn't
hurt any of us to understand ourselves a bit better – let alone
other people.

We'll begin our investigation of psychology by looking at
psychology in general – how it has developed and some of its
main areas. Then we'll go on to look at ourselves: in particular,
how we connect with the social world in which we find
ourselves, and how we understand other people. After that we
will go on to explore more personal matters – emotions, states
of mind, motivation and cognitions, and then we'll look at
how our biological heritage influences us, in terms of evolution,
genetics, and also in terms of the many different ways that
human beings are able to learn. After that, we will look at some
of the broad patterns of development which are apparent during
childhood and adolescence, and on throughout our lifespans.

The first 11 chapters, therefore, mainly cover psychological
knowledge obtained from academic research. In the following
five chapters you will have a taste of applied psychology –
enough to get a general idea of how psychologists have looked
at different aspects of our lives. Finally, Chapter 17 explores
how psychologists go about their research, and what is involved

in becoming a professional psychologist. This book can't possibly tell you everything about psychology – it would need to be far more massive than it is to do that – but it will give you a taste of what psychology is about.

Speaking personally, I have always found psychology to be a fascinating subject, ranging as it does from brain chemistry to social cultures, and covering so much personal stuff in between. I know that a lot of other people share my interest too, without necessarily wanting to become professional psychologists themselves. So do enjoy this book, and have fun!

Nicky Hayes

1

Introducing psychology

In this chapter you will learn:

▶ *how 'psychology' can be defined*
▶ *the importance of levels of explanation*
▶ *about some major areas of psychology.*

What is psychology? Different psychologists would answer that question in different ways. But the most straightforward answer is probably that psychology is about understanding people: how we think, what we say, and why we do what we do. It's about finding out what motivates people: what is important to us, and why we are all so individual. Not every psychologist would say that, because psychologists work in lots of different fields, and for some their main interest is in understanding animals, or brain cells, or something else altogether. But in essence, psychology and psychologists are all about understanding people.

Understanding the mind

The problem with trying to understand people, though, is that people are complex, and change all the time. We learn from our experiences, we form good intentions, and we are affected by circumstances. So what we do can be influenced by a great many different factors. Also, everyone has their own ideas and opinions about what people are really like. Those ideas influence what we do far more than we realize, and they also determine how we interpret what other people are doing. Since each of us has had a different life, with different experiences, these ideas can be very different from one person to the next.

Key idea

There's never just one reason why somebody does something. People do things for lots of reasons, some of which are completely unconscious. So looking for a single reason for someone's actions is always a misjudgement of some sort – and sometimes it can be quite a serious one.

The first part of the word 'psychology' comes from the Greek word *psyche*, which means 'the soul', or 'the essence of life' and is sometimes portrayed as a female figure representing the mind. The second part of the word also comes from the Greek language, *logos*, and indicates knowledge or science. So combining the two gives us the idea of psychology as being the science of the mind and this is what modern psychology is mainly focused on.

The human mind, though, is more complex than people realize, and it is easy to over-simplify what it is really like. People often say, for example, that the brain is like a computer, which works by lots of neurones switching on and off and producing thoughts as a result. This is partly true, but it doesn't explain how the human mind itself works – or at least, only on a very simple level. Which neurones fire, and what thoughts they produce, is affected by our physiological state, our physical experiences, our social situations, our past experiences, and the different human cultures and groups which we encounter in our lives. A science which tries to understand the human mind has to deal with many levels of understanding, and bring together an unbelievable range of different factors.

What this means is that there are no easy answers to understanding people. Any one person's mind is so complex that we could only understand it by knowing everything about their whole life – and also knowing how their previous learning had led them to interpret and make sense of the experiences that they have had. What we can understand, though, are some of the ways that the mind works, and how different factors combine together. As the science of psychology has developed over the past 150 years or so, psychologists have taken many different approaches to understanding the human mind – often believing that their particular approach would provide all the answers. Nobody has managed that, but each approach has helped to throw light on different parts of the puzzle, and so contribute to the whole picture.

Psychological knowledge, then, is more about processes than predictions. We know, for instance, what is happening when we dream – how the mind takes the jumble of information, memories and thoughts which constitute our experience during the waking day, sifts through it all, making connections with what we already know, and files it away in our memories. That doesn't mean we know what someone is going to dream about, or what dream objects stand for, because everyone is different and symbols mean different things to different people. But it does help us to make sense of real dreams that people have had, and to identify anxieties and concerns reflected in the dreams' content.

STUDYING THE MIND

Early psychologists explored how the mind works by thinking about it, and trying to analyse the thoughts and feelings they were experiencing. This is known as introspection, and this method gave us quite a few insights into memory, attention, how our emotions affect us, and other aspects of our experience. But the mind has many layers, and we are not directly aware of a lot of what it does. Some – probably most – of what it does happens unconsciously, so thinking consciously about our experiences can't tell us everything. Psychiatrists like Freud, at the beginning of the twentieth century, showed how unconscious experiences and memories can lead to disturbances in adult behaviour, and even to mental illness. But they, too, are only a small part of what goes on.

The first half of the twentieth century was strongly influenced by the general social movement known as modernism – a rejection of traditional thinking, and an emphasis on building a new society by starting from the basics. Science, it was felt, could sort out most of the world's problems, using knowledge it had developed from understanding how basic building blocks such as cells, genes, atoms or elements combined to produce the world we live in. The American psychologist J. B. Watson argued that psychology too had its basic building block: the learning unit, or the link between stimulus and response. Psychology, Watson argued, should be objective, dealing only with information which can be directly observed and measured – in other words, with people's behaviour, not their minds. Watson called this behaviorism, and as the approach developed, it became a powerful force within psychology. Some behaviourists, such as B. F. Skinner, insisted that behaviour was the only thing that mattered, and that thoughts, feelings or personal experiences were unimportant – even illusions – because you couldn't study them directly.

Over time, other psychologists objected to this mechanistic approach, and began to explore more holistic or social aspects of human experiences. Gradually, psychologists became better at studying experience as well as behaviour. They began conducting research which allowed them to investigate in a careful, scientific way how people think, and how we make sense of our experience. In the last few decades of the twentieth century, psychology underwent what we now refer to as the cognitive revolution. This brought a new emphasis on understanding our cognitions – perception, thinking, remembering, attention and so on – partly as a reaction to the mechanistic approach of behaviourism, and partly also because the computer age had made people more curious about how the mind works.

Later, there was an increased interest in developing research methods which could look at people's beliefs and experiences, rather than just observing their behaviour. All of which means that, although present-day psychologists don't use the same methods as those early psychologists, they are as interested in understanding the human mind as they are in understanding people's behaviour.

More recently, too, psychologists have begun to understand the importance of the social influences in our lives – both directly, through the groups, families and communities that we participate in, and indirectly, through our social experience and understanding. And our understanding of the way in which the mind works has taken a great leap forward with the development of brain scanning techniques. Early neuropsychologists had to be content with quite clumsy research methods, like post-mortems to identify the location of brain damage, or electrical stimulation of the brains of people who already had clinical reasons for undergoing open brain surgery. The use of brain scanning, though, means that we can see how different parts of the brain react to thinking, memories or ideas, even in normal people, so we are much better placed to understand how the brain works. As psychologists, we need to put all these types of knowledge together if we really want to understand human beings.

A modern definition of psychology would probably refer to it as the scientific study of experience and behaviour. That means that as psychologists we are interested in what people experience as well as what they actually do. Psychologists, of course, aren't the only people who are trying to understand human beings. A sociologist, for example, will try to understand human beings from the point of view of people in society, and how groups of people and social trends emerge, whereas a psychologist is interested mainly in the individual person. That doesn't mean that, as psychologists, we can ignore society: as we will see in the next chapter and elsewhere in this book, it simply isn't realistic to try to understand an individual person as if their society or culture has nothing to do with what they are like. But it means that in psychology we take the individual person, rather than society as a whole, as our starting point.

Levels of explanation

One of the most important lessons that we have learned from the history of psychology is that just looking at one single aspect of experience or behaviour isn't enough. People do things for lots of different reasons, and usually for several reasons at once. If we try to single out just one of those reasons, as if that were the only explanation, then we hit problems straight away. Saying, 'Oh, they're really intelligent' to explain why someone became a research physicist doesn't answer the whole question, because it doesn't tell us why they became interested in science in the first place – or even why they went into an academic career at all, instead of becoming a politician or going into business. Instead, we have to look at what people do from several different angles, to see how all the different factors and influences work together to produce the final outcome.

This is where we come to the idea of levels of explanation, or levels of analysis. Anything that we do can be studied from several different levels. Imagine, for instance, that you came across someone reading this book. If you wanted to understand what was going on there, you could look at it from a number of different levels. You might ask what is going on in the actual process of reading. How do people look at a set of marks on a printed page and respond to them as if they were words that someone has spoken? Understanding that would be part of an explanation of what was going on.

But it wouldn't be the whole answer. There would also be the question of why the person was reading this particular book, rather than, say, a book about car mechanics. This would lead us into questions about their own personal experience and why they had developed some interests rather than others. We might also ask why they were reading in the first place, rather than, perhaps, cultivating rice or watching TV. This would lead us into a different set of questions, which would include questions about their particular culture as well as questions about personal habits, beliefs and moods.

Key idea

Understanding what the pieces of a jigsaw puzzle are made of won't tell you anything at all about what the picture represents. In the same way, understanding how brain cells work won't tell you what someone is thinking.

In other words, we can look at the same thing using different levels of explanation. One psychologist studying reading might use a very general level, such as looking at cultural influences on human behaviour. Another might approach it at the level of social influence, by looking at how family or similar groups affect what we do, and also how we conform to social expectations – or don't, as the case may be. Some psychologists might look at it in terms of personal habits and past experiences, while others would seek to understand how the visual information is processed in the brain. All of these, and many others, are levels of explanation that we can use in our attempt to understand human beings. Psychologists know that no single level of explanation is going to be enough in itself, but researchers focus on one single level in their work because trying to deal with everything all at once would simply be too much.

Table 1.1 shows some of the main levels of explanation which psychologists use in analysing problems.

A professional psychologist dealing with real people needs to be aware of how all of these levels of explanation interact. This is partly why training as a professional psychologist takes so many years. Academic psychologists, though, use a more limited number of levels of explanation at any one time, because they are trying to analyse and understand psychological processes, rather than people as a whole.

Table 1.1 Levels of explanation.

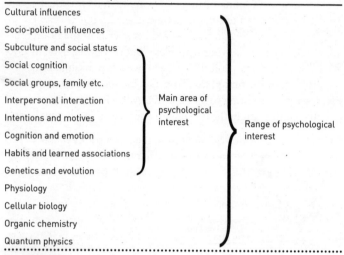

Cultural influences
Socio-political influences
Subculture and social status
Social cognition
Social groups, family etc.
Interpersonal interaction — Main area of psychological interest
Intentions and motives
Cognition and emotion
Habits and learned associations
Genetics and evolution
Physiology — Range of psychological interest
Cellular biology
Organic chemistry
Quantum physics

EMERGENT PROPERTIES

Understanding everything about one level of explanation couldn't give us the whole answer, because each level of explanation is more than just the sum of the lower levels. Sometimes, for instance, you hear people claiming that once we know about all the different nerve cells in the brain, then we will know all there is to know about how the brain works. But this isn't true, because there are often entirely new properties which emerge when the different parts are combined into a whole system. And these emergent properties can make all the difference.

Perhaps this will be clearer if I take an everyday example. A cake is made up of everyday ingredients: flour, eggs, butter, and so on. To understand what a cake is, you would have to know about these. But knowing about them wouldn't tell you everything about the cake, because a cake has properties which the single ingredients on their own don't have. At the simplest level, it has a taste and texture which are not present in the single ingredients. At higher levels, it may have cultural or symbolic significance. It might be a birthday or a wedding cake, or symbolize a particular religious festival. None of these can be deduced simply by studying the ingredients.

It's the same with human beings. We can learn a great deal about people by studying the brain and how it works, but we can't learn everything. We can trace which nerve cells in the brain are active when we are solving a problem, but this doesn't tell us how we are working out a solution, or why we are thinking about the problem in the first place. To make any sense of the human mind, we need to bring together as many levels of explanation as possible, and to study the emergent properties of each new level.

Understanding the individual person, then, is a pretty massive task, and it would be unrealistic to think that we know everything there is to know. When it comes to human beings, there aren't any easy answers. After reading this book, you won't find that you can understand everyone you've ever met. But what you will find, I hope, is that you know a great deal more about people than you knew before, and you may also find that it sometimes helps you to understand the people around you a little better.

Areas of psychology

Psychology, as we've seen, is about people. But people have complex lives, and we need to gather information about them in many different ways. So professional psychologists need to understand the different areas of psychology, and how each of them contributes to our understanding. There are six of these, roughly speaking, and each one gives us a different kind of information.

Key idea

The wealth of psychological knowledge which has been accumulated over the past century is so extensive that modern psychologists have to specialize – nobody could know everything there is to know about psychology because there's just too much of it.

One of the areas of modern psychological knowledge is known as cognitive psychology. This has to do, in essence, with how we think. It includes mental processes such as taking in information and making sense of it (a process we call perception), remembering things, or recognizing them, and also thinking, decision-making and reasoning. These mental processes are known as cognition, which is how cognitive psychology gets its name. Psychologists studying cognition have discovered a great deal about how people's minds work, and that information is often useful when we are trying to understand why someone is acting in a particular way.

Another important branch of modern psychology is concerned with other people – how they influence us, and how we influence them in turn. This is known as social psychology. It ranges from looking at our body language to understanding cultural norms and expectations, or why people obey those in authority, or when someone will or won't help a person in need. Social psychologists are also interested in how we make sense of our social experience. That part of social psychology is about the mental side of social life, so it is known as social cognition.

Some psychologists focus on what makes people different from one another. Some people seem to be more intelligent than others; some people are highly creative while other people are not, and each of us has our own special personality. We also differ in motivation: some of us are keen to get ahead in life, while others are concerned mainly with establishing a happy home and family. Individual psychology is concerned with what motivates people, as well as with how people are different from one another.

All this makes it seem as though understanding people is really just about looking at what they do, or how they process information. And that is a large part of it. But, sometimes, what we do or how we think is also influenced by our physical state. If we are tired or stressed, for instance, we often don't make decisions very well, or we can become irritable with the people around us. So an important part of psychology is concerned with understanding how our physiological state influences us, and this is known as physiological psychology or, sometimes, bio-psychology. Physiological psychologists look at areas such as the effects of brain damage, how drugs work, sleep and dreaming, and stress.

Each year that passes adds its store of experience and knowledge, but how do we use that experience? And do we inevitably decline as we get older? Developmental psychology is concerned with understanding how changes in childhood, adolescence, adulthood, and old age affect us, and what those changes actually involve. Interestingly, the picture which emerges when we really begin studying the processes of maturity and ageing is much more optimistic than society often assumes – but we will look into that in more detail in Chapter 11.

Comparative psychology, as its name suggests, is all about making comparisons. But what are we comparing ourselves with? As we know from evolutionary biology, human beings are a kind of animal – even if rather a special one. So that leads us to some very interesting questions about how close we are to other animals, and whether we have anything in common with them – or whether they have anything in common with us. Comparative psychologists are interested in animal behaviour in its own right, but they are also interested in studying how animals interact with one another because this might give us some clues to understanding human beings.

So what do we do with all this knowledge? Well, as we've seen, finding out about human beings is a complicated and wide-ranging task, and we're not really very likely ever to know everything. But we can apply a lot of the insights that psychological research has given us in the real world. Most psychologists work in one area of applied psychology or another: some work in large organizations, some work in the prison or justice services, some work in the health services – in fact, psychologists work in just about any field which involves human beings. Working as an applied psychologist involves bringing psychological knowledge to bear in real-world situations. Applied psychologists sometimes work directly with clients, sometimes train other professionals in some aspect of their work, and almost always undertake research of their own. As psychological knowledge broadens and develops, psychological insights become increasingly useful in everyday living.

We can see, then, that psychology is really quite a broad topic. It covers a great many levels of explanation, ranging from research at the molecular level as physiological psychologists investigate how drugs work in the brain, to research into the shared beliefs of entire cultures, as social psychologists investigate social representations. And it tries to bring together the insights obtained from these levels, and from the different areas of psychological research, to make sense of what people do, to see how they understand their worlds, and to help those who are finding life difficult.

Focus points

Psychology is about understanding people. People are complicated and there are no simple answers.

Psychologists use a wide range of methods to study cognition, social influences, and brain activity. Modern psychology includes the study of experience as well as behaviour.

Psychology can be studied at many levels, ranging from molecular to societal, but most psychologists conduct research on just one level of analysis at a time.

There are emergent properties at higher levels which cannot be predicted by studying lower ones.

Psychology has six major research areas: cognitive and social psychologists explore how the mind and our social influences affect us; individual and physiological psychologists explore abilities and mechanisms of the body; developmental and comparative psychology are both concerned with aspects of development.

Self and others

In this chapter you will learn:

▶ *why sociability in human babies is so important*

▶ *how other people can change the way we feel about ourselves*

▶ *to identify three different cultural approaches to understanding ourselves.*

This chapter is about who we are and how we come to be that way. Each of us has different life experiences and we are each born with our own particular temperament and physique, which have shaped those experiences. These things all help to make us different from one another. Even newborn babies differ in their likes and dislikes. So we are all different from the start. But we also live in society, and as part of that, we learn how to act with other people, and how to recognize experiences that we have in common. We inherit a powerful tendency to be sociable and to learn from other people who matter to us. And that, just as much as our physical characteristics or temperament, is crucially important in who we are.

The first relationships

All over the world, babies are brought up in different ways. The experiences of an Inuit child, living in a traditional community in the Arctic regions of northern Canada, are widely different from the everyday experiences of an infant growing up in Papua New Guinea, and both of these are different from the experiences of a child growing up in modern Britain. In some communities babies are kept tightly wrapped up (swaddled), while in others they wear few if any clothes; in some communities they are carried around continuously, while in others they spend most of their day in cots or beds. And in some communities they spend all their time with their mothers, while in others they are looked after by relatives, friends, or even older children.

Yet despite all these different conditions all over the world, babies grow and, if they survive, generally develop into mature, balanced adults. Human babies can adapt to a tremendous range of different environments and conditions. These differences in how they are looked after don't really matter, as long as a baby gets what it really needs for healthy development. And what it needs most of all is other people.

Key idea

Humans are the most widely adaptable creatures on Earth, but we adapt by modifying our environments rather than our bodies, and passing on that knowledge to the next generation. So being able to learn from others is our most important survival skill.

Human infants, when they are first born, are totally helpless physically. They have to be fed, cleaned and carried around by other, older humans, and without this they would not be able to survive. This physical helplessness continues for a very long time – far longer than in any other animal. On the face of it, it would seem as if luck, as much as anything else, is what helps babies to get through. But nature doesn't really work that way. As we will see in Chapter 8, the process of evolution means that we would only develop in a certain way if it gave us an increased chance of surviving. And the human infant is actually a long way from being as helpless as it looks.

Human infants are born supremely adapted for sociability. Being unable to move themselves, as well as being unable to cling to their mothers as many animals do, they depend completely on other people. Because of this, they are very strongly predisposed to interact with people – and this is true of babies all over the world. For example, when an infant is first born it is unable to change the focus of its eyes. However, those eyes have a fixed focus at just the right distance to allow the child to look at its mother's face while it is breastfeeding – and this is from the first day after birth.

Human infants also begin to make facial expressions very soon after birth. These movements are often quite tiny, but their parents, who are used to the baby's face, can recognize them. A human infant inherits a tendency to smile when it sees something which resembles a human face – and as it gets older, the resemblance needs to be more and more exact. Ahrens (1954) showed that very young babies, in their first month or so, would smile when they saw an oval shape with two dots in it for eyes. As the baby grew older, though, more detail was needed until by four months the infant would smile only at a real human face, or a very realistic picture.

For a parent, of course, being looked at and smiled at by your baby is an extremely special experience. It is very rewarding and so it means that the parent is more likely to want to spend time with the baby, playing with it and talking to it. And that interaction, as we will see, forms a strong foundation for the future relationship between a parent and its child.

Key idea

When infants smile and respond to people they are increasing their chances of survival. If the person looking after the child is rewarded with a smile, it will be a satisfying experience, and they are more likely to stick around and care for the helpless infant.

Babies also have a very good way of summoning help when they need it. Since the human infant can't run for help itself, it needs to have a way of summoning help from its caretaker quickly. And it has. A baby's crying can carry for a very long distance, and parents quickly learn to recognize the sound of their own baby's crying, as opposed to that of any other infant.

Some psychologists believe, too, that there are special harmonics in a baby's cry which activate the autonomic nervous system, so that adults find it particularly disturbing. This means that they are particularly likely to hurry to the baby and try to calm it down. It might also account for the intense degree of frustration on the part of parents living with a continually crying child: they may sometimes become so frustrated and upset, and feel so helpless, that they end up injuring the child. We don't know whether this is really the case – that is, we know that people find baby cries extremely disturbing, but it is possible that they disturb us because they are associated with pain and distress, and not because of the harmonic qualities of the sound. In either case, though, very few people can really ignore a crying baby. And this makes it a good way for the infant to let other people know that it needs help.

Moreover, infants can communicate more than one message through crying. In the 1960s, Wolff recorded baby cries and analysed them using a sound spectrograph. This showed that there were at least three different types of cry, with three entirely different sound patterns: one for pain, one for hunger, and one for anger. Wolff also found that the babies' mothers were perfectly able to recognize the message in their own baby's crying.

Key idea

Crying is a powerful survival mechanism, because it lets a helpless infant summon assistance from a long distance away. Since the infant can't defend itself, only other people can help if it is in pain or frightened.

So even an apparently helpless infant is equipped to interact with other people – in other words, to be sociable. Babies will respond to the sound of people's voices, they show pleasure when people are nearby and socializing with them, and they can summon help if they need it. The baby's physical survival depends on the people around it, and the baby's ability to communicate helps people around it to know what to do. But babies are even more sophisticated at interacting with other people than just communicating pleasure or discomfort.

PARENT–INFANT INTERACTION

As it grows older, the baby's tendency towards sociability becomes even more apparent. Babies delight in even the simplest repetitive games with another person. As any parent knows, they will play games like 'peek-a-boo', or 'throw-your-teddy-out-of-the-cot-and-see-daddy-pick-it-up' for as long as the adult is prepared to carry on playing, although they rarely show so much persistence with the games that they play on their own, such as with rattles or toys.

Parents and other adults seem to automatically adapt themselves to these baby games. Psychologists have conducted many observations of parent–child interaction, and found that most of the things which parents and infants do when they are playing together help the baby to learn skills it will need in childhood and later life. But for many people, this is entirely unconscious: we do it automatically, without thinking.

One thing which people do when they are playing with a baby, for instance, is that they make faces. Carefully analysed videotape of these games shows that the babies make faces too. Parent and infant imitate one another, and these exchanges can go on for some time. It is games like these which set the foundation for later social experience. Infants learn how to take turns and how to wait for the other person to respond before doing their action – which is like the turn-taking that occurs in conversation, and which even involves the same kind of timing. Moreover, they learn it very quickly: we are strongly predisposed to learn that kind of thing.

Infants are also strongly predisposed to learn to communicate. They want to do it, and try very hard to do it. Again, we help them automatically. Psychological studies of baby-talk have shown that the special way in which human beings talk to babies, so often ridiculed by comedians, actually helps the baby to notice speech. The softened tones and higher notes that we use are particularly easy for the baby to hear, and the repetition of vowel sounds ('baa-baa') draws attention to the part of the language which the child learns to produce first.

What all this adds up to is that other people are the most important thing in a child's world. A human baby may be physically helpless, but it is not at all helpless in terms of its social abilities. It is already equipped with some social skills, and learns new ones even faster than it learns physical co-ordination. People are the most important thing in an adult's world too – except a few very exceptional individuals. And what infant sociability does is to form the foundation for the personal attachments and relationships which we all need in later life.

DEVELOPING ATTACHMENTS
It was once believed that infants developed attachments with the people who looked after them purely because of the association with physical care and satisfying hunger. This led to a number of debates, such as whether mothers should go out to work, and similar issues. However, as a result of these debates, psychologists began to study relationship development

very carefully and found that things weren't nearly as simple as that. For one thing, many babies develop special attachments to more than one person, and sometimes they will develop a special relationship with someone who they only see for a relatively short period each day. In the pioneering study by Shaffer and Emerson, conducted in 1964, the psychologists found that many of the infants in the families that they were studying had special attachments with their fathers, who were out at work all day, as well as with their mothers, who in this particular study were at home. Other babies though, didn't form attachments with their fathers, and some formed attachments with the fathers, but not their mothers, even though it was the mother who was with them most of the time.

What made the difference? Shaffer and Emerson found, as have many psychologists since, that it was the quality of social interaction between parent and child which affected the infant's response. Babies become especially fond of parents (and other people) who are sensitive to the signals they are giving out – smiling and other facial expressions, movements, and so on – and who are prepared to interact with them in their playing. They don't develop such strong attachments to people who just care for them physically but don't play or talk with them.

Key idea

Bonding to the person who interacts most sensitively with an infant gives that baby the greatest chance of survival, because that person is most likely to be able to read its needs accurately.

Even though parents can become attached to their infants very quickly, it takes longer for the infant to develop its own attachment. Although infants often prefer to be with one particular person in the first few months, they are rarely distressed if their special person is not present. Psychologists have found that the full attachment appears at about seven months. Then, the baby might cry if the person has to leave – although of course babies can usually be distracted quite quickly.

This attachment forms the basis of the loving relationship between parent and child which persists throughout life (if it is not actively disrupted). And that attachment, in its turn, has been based on the quality of the interactions between the parent and the baby. Of course, that doesn't mean that an attachment has to be based on infant interactions – as adopted children know, a relationship which begins later in life can be just as special. But a predisposition to interact with people, and to form relationships with the people who respond to you sensitively is one which is common to human infants all over the world. It is, quite literally, part of our heritage as human beings.

The self-concept

In later life, too, other people are more important to us than we sometimes realize. Each of us has our own, personal idea of ourselves, known as the self-concept. This is our ideas about what we are like, what we are good or bad at doing, and how we think. On the surface, it seems as if we should develop that knowledge of ourselves just from our own personal experiences of what we can do, and what we like. After all, we see ourselves from the inside! But when psychologists have studied the self-concept, they have found that, actually, one of the most important factors in how we see ourselves is how other people see us.

SOCIAL RELATIONSHIPS

As early as 1902, Cooley described the self-concept as the 'looking-glass self'. What Cooley meant was that we see ourselves as if we were reflected in the eyes of other people. We don't just think of ourselves in terms of our own personal knowledge: we judge what we are like by the way that other people respond to us, and what we think they may think. Another early psychologist, Guthrie, related a story about a group of students who decided to play a joke on a class member – a girl who was very plain and unattractive. The male students in the class took it in turns to ask her out and to treat her as if she were attractive and interesting. Guthrie observed that the students who were fifth and sixth on the list actually became quite interested in taking the girl out, because by that time, she had changed considerably. The social interest that she was receiving had raised her self-confidence, and now she really was interesting to talk to and took pains to make herself look attractive.

✳ ▶ The self-fulfilling prophecy

What this shows is that sometimes other people's ideas about us may become a self-fulfilling prophecy. In other words, what we think about someone may come true simply because we think it. One of the most striking illustrations of this mechanism was reported by Rosenthal and Jacobson, in 1968. They had gone into an ordinary high school in America, ostensibly to test out a new kind of intelligence test. On the basis of the test they gave (which was really just a standard one) and class marks, they chose a number of ordinary children whose performance in class was only average. They didn't speak to the children directly – instead, they let the teachers 'overhear' a conversation in which these children were named as being likely to show a sudden spurt in their academic work over the next year. The teachers also believed that the intelligence test the researchers had used was a special one, designed to pick out these late developers.

When Rosenthal and Jacobson returned to the school a year later, they found that the children they had chosen were up at the top of their classes. Because the teachers believed that they would do well, they had given them extra encouragement. The children didn't know anything about the teachers' beliefs, but they had felt the encouragement, and worked harder. They had also become more confident about their ability to learn. So the prophecy which Rosenthal and Jacobson had made – that the children would improve during the course of the next year – had come true simply because they had said it.

Many other psychologists, too, have found that our self-concept depends on the type of interaction we have with other people, and the expectations they have of us. The self-concept is often thought of as having two different parts. One of these is a descriptive part, which is just about what we are like: tall, being good at languages, liking sport, and so on. That part is known as the self-image. The other is an evaluative part, which makes judgements about whether we are good, bad, worthwhile and so on. That part of the self-concept is known as our self-esteem. And that is the part which can be most influential in shaping our relationships with others.

Remember this

The judgements we make about others can come true simply because we have made them. If we decide that someone is unpleasant, we treat them as such and they are almost bound to respond unpleasantly. Then we feel that we were justified, because we knew they were unpleasant all the time. Is that fair?

PERSONAL RELATIONSHIPS

Carl Rogers, the famous psychologist who is known as the father of counselling psychology, argued that our level of self-esteem depends on the type of personal relationships that we have had. People, Rogers argued, have two basic psychological needs, and will suffer psychological damage if those needs are not met. One of those needs is that for positive regard from other people – affection, love, trust and so on. Everyone, Rogers argued, needs positive regard of some kind. Even people who avoid close relationships find it important that other people should respect them. To have some kind of positive regard from other people is a very fundamental need, which has to be satisfied.

The other fundamental need which has to be satisfied is the need for self-actualization. Self-actualization means making real ('actualizing') the different parts of the self – in other words, exploring and developing our ideas, abilities, interests and talents. This is a fundamental need in people too: without any way of developing our abilities or skills, we can become psychologically damaged.

People self-actualize in many different ways. Many people have a hobby or an interest which takes up some of their leisure time, and this usually involves some kind of skill, or problem-solving.

Fiddling with a car engine, playing video games or darts, baking, sewing clothes, or conducting a successful children's party are all highly skilled activities: we enjoy doing them, and doing them well gives us a sense of achievement and satisfaction. It helps us to feel good about ourselves.

So far, so good. Most people have family, friends and working colleagues who provide them with the positive regard which they need, as well as hobbies, interests and, if they are lucky, challenging jobs to satisfy their need for self-actualization. And for that reason, Rogers argued, most people have a reasonably high level of self-esteem. While they don't see themselves as being perfect, they are reasonably content with being who they are.

However, Rogers was working as a clinical psychologist and came across a lot of people who weren't in that position. In these people, Rogers found that the two needs contradicted one another. Their need for positive regard or approval from other people was in direct conflict with their need for self-actualization. These people had come to Rogers because they were suffering with neurotic problems. From his clinical observations and treatments, Rogers concluded that their problems occurred because they were suppressing an important psychological need.

When Rogers explored the childhood which these people had experienced, he found that they all had one thing in common. They had all grown up with parents or caretakers who had made their positive regard conditional on good behaviour. In other words, when they were naughty or had misbehaved – as children often do – they had received a very clear message that they were unloved and unwanted. 'Normal' people, though, had parents who, even if they were strict, always made it clear that they still loved their child.

Those children who had grown up with conditional positive regard were actually being given a message that it wasn't really them who was loved – it was some ideal, perfect child who was never naughty. So they grew up believing that they had to be ideal and perfect, and that if they were not, nobody would like them. What this meant was that they needed approval from other people so much that they wouldn't risk exploring their own interests, in case other people didn't like it or didn't approve. They stifled their own personal ambitions, interests or talents – in other words, their need for self-actualization – in order to be sure of social approval.

These people, as we can see, had very low self-esteem. They had developed unrealistic conditions of worth – that is, unrealistic ideas about what they needed to do to gain social approval or respect. And they applied these unrealistic conditions of worth when they were judging their own behaviour. Even if they were really quite successful, they still thought of themselves as failures, or as inferior to other people. Naturally, all this had made them very anxious and, eventually, neurotic.

The solution which Rogers found was very simple. He argued that everyone needs some kind of secure psychological base from which they can develop. That base will be found in a relationship which gives them unconditional positive regard – positive regard which doesn't depend on how they act. If you really love, trust or like someone, then you accept the decisions they make about how they live their life. That doesn't mean, of course, that we have to condone things which are morally wrong. But we can dislike what someone does, and make that clear, without disliking that particular person. As parents do all the time.

However, Rogers found that it isn't only parents who can provide this kind of relationship. In fact, we can experience this kind of relationship at any age, and it can provide us with the security we need to begin to self-actualize. Many people in adult life find relationships which give them that security, and begin to explore aspects of themselves which they have ignored before – like people who go to college for the first time in their 30s or 40s. The important thing is to have a relationship of that kind – it doesn't have to be in childhood.

Key idea

Unconditional positive regard doesn't only have to happen in childhood. A warm and accepting relationship in adulthood can let people recover from an awful lot of childhood trauma.

Rogers developed an approach to psychotherapy based on this principle. The role of the therapist, he argued, should be to provide an accepting and warm relationship for the client (he didn't approve of the word 'patient') – in other words, a relationship based on unconditional positive regard. This would give the client the psychological freedom to make their own life decisions and to develop solutions to their own problems, because they wouldn't be risking disapproval. Rogers called this client-centred therapy, because it is based on what the client wants and needs, and not on what the therapist thinks they should do. Many counselling psychologists still use this approach today.

Cultural and social influences

We can see, then, that both our social interaction and our personal relationships can have a considerable effect on how we see ourselves – on the self-concept. But our ideas about ourselves and how we are linked with other people are also shaped by the social groups and cultures that we belong to. And different cultures make very different assumptions about individuals and what it is to be an individual human being.

THE INDIVIDUAL SELF

In the Western world, it is quite common to see each person as a separate individual, who may choose to link him/herself with some kind of social group if they want to. This model of the individual person has a long history: ultimately, it goes back to the philosophical systems of the ancient Greeks, and was reinforced by later philosophers such as Descartes, in the seventeenth century. The idea is also apparent in European history. The Protestant Reformation, for example, emphasized the individual's own direct responsibility and conscience in religion, rather than the responsibility of the priesthood to interpret religion for the community.

It is open to question, though, whether any human being really can be such an entirely separate individual as all that. In fact, the idea of the individual as totally independent of others around them is almost unique to the USA. Just about every other culture, even Britain, recognizes the importance of social factors and group memberships to the self-concept. Most of us exist within a network of communities and social expectations: family, friendship groups and occupational groups. Many people seek out communities to belong to, like religious groups, hobby or sporting clubs or volunteer groups. In other words, we don't really exist as independent individuals: we live within social networks and groups. As we will see later in this chapter, belonging to such social groups can form a very important part of our sense of identity.

Key idea

Individuality doesn't contradict the notion of social embeddedness. For instance, it is quite easy to be a unique person and still a member of your family.

We do, though, tend to believe that it is important to be an individual, in the sense that being an individual involves making one's own decisions about one's life, partners, friends and career. And it is this belief in an individuality that is separate from the other people around us which makes the Western approach rather different from most of the other cultures in the world.

SELF IN COMMUNITY

In most of the traditional African cultures, and in Native Australian cultures as well, the person is seen as being primarily a member of the community. This doesn't mean that they are not regarded as an individual person, but it does mean that how they live their life concerns the rest of the community and isn't just their own responsibility. Individualism which doesn't concern itself with the community as a whole is seen as irresponsible, and pretty well uncivilized.

When the Native Australian rock group Yothu Yindi began to have commercial success with their records, for instance, the decisions about how the group's career should go were all taken by the group's tribal community. As spokespeople for their culture, the members of the band had no wish to do anything else. The prominence of the band had brought increased acknowledgement and recognition of Native Australian culture to white Australian audiences (and later to worldwide ones). To the members of the group, it was important that they remain a part of their culture, rather than abandoning it and chasing success as individual musicians.

In other words, they regarded being part of their community as an important aspect of being themselves, not just an optional extra. To people from such cultures, the idea of acting as an individual, separate from family, community and social group is seen as simply unrealistic – and selfish, too. According to Mbiti (1970), the individual self is firmly located within the collective self of the tribe or people, and to try to separate them is to imply that the person operates only with half an identity.

LAYERS OF SELF

A different concept of the self is apparent in Hindu belief systems. Bharati (1986) described how Hindu belief is centred around the idea of the self – but not the individual self-concept as it is in Western cultures. Instead, according to Hindu thinking, the innermost self, or *atman*, is at one with God: it is a central, spiritual self which everyone possesses, but which can be reached only through meditation and other techniques. Other, more superficial parts of the self also contain more superficial qualities like personality, and negative emotions such as jealousy or greed. For the most part, therefore, what someone sees as their self-concept is really these outer layers of personality, and not their true, inner self. Only those who have disciplined themselves, through yoga or meditation, have access to the *atman* and can experience the true unity of the self and God.

So this idea of the self, too, is very different from the idea of the individual which is maintained by Western cultures. Although this view is not based on the importance of the culture and community, it still maintains the idea that there are other dimensions to the self: that there is more to being human than simply our own individual wishes and emotions.

THE PRIVATE SELF

Even within highly industrialized societies, there are different ideas of the self. Japanese people, for example, see the self as operating within a social context – but not a context of traditional family or tribe. Like city-dwelling Westerners, Japanese people may be meeting strangers all the time, but Japanese society places a great deal of emphasis on social consideration and social harmony. In order to maintain this, people are expected to keep inner emotions private, and to act in a socially acceptable manner at all times. Azuma, Hess and Kashiwagi (1981) described how this idea is apparent even in the experiences of a very young child in Japan.

At the age of two or thereabouts, as many parents know to their cost, children often become very wilful, insisting on getting their own way at every opportunity – or trying to. It is at this time that they have to learn social responsibility – or at least, that they cannot always have their own way in everything. Different cultures go about teaching this in different ways. Among traditional families of the Shona people of Africa, for instance, children of this age go to live with their grandmother, and stay with her until they are about five. So the most experienced family member is the one who tackles the most difficult part of child-rearing.

Western parents tend to confront their children, refusing to co-operate until the child eventually learns that it must moderate its behaviour. A Japanese mother, though, doesn't tend to confront an egocentric two-year-old directly. Instead, she 'suffers' her child, making it very clear that its behaviour is causing her pain and distress. In this way, the child is brought to realize that its actions have social and emotional consequences for other people, even from a very early age. It is encouraged to feel responsible for the suffering that it has caused, and also guilty, so it learns self-control as a way of not causing the suffering and not having to feel the guilt. These messages are consistent throughout childhood and have a powerful influence on the adult's behaviour.

A Japanese person, then, is still regarded as an individual, but in a different way from a Westerner. The self is essentially private, and the person has important social responsibilities which cannot be avoided. This means that, for the most part, personal wishes, emotions, and impulses need to be kept in check. The self is not independent of other people because it is easily able to cause grief or pain to them, through inconsiderate behaviour. So social interaction has to be managed in such a way as to minimize that grief or pain, and so minimize the guilt which the individual would feel for having caused it. The self exists in a social context, with social requirements, meaning that it often has to be kept private, or even secret.

Key idea

Many people maintain public and private selves. For example, someone who wears make-up every day may be creating a 'public' self, which hides the private self underneath.

We can see, then, that people in different parts of the world – and also in different subcultures within Western countries – have very different ideas of what it is to be an individual person. The idea of the individual as entirely separate from others is really quite an uncommon one. And even in Western cultures, we are not quite as immune to the influence of other people as all that.

Social identification

There is another way, too, in which other people affect how we see ourselves. We are all part of society, and each of us belongs to social groups of some kind. Social groups can be large-scale, like gender or ethnic background groups; they can be medium-scale, like being an accountant or a machinery tuner in a mill; or they can be small-scale, like being a member of a local astronomy club. But whatever the size, belonging to different social groups has an influence on our sense of identity.

Social identity theory began in psychology with the work of Henri Tajfel, and has become a very useful way of understanding many important things about how human beings act. Tajfel pointed out how the social groups which we belong to exist in the real world, and vary in terms of things like how powerful they are, how widely known they are, and how much prestige there is in belonging to them. Because we all live in the real world too, we are aware of these differences. So, for example, if we belong to a local astronomy society and are aware that the astronomy society is quite respected in our local town, then we would feel proud of belonging to it.

Key idea

We belong to more social groups and categories than we realize. Age-groups, gender, family, interests and hobbies, social class are only a few of the possibilities. See if you can count all yours.

After a while, belonging to that particular social group becomes part of our own identity – part of who we are. At times we will interact with other people as if we were a representative of that group – for example, speaking up for the group, or giving the members' point of view if we are talking with someone who doesn't belong to it. We don't always realize when we're doing it, because it's just part of how we identify with the group. At other times, we will interact with other people just as ourselves, or from some other social identification. We can slip into any particular social identity when it seems to be relevant.

We can even slip from one to another without realizing. For example, an argument about who should do the washing-up might begin as just a discussion between two partners. However, if one of them makes a remark about gender, it can rapidly change from being a personal argument, to a confrontation between 'men' and 'women', with each person arguing as a representative of their gender group, rather than as their individual self.

CATEGORIZATION AND SELF-ESTEEM

We all have a number of different social identities. According to Tajfel, social identities come from our basic human tendency to sort things into different categories. We categorize other people as well as other things: this person is a typical Volvo driver, that person is a rock fan, and so on. And we include our own groups – the ones that we belong to – in the classification.

However, there is more to it than that, because it is also a basic human tendency to look for sources of positive self-esteem. In other words, it is important for us to feel good about our own groups – we need to be able to feel proud of belonging to them. If our social group doesn't have much status, then we may try to redefine it so that we can see it as more important. But if we can't do that, then we may try to leave the group, or at the very least, pretend that we are not like the other members of it.

For example, imagine that you are a teenager and have a particular hobby, say, trampolining, which you really enjoy. Moreover, you are really getting quite good and have passed various certificates. But then you join a new school and it becomes apparent that your new friends there see it as an inferior kind of sport. What would you do?

Actually, there are several possibilities which are open to you – and all of them amount to ways of keeping positive self-esteem. You might leave the trampolining group altogether and look for some other hobby which will be a bit more respected. You might claim that you only go because of parental pressure, or because your younger brother likes to go and you have to take him, or something like that. That would be distancing yourself from the group – implying that you aren't really like the others.

CHANGING THE STATUS OF THE GROUP

Alternatively, you might try to get your friends to change their view of it, for example by pointing out that it actually involves a very high level of skill. Or you might argue that it is a great deal better than other kinds of recreational activity. Both of these are attempts to change the perceived status of the trampolining group, so that it becomes more respected. Or you could change your friends and associate only with other people who also do trampolining and know how skilled it is.

This is a fairly small-scale example, but exactly the same processes take place in larger social groups too. It is now much easier for a black child in the UK, for example, to grow up being proud of being black than it was 50 years ago. There are far more black people doing responsible, professional jobs, or holding highly respected positions in society than there used to be, which helps. There are also many people in the public eye who are proud of being black, and ready to say so.

This is because over the past 50 years a great many black people have been deliberately changing the perceived status of their group, by challenging stereotypes and discrimination whenever they encounter it. This has had its effect. There is still racism, of course, and still a lot to do, but the general view in Western society is very different from the view which was commonly held – even by black people – 50 years ago.

Another example is the difference which the Paralympic movement has made to the social status of disabled people. The increased respect which disabled athletes have earned from their achievements has done a great deal to change the way that disabled people in general are perceived in society. In particular, people with disabilities are now much more likely to be perceived as individuals, with their own personalities, interests and ideas, where before they were more likely simply to be stereotyped on the basis of their disability, with other people largely ignoring their individuality.

We can see, then, that who we are and how we see ourselves, is very closely linked with the ways in which we interact with other people. We all have our own personal likes, dislikes, talents and personalities. But we also exist in a network of social interaction, and have done so since we were very small babies. Other people's reactions and ideas matter to us, and they influence how we go about acting in life. Our cultural background also shapes how we see ourselves, and so do our social identities. None of us is totally moulded by these social influences – after all, everyone is different – but we are not totally independent of them either.

Focus points

Human beings are social animals from birth, and they learn best from other people.

Smiling, crying and responding to others are all ways in which infants interact with other people, and adults respond strongly to these behaviours.

Infants develop their strongest attachments with people who interact sensitively with them.

The self-concept is how we see ourselves, and is strongly influenced by feedback from and interactions with, other people.

Ideas of the self vary greatly from one culture to the next. Most human cultures see the self as being deeply embedded in the community.

The social identifications we derive from our memberships of social groups are important in defining who we are. We need to derive positive self-esteem from our group membership.

3

Understanding other people

In this chapter you will learn:

- ▶ *how people prefer to co-operate rather than disagree with one another*
- ▶ *how people develop social understanding*
- ▶ *to identify at least two ways of analysing communication between people.*

In the last chapter, we looked at how belonging to social groups can influence our sense of identity, and our dealings with other people. In this chapter, we will look more closely at the branch of psychology known as social psychology – the study of how we interact with other people. We will look at when we are likely to co-operate or obey, how we communicate with other people and why we sometimes help others and sometimes don't. There are other aspects of social psychology in later chapters, as well – for example, in Chapter 4 we will look at some of the social influences involved in our experience of emotion, and in Chapter 6 we will look at social motivation. Human beings are social animals and so social influences affect just about everything we do, in one way or another.

Co-operation, compliance and obedience

In some ways, we have a very good social understanding. But when it comes to modern living, the predictions we make aren't always accurate. For example, people often avoid disagreeing openly with someone else because they imagine that doing so will have more dramatic consequences than it really would. They think the other person might become upset or angry. In fact, we seem to spend a lot of time avoiding other people's imaginary anger, although if we do actually confront someone and disagree with them, it usually isn't nearly as difficult as all that.

Key idea

It is sometimes said that humans are naturally aggressive. Actually, we're quite the opposite, which is why even disagreeing with other people face-to-face is so stressful. Part of our heritage as social animals is that we place a high value on consensus and agreement within the group.

CONFORMING TO THE MAJORITY
Asch (1952) showed just how hard we try to avoid openly disagreeing with other people. He set up a situation in which several people were asked to sit in the same room and to

compare various lines with a test line, saying whether they were shorter or longer. The task was very easy, but most of the people in the room were actors who had been told to give obviously wrong answers. Only one unsuspecting person was the real research participant on each occasion. That person could see what the right answer was, but also heard all the other people in the room giving the wrong answer – and the same wrong answer at that! So the participants were forced into a situation where they either had to disagree with the others or lie.

Asch found that about a third of the time the research participants would give the same wrong answer as the others. And even when they gave the right answer, they became extremely nervous and tense just before it was their turn to speak. Later, they said that they had given the correct answer only because they knew it was an experiment and they felt it was their duty to report it accurately. Clearly, disagreeing openly with other people is something they found very difficult.

A later study of the 'Asch effect', conducted by Perrin and Spencer (1980) found that fewer people actually lied, but that they all became just as anxious. Perrin and Spencer suggested that perhaps modern people are more independent and less worried about confronting other people. But other researchers challenged this idea on the grounds that when they, too, had repeated the study, they had found the 'Asch effect' to be as strong as ever.

The debates about how much people actually conform and how much they don't, continue. But all of the researchers, no matter when they did the study, found that openly disagreeing with other people is deeply stressful. Their research participants said that they only did it because they believed it was important to tell the truth for the experiment. It isn't at all easy for us to challenge the majority.

Key idea

Disagreeing with other people calmly and reasonably is a learned skill. Like other skills, it is easy once we have learned to do it, but quite challenging to acquire.

As we can see, co-operating with other people is something which we tend to do almost automatically – at least when those other people are present. When we're away from other people, or after we've had time to think about it, whether we co-operate or not may be quite another matter. But the tendency to avoid disagreement and confrontation is strong, and some studies show that even if other people aren't present, we may still be likely to go along with what we think other people might say.

In 1954, Crutchfield reported a study that was conducted during a management training session with a number of military officers. It was based on the same idea as Asch's study, in that people were asked to give answers to a set of very easy problems, while believing that other people also taking part were all giving the same wrong answer.

In Crutchfield's study, though, the other people were not physically present. The research participants worked in booths, with a display of lights in front of them which supposedly told them what the other people had chosen. (The lights were rigged, of course, so that they implied that the others had got the answer wrong even if they hadn't.) But even though the other people doing the study weren't actually there, so there was no need to confront them face-to-face, the research participants still conformed to the majority view half of the time.

Of course, it is always possible that this is a higher figure than we might normally get in those circumstances because the research participants were all military people. It's possible that, because of their training, they valued conformity more than other people would. But at the same time, they also valued accurate perception and knew that the answers they were giving were wrong. So it does seem as though our tendency to conform to other people is more than simply avoiding face-to-face interpersonal conflict.

OBEYING AUTHORITY

What happens, though, when such a situation could mean that we end up doing something which is morally wrong? We usually obey authority figures, even if we disagree personally with what they are asking us to do. But would we obey them if they were asking us to, say, give someone a lethal electric shock? The social psychologist Milgram asked that question to a sample of psychologists, psychiatrists and other people in the early 1960s. All of them were certain that only a very small minority of people – fewer than three per cent – would be prepared to kill or seriously harm another person in obedience to the demands of a psychological experiment.

So Milgram decided to set up the situation. Not to kill people, but to set it up so that people would believe their actions were being seriously harmful, even though nobody would actually be hurt. He advertised for volunteers and, when they arrived, they were told that it was an experiment about punishment and learning. The volunteers were to act as 'experimenters', and to give increasing electric shocks to a 'subject' in the next room by pressing switches each time the 'subject' got an answer wrong.

The switches were clearly labelled with levels of increasing severity, going up to 450 volts, and the 'subject' (who was an actor) said at the beginning of the study that he had a weak heart. Both the labels on the switches and the sounds made by the actor in the other room implied that the person was in serious pain as the voltage increased. When the voltage level reached 300v, the victim fell ominously silent. Even then, the 'experimenter' was told to keep giving the shocks by a grey-coated supervisor who oversaw the whole operation and insisted that they should continue.

Milgram found that nearly two-thirds of the people he tested would carry on obeying the supervisor even to the very highest shock level. That didn't mean they liked doing it: they would argue and point out that the 'subject' needed help, and try to refuse to do any more. They became very distressed indeed. But the supervisor would insist that they continue, and in the end they would obey.

There were a lot of things about the situation which encouraged obedience, such as the way that each electric shock was only a little bit stronger than the one before. That made it very hard for someone to draw a line and say, 'I won't go any further', because what they were being asked to do next wasn't very different from what they had already done. The people who were aware of the dangers of unquestioning obedience, though, stopped anyway when they felt they had gone far enough. They knew, in their own minds, that to go further would be wrong and that was enough. They didn't feel any need to justify or rationalize what they were doing.

Unthinking obedience happens in real life, too. Hofling and others (1966) set up a study in a hospital, in which nurses working on the night shift were telephoned by a doctor whom they didn't know and asked to administer medication to a patient. They were told to go to the drugs cabinet and find a medication, which was labelled 'Astroten'. On the label it said very clearly that the maximum daily dose was 10 mg but the doctor asked the nurse to administer 20 mg.

Even though it violated several hospital rules – doctors were not supposed to give orders by telephone, for instance – 95 per cent of the nurses in the study were prepared to administer the medication. They were stopped at the last minute by a staff psychiatrist who had been secretly observing what was going on. The problem was that in real life, the hospital doctors were accustomed to breaking this type of rule, and because of the hierarchy of power and their training, it was very difficult for a nurse to disobey a doctor.

Assertion and rebellion

So why is it, then, that people will sometimes stand up for their own beliefs and at other times simply go along with what they are told? One of the answers has to do with social expectations. In Chapter 2, we saw how powerful expectations can be, and how simply expecting something to happen can sometimes become a self-fulfilling prophecy. A self-fulfilling prophecy comes true simply because we expect it to, and therefore we act as if it already is true. That is one factor which is at work here.

Our previous training is another factor. We learn to obey people who are in charge and to do what we are told. This is a powerful form of social conditioning: many people become very distressed at the thought of disobeying someone who is in authority, even when they know it is the right thing to do.

Our early learning has taught us that, and it remains a powerful influence throughout our adult life. It is reinforced, too, by the way people communicate. How people use words, and the actual words they use, encourages us to see possibilities in certain ways. Non-verbal dimensions of communication also reinforce those messages. It was no accident that the supervisor in Milgram's study wore a grey lab coat and acted in a distant, official manner. It made his authority seem even stronger.

Milgram showed us how easy unthinking obedience is for many people. But a third of the people in his study refused to obey the supervisor once things reached the point where they felt that the 'subject' was in danger. Before they made the decision to refuse, these people showed just as much stress and discomfort as the other participants. But once they had reached a critical point, and made their decision, they became very calm and simply refused to continue. When they were interviewed afterwards, these people generally turned out to have had some previous experience with unthinking obedience and what it could do. One of them had been brought up in Nazi Germany, for instance. These people made disobeying, and acting in accordance with their own conscience, seem a very ordinary thing to do. They simply made up their minds that to go any further would be wrong and ignored all of the pressure which was put on them to continue.

WHEN WILL PEOPLE ASSERT THEMSELVES?
Gamson, Fireman and Rytina set up a study which more or less encouraged people to rebel. Their research participants were asked to take part in a marketing research exercise. This involved filming a group discussion about a manager of a petrol station who was in dispute with the franchise company. The research participants were told that the company said they wanted to revoke his franchise because he was living with someone and was not married to them, but the manager said it was because he had publicly criticized their pricing policies.

As the people in the study discussed the case, they were frequently asked to argue a particular case in front of the video camera. For instance, at one point, three members of the group were asked to argue as if they were personally insulted by the manager's behaviour. It soon became apparent that the group was actually being asked to provide videotaped evidence which could be used by the company to discredit the manager. At the end, they were all asked to sign an affidavit giving the company the right to use the videotapes as evidence, in any way it wanted to.

It became obvious to the groups that they were being manipulated and most people, at that point, refused to co-operate and sign the affidavit. In 16 of the 33 groups, all of the group members refused to sign, and in eight more groups most of the members refused. Even in the groups where most people signed, there was a strong minority who refused to co-operate any further. So it's apparent that we will refuse to obey other people if we are clear enough about what is going on and how we are being manipulated.

Key idea

We are all trained to obey authority, but unthinking obedience can lead to terrible injustices. So, sometimes disobedience is the only right thing to do. That's why we need to understand the psychology of rebellion as well as obedience.

Sometimes, as we've seen, it's important to disagree. All the great social reforms which took place in the eighteenth century, for instance, began with the dedicated campaigns of a handful of people who saw something wrong, and did not let it rest. Slavery was widely accepted in Europe in the eighteenth century, but as a result of consistent campaigning the slave trade was made illegal near the beginning of the nineteenth century, and the owning of slaves became illegal a few years later. Moscovici and Nemeth (1974) showed that if just a few people stick to a particular view, which they are convinced is right, then over time they can have a great deal of influence on a larger group. The important thing, though, is that those people who are in the minority and trying to influence the majority should be seen to be genuine, consistent and resisting social pressure. If we see people acting like that, over time we become curious about why they are doing it and so are likely to think more seriously about what they are saying.

It's evident, then, that we have choices. We can do as we are told, or we can act as independent people in accord with our own conscience. But in many ways, people in modern society are not trained to act independently. Throughout school we are expected to do as we are told, and trained to obey. In later life, too, there are people whom we are expected to obey without question, such as police officers. When this goes together with our natural tendency to conform to other people, we can see why most people obey in a situation like that, even if they didn't want to. Experiences like Nazi Germany show us just how dangerous that kind of acquiescence can be.

People who stand up to authority and do what they believe is right have a difficult task, which we should respect. But we live in a world which isn't always consistent in what it expects. Whistleblowers, for example – people who 'leak' important documents or inform authorities of breaches of the law – are people who are acting according to their conscience, and trying to do what they believe is right. What they do is often difficult, because of the social pressures for conformity and obedience. Yet they are often penalized for their actions, or blamed for causing trouble, which makes it even more difficult. A better understanding of the social processes underlying these actions might help society to behave more reasonably towards such people, and to make sure that they get the support they deserve.

Understanding other people

We actually spend quite a lot of time thinking about what other people think. In other words, we are aware that other people have minds of their own, and we use our social experience to guess how they will use those minds. From a very young age, we develop what is known as a theory of mind – an awareness of other people as thinking, feeling individuals – which we use to interact effectively with other people.

But how does that theory of mind develop? As most mothers know, a two-year-old isn't really aware that other people have minds or needs of their own. Bringing up children at that age can often become a battle of wills, as the infant insists that the world must conform to its own demands, while the parent insists that the child must learn to act in socially acceptable ways. It can be an exhausting time, particularly because the child doesn't seem to have any idea about how the other person might be feeling.

Remember this

Parents have known for years how toddlers can deliberately wind up their older siblings. Their social understanding is often much more subtle than we realize. But although the toddlers know that what they are doing produces a reaction, they don't fully understand what it means for the other person.

Yet by the age of five, children are very well acquainted with the idea that other people may think differently from them, that they have good and bad moods, and can be upset or made happy by the child's actions. It's obvious that something happens during this time which allows the child to become much more socially sensitive. Psychologists have found that most children develop a theory of mind some time between the ages of three and four. At this point, the child becomes aware that other people think and see the world differently and that its own experience isn't necessarily shared by everyone else.

In one study, Perner, Leekam and Wimmer (1987) worked with pairs of children. One child was in a room while their friend waited outside. The child in the room was shown a Smarties tube and asked what was in it. The child, naturally, would answer 'Smarties'. The tube was opened and the child saw that it actually contained a pencil. Then it was closed again and each child was asked what their friend would think was in the box, if they came into the room now.

There was a difference in children's answers, depending on how old they were. The younger children, who were only just three years old, said that their friend would think the box contained a pencil. Because they hadn't yet developed a theory of mind, they couldn't imagine that the friend would think differently. But the children who were nearly four gave a different answer. They could predict what their friend would think, so they said that the friend would believe the box contained Smarties.

Having a theory of mind – being able to imagine ourselves in someone else's place – is the basis for most of our social interaction. Harris (1989) suggested that this might be the problem with severely autistic children. They can often talk and do everything that is needed for social interaction, and yet they don't interact socially with other people, and they also fail on tests like the Smarties experiment. Harris believed that autistic children simply haven't developed a theory of mind, which is why they often don't communicate well with other people.

NON-VERBAL COMMUNICATION

The experience of autistic children shows us how important communication between people is. Deliberate communication depends on being able to guess what the other person will think, so that we can make our messages clear. If we don't know that the other person is thinking independently, we can't engage in the give-and-take which conversation needs.

Communication isn't always deliberate, though. We pass information to one another in all sorts of ways, and sometimes we may not even realize that we have done it. We influence other people by what we say, of course, but also by how we say it, and the context in which we say it. This type of communication is known as non-verbal communication, which means communication without words.

As a general rule, we use non-verbal communication without even thinking about it. For example, imagine that one day you came into work and were told to go to the general manager's office. Straight away, you'd be curious, especially if that sort of request was unusual. The first thing you'd want to know, of course, is whether there was trouble coming. So you'd be looking for any non-verbal cues from your colleagues, or from the message, to get a hint as to what it might be about. The actual words that people used would be only a small part of what was being communicated. You would listen to them, of course, but you would also be taking notice of all of the other messages which were being transmitted as well. We are all experts at non-verbal communication, even if we don't always realize it.

From the moment you walked through the office door, you would be getting messages – consciously or unconsciously – from the manager's body language. You'd notice whether she seemed angry, or tense, or worried, and you'd pick up on that without any words being said. If she smiled at you as soon as you came through the door, you would be reassured because that would be a non-verbal message to tell you that you, personally, weren't in trouble. If she looked serious, you'd be wondering what was up. You'd also be taking notice of the tone of voice which she used because that's another important signal, and whether you were asked to sit down or not. Facial expressions, posture, gestures and tones of voice are all important indicators of our feelings and attitudes. In any interpersonal situation it is important for us to pick up on feelings and attitudes, if only so we can get some idea as to how we should be responding to them.

Key idea

We all understand non-verbal messages without really trying. It's something we share with many other mammals, especially primates and dogs, and goes back a long way into our primeval past.

▶ Signs and symbols

Human life is full of signs and symbols which convey meanings to us. For example, the fact of being summoned to the general manager's office is in itself a message. Who says and does what and to whom is often a communication about power. If the manager had come to see you at your workplace, that would have given an entirely different message, and would be a signal that, on this occasion, the manager wanted issues of power left out of the discussion, or at least minimized. In the normal run of things it would signify that she wanted to consult with you, or gain your opinion.

But being summoned to the office is quite different. It is a message about who is in control of the interaction: who has the power. Similar messages are also communicated by the layout of offices and where people sit. Typically, a general manager sits behind a large desk in their office – a symbolic barrier, as well as a symbol of power – and has access to all sorts of devices which can be used to control the situation: telephones, computer, intercoms and the like. The person who has been summoned, however, has nothing like that to hand.

This example is only the tip of the iceberg. Non-verbal communication has been studied extensively by psychologists because there are so many different ways in which we communicate messages to one another, and so many messages contained within any episode of human interaction. For example, we communicate information even by how close we stand to other people. Friends will tend to sit closer to one another than strangers, and people in powerful positions, like managers or teachers, tend to have a much larger share of the space in a room than other people do. The study of how we use the space around us is called proxemics. There are also cultural differences in proxemics, particularly for what is considered acceptable personal distance in conversations. Some cultures, particularly Northern European ones, have a much larger personal distance than other cultures, such as Middle Eastern ones. If they are not aware of it, it is easy for people from different cultures to feel uncomfortable in conversations: one person may feel the other is being too unfriendly and distant, while the other person feels uncomfortable because the first person wants to stand too close to them.

One of the most interesting findings has been that people tend to believe non-verbal communication far more than they believe the words are actually said. In one study, Argyle, Alkema and Gilmour (1971) asked actors to communicate different messages to people. Following that, the people (not the actors) were asked to report what they had been told. The actual words of the messages were either friendly, hostile or neutral. The non-verbal manner in which the actors delivered the messages could also be friendly, hostile or neutral, but the two didn't always match up.

When the actor's manner and words carried the same implications, there was very little misunderstanding of the message, which wasn't surprising. But it was different when the actor's non-verbal communication contradicted the words that they actually said – when, say, they were acting in a hostile manner but delivering a friendly message. When that happened, the researchers found that people were four times more likely to take notice of the non-verbal communication than the actual words which were used.

Key idea

We believe people's non-verbal signals much more than we believe their words. That's how con artists, who have excellent control of their non-verbal signals, can be so successful, and why young people who adopt casual postures and attitudes are so often misunderstood.

VERBAL COMMUNICATION AND DISCOURSE

It's apparent, then, that we are very prepared to take in non-verbal information, and that we consider it important. But we do listen to what people say as well, and again we may take in more than we realize. People often convey quite a lot of extra information in the actual words that they choose, as well as the way in which they say them. Looking at how people express themselves has become a major source of interest in modern psychology. It's known as discourse analysis, because the researchers who are doing it are analysing the patterns of discourse or conversation.

For example, Beattie and Speakman (1983) looked at how discourse happens when we are discussing complex topics, like politics or the state of society. They found that we often try out different images, and then, as the conversation progresses, settle on a single metaphor. Using the same type of image helps the people in the conversation to frame the problems that they are discussing, and also to identify possible solutions. One common metaphor, for example, involves describing the country's economy as if it were a sick person, by using phrases like 'an ailing economy' or the need for an 'injection' of capital, as if capital were a kind of medicine which would help to 'cure' the problem.

The sickness metaphor isn't the only one people use. A different group of people might refer to the economy as if it were a garden, and talk about 'cultivating growth', or 'pruning surplus expenditure'. That particular metaphorical frame would lead to different conclusions than a metaphorical frame based on illness, because a garden is something which has to be continually cared for and looked after, while an illness has to be cured. The metaphors which people use actually contain different theories about what a 'normal' economy is like. So by listening to the pattern of words which people use, we can get an insight into how they understand or make sense of the problem that they are discussing.

Key idea

Politicians are particularly good at using words or metaphors to mislead others without actually lying. Try looking very carefully at the actual words that they use. What they say often contains hidden meanings which don't show up in the general impression that they give.

▶ Attributions and explanations

Another part of discourse analysis involves looking directly at the explanations which people give for why things happen. We all have to make sense of our social experience, and explanations are an important part of that. We don't just passively accept what happens to us– we try to work out why it has happened, and whether we could have done anything about it.

Finding a reason why something has happened often involves making decisions about intentionality: did so-and-so do that deliberately, or was it just an accident? We draw on our knowledge of other people and on more general social explanations and assumptions in forming these explanations. The process of ascribing reasons for why things happened and why people acted in certain ways is known as attribution.

In Chapter 4 we will look at how the different kinds of attributions people make can influence our behaviour. Some people have attributional styles which mean that the explanations they give for why things happen make them feel helpless and out of control. Other people make attributions which allow them to see themselves as able to act positively and to be in control of things. The types of attributions we make can make a lot of difference to our own lives. But they also influence the way we judge other people.

One of the interesting things about how we use attributions is that we almost always judge other people's actions differently from the way we judge our own. When we are giving reasons for what we do, we make what are known as situational attributions – in other words, we give reasons which are to do with the situation. For example, Nisbett *et al.* (1973) asked college students to write a paragraph explaining why they had chosen to study their particular course at college. The students all gave situational reasons, such as saying that doing the course would help them to get a better job. But when we are judging someone else's actions, we generally use dispositional attributions – we conclude that their reason for doing something is because of their personality or character. When the same students were asked to explain why their best friend had chosen to study that particular course, they gave dispositional reasons, such as 'he's good at maths', or 'he likes studying rocks'.

Our tendency to make dispositional attributions about other people is very strong. It's known as the fundamental attribution error, and we do it even when we know that the situation is really the most important thing. Ross, Amabile and Steinmetz (1977) asked people to observe a quiz game. They saw how the people playing the game were chosen: it was entirely random whether someone acted as a contestant or as the quizmaster. The quizmasters had free choice of subject, so they could choose topics that they knew about. But even though the observers knew that, they always judged the person asking the questions as being generally better informed than the contestant. They knew about the situational factors, but still believed that the person's disposition was more important.

Key idea

We almost always underestimate how much people's behaviour is driven by situations. If we judged their behaviour the way we judge our own, we wouldn't make that mistake.

SOCIAL REPRESENTATIONS

Other people are important to us in all sorts of ways, even when they aren't actually present. For example, we often regulate what we do by imagining what other people would think if they knew about it. That type of social influence is very strong, even when we are alone and nobody else would know. Our social beliefs have become internalized, as part of the way that our minds work. We don't actually have to see someone react to what we are doing: we use what we know about people to predict or imagine how they will respond.

We all develop our own ideas about why things happen, and we will be looking at personal constructs in Chapter 6. But a lot of our thinking is shaped by the shared explanations held by our own social groups, or by society in general. These shared explanations are known as social representations and they can be a very powerful influence in society. A social representation is a kind of theory about why things happen which is shared by a lot of people, rather than held by just one individual person. Social representations have a strong influence on how we act. For example, in a study of medical social representations, Herzlich (1973) showed how some doctors tend to see all problems which are brought to them as having physical causes, while other doctors see many problems as having psychological causes. They recommended entirely different forms of treatment for the same kinds of problem, depending on which social representations they held.

Key idea

Social representations are powerful shared beliefs which can direct the actions of whole societies. You can see this working very clearly in the various explanations which different groups of people use for Middle Eastern conflicts.

▶ Cultural differences in social representations

Social representations are also influential in determining social policy. For example, in Britain, a common social representation used to be that people become criminals because of something inside themselves – because they are inherently bad in some way. This means that we tend to discount serious attempts to rehabilitate criminals, because we don't believe they will work. And even when we try a rehabilitation scheme, we don't usually give it enough time or resources for a long-term effect.

However, other societies have different social representations. Unlike Britain, for instance, American society has a general social representation that people can change – that they don't stay the same all their lives. (This doesn't mean that everyone in the USA believes that, of course, but it means that most people do, or at least that many social policies have been based on that idea.) So in the USA, rehabilitation units attempt to develop re-education programmes which will help criminals to change their ways.

I remember once being at a conference on child abuse and watching an argument between an English and an American professional working in this area. The American woman ran a rehabilitation centre for young men who were sexual abusers of children. The centre had a very intensive treatment programme which took a couple of years to complete. It was carefully worked out and was very arduous to go through, but it also had a very high success rate.

The argument between the English woman and the American, though, wasn't concerned with exchanging information about the programme. Essentially, it was a clash of social representations. The English woman simply did not believe that child sexual abusers could change their ways, and the American woman knew, from her own experience, that they could. So she became very frustrated with the discussion and ended up almost jumping up and down (though not quite – it was a professional conference, after all!) because she couldn't understand why she was unable to get her point across.

People with different social representations often end up talking past one another, like those two women. Di Giacomo (1980) looked at the social representations held by student political leaders in a Belgian university in the 1970s, and compared them with the social representations shared by most of the ordinary students. Di Giacomo found that the two groups had very different social representations, and so they entirely failed to understand one another. In some ways, Di Giacomo reported, it was almost as if the student leaders were talking a different language from the ordinary students. They would use phrases like 'student–worker solidarity', but the majority of the ordinary students couldn't see what students and workers had in common at all. To them, the idea of solidarity between students and workers didn't make much sense. As a result, when the student leaders tried to mobilize the students in a protest movement they failed to get enough support for the movement to be successful.

Social representations, then, are all about how we explain what is going on to ourselves. Wagner and Hayes (2005) showed how we draw from social influences and factors to make sense of our lives – to tell ourselves the 'stories' which shape and direct our actions. Those stories are closely influenced by the social groups we belong to, and the cultures that we come from, and understanding them is important in understanding why human beings – and societies – behave as they do.

HELPING OTHER PEOPLE

How we explain things to ourselves also has quite an influence on how we interact with other people. For example, if we come across someone who is asking for help, whether we actually step in and help them or not depends on how we define the situation – and that in turn will depend on the social representations we are using. If we conclude that the situation isn't really serious, or that it is the person's own fault that they are in that situation, then we are much less likely to help out than if we define it differently.

Darley and Latané (1970) conducted a study in which an actor went up to people passing by on the street and asked them to give him ten cents. People responded differently, depending on what the actor said about why it was necessary. As you can see from Table 3.1, the more 'worthy' the person's cause seemed to be, the more likely people were to give him the money.

Table 3.1 Reasons for helping.

Reason	Percentage of people asked who gave money
No reason given	34%
Money needed for a phone call	64%
Wallet stolen	70%

(adapted from Darley and Latané, 1970)

The way other people act – other bystanders, that is – also
influences whether we are likely to offer help to strangers. The
same psychologists set up a situation in which people who were
sitting in a waiting room heard a crash from the next room,
and a woman's voice crying out for help. When someone was
waiting alone, they were very likely to go into the next room
to see if they could help – in fact, 70 per cent of the people in
that situation did so. But if there were three other people in the
waiting room as well, then they were much less likely to go and
help. Only 40 per cent of the research participants offered help
under those conditions.

When they were interviewed afterwards, the people
participating in the study said that they had taken their cues
from the other people around them. Because they seemed to be
reasonably calm, the person had come to the conclusion that
the situation wasn't really serious and so hadn't bothered to
do anything. They had redefined the situation to themselves,
so that it seemed as though help wasn't really needed after
all. Also, they felt that the responsibility was somehow shared
with the other people around them, so it was less important
that they offered their personal help than it was when they
were alone.

We can see, then, that whether we actually exert ourselves to go
and help someone depends on our social representations – how
we explain to ourselves what is going on. Having an unclear
situation, or having other people around, can make a difference.
Nonetheless, if we are sure that someone really does need help,
we do tend to help them. In a study on the New York subway,
Piliavin *et al.* (1969) found that commuters would usually help
someone who had collapsed on the train. If the person seemed

to be ill, he was helped 95 per cent of the time, and even if he seemed to be drunk, people helped out on half of the occasions that he 'collapsed'.

Key idea

Our natural tendency is to help other people who seem to need it. But social representations can interfere with this, so that we end up ignoring people because we think they don't deserve our help.

SOCIAL SCRIPTS

We also have social scripts which tell us what to do in most situations. As we grow up, much of what we learn is about acting in the ways that society expects. We learn about social roles and how to behave in a way that fits in with the part we are playing, and we also learn about social scripts – what would be expected in a given situation. If we go to a restaurant, there is a definite script which tells us when we should do certain things and when we can expect things to happen. We'd be deeply disconcerted if the waiter brought coffee before the main course, for instance, and we would wonder what was going on.

Other social situations, too, have their own scripts, and sometimes these can cause us to act in unusual ways. In one study, Orne (1962) showed how powerful scripts can be. Normally, if you ask people to add up a set of numbers on a piece of paper and then tear the paper up and throw it in the bin, they will refuse. They might do it once or twice, but no more. But if you tell them that it is part of a psychology experiment, they will do it over and over again. In Orne's study, one research participant even had to be stopped after several hours because the experimenter wanted to go home!

So we weigh up the situation that we are in and match what we do to what we think the situation requires. The attributions and explanations that we make influence how we understand what is required, and our social representations guide our choice of actions. We interpret and analyse the situation we are in, and that, too, influences how we behave.

Social scripts are closely linked with social representations, but they operate at a more specific level. Where social representations tell us the overall 'story' of why things are happening, social scripts tell us what behaviour seems to be appropriate in a given situation. It is for this reason that so many psychologists are concerned about the large amount of negative drama on TV and in film. It isn't about people copying behaviour directly, although that can happen occasionally. It is more because these dramas provide people with social scripts which suggest that this is an appropriate or normal way to behave. In doing so, they place an unrealistic emphasis on the less pleasant options for human interaction, and encourage people to think it is normal to deal with other people aggressively or vindictively.

Our social behaviour, then, is complex, drawing from many levels of explanation and different kinds of experience. We are influenced by our early conditioning, by non-verbal and verbal communication, by our social roles and social scripts, by our personal attributions and by social representations. And we are also influenced by the emotions that we experience. We will look more closely at these in the next chapter.

Focus points

Social pressures can produce unthinking obedience to authority which can even result in ordinary people committing crimes.

People who disobey social pressures and act according to their conscience have often learned by past experience how important this disobedience is.

Communication can be either deliberate or accidental, and much of it is non-verbal – not involving words. Non-verbal communication, both in human actions and in symbols, is generally more powerful than verbal communication.

Attributions are the reasons that we give for why things happen.

Social representations are explanations for why things are the way they are, and these are shared by groups of people.

Social scripts establish expectations which guide our everyday behaviour.

4

Emotional living

In this chapter you will learn:

► *eight different types of positive emotion*
► *how fear and anger affect us*
► *the principles of positive psychology.*

If you were to survey a large number of people about what makes a human being different from a computer, the chances are that one reply would overshadow all the rest. Human beings are very different from machines, because we can feel emotion. We become happy, upset, thrilled or furious – and we're not always particularly rational about how we do it. In this chapter, we will look at the psychology of emotions and at how psychological knowledge has been used to help people to cope with anxiety and stress.

Emotions

When we think of emotions, it is generally the unpleasant ones which come to mind: fear, anger, anxiety, and so on. Partly, that's because we live in a society which tends to emphasize those much more than the positive ones. Films, news and TV dramas all emphasize negative emotions and ignore positive ones. So we tend not to notice the positive emotions that we feel, or to dismiss them as not really important.

People who give up smoking, for instance, often notice that they become more easily irritated. But they overlook the fact that they also become more able to smile, and that they laugh more easily. Both of these have the same physical origin – they are to do with getting the nicotine out of the body (we will look at this more closely in Chapter 5) – but we notice only the unpleasant side, because that's how our perceptions have been shaped by modern society.

POSITIVE EMOTIONS

In the later part of the twentieth century some researchers began systematic investigation of our positive emotions. For example, Argyle and Crossland (1987) asked people to imagine how they would feel in each of 24 different situations, which are listed in Table 4.1. They also asked them to compare those feelings with the feelings produced by any of the other situations on the list.

Table 4.1 Situations producing positive emotions.

Spending a good social evening with friends.

Receiving an unexpected compliment which means a lot to you.

Getting involved in a thriller on TV.

Feeling overwhelmed by the beauty of nature.

Getting on well with your loved ones.

Solving an important personal problem.

Listening to a beautiful piece of music.

Engaging in a favourite hobby (not sports).

Having a rewarding conversation.

Doing some sort of commitment activity (e.g. charitable work, etc.).

Feeling popular at a social gathering.

Being a success at something important to you.

Being absorbed by your work.

Meeting an interesting new person or people.

Engaging in a favourite sporting activity.

Being successful at work.

Reading a good book.

Doing some enjoyable physical work.

Buying yourself something you have wanted for ages.

Spending some time thinking about the good things in life.

Being given a valuable present by someone dear to you.

Having a long hot bath, or pampering yourself some other way.

Spending a memorable evening at a cinema/theatre/concert.

Having a quiet drink with friends (non-alcoholic or alcoholic).

(adapted from Argyle and Crossland, 1987)

As you can see, each of these situations involves an experience which we would describe as pleasant or positive, but some are very different from others. By combining the different descriptions and analysing what they had in common, Argyle and Crossland found that there seem to be roughly eight kinds of positive emotion, which are listed in Table 4.2.

Table 4.2 Types of positive emotion.

Potency	Feeling capable and able to do whatever is needed.
Spirituality	Feelings of wonder or awe, such as when listening to a particularly beautiful piece of music, or enjoying nature.
Contentment	Feeling pleasantly satisfied with circumstances.
Relaxation	Feeling unstressed and mentally calm.
Self-indulgence	For example, pampering yourself. Not selfish, but a pleasure which is personal rather than shared.
Altruism	Sharing, or caring for other people.
Absorption	Feeling interested in a topic or a hobby.
Exhilaration	Being excited about something, or thrilled by an unexpected pleasant experience.

Using these eight types of emotion as the basis for further research, Argyle and Crossland concluded that they could be distilled into four basic dimensions. The first of these dimensions is involvement – how involved we are in what we are doing. When we are having a quiet drink with friends, we tend to be less absorbed than if we were reading a good book or solving an important personal problem. We take things more lightly, and don't plunge into them as deeply.

The second dimension is potency – how effective we feel ourselves to be. Some experiences require us to use our abilities fully, in order to achieve success, and those can be very satisfying. But other equally pleasant experiences, like socializing with friends or going to the cinema or a music concert, don't require the same kind of personal effectiveness. That type of experience simply isn't relevant in these situations. So positive emotions can vary depending on how much they involve a feeling of potency on our part.

The third dimension is social – whether our attention is focused on social events, as it might be when we are in conversation with friends or meeting new people, or whether our current experience is simply personal and/or self-indulgent. Some positive experiences seem to direct our attention outwards, to other people, while others direct it inwards, towards our own selves.

The fourth dimension is intensity. Some experiences are really quite lightweight: having a hot bath or watching a TV thriller are pleasant, but they are not desperately serious activities. Some positive emotions, though, produce much deeper emotions, such as solving an important personal problem, getting on with loved ones, or feeling overwhelmed by the beauty of nature.

We can see, then, that there is a much wider range of positive emotions than we sometimes realize. There are others, too, which aren't on this list. But modern society's tendency to notice only the unpleasant emotions like anger or fear, or to regard them as somehow more important than the positive ones, means that these aspects of human experience are often ignored or neglected.

Key idea

Modern society tends to exaggerate unpleasant emotions, through the media and everyday discussion. But we have a rich and varied array of positive emotions too, and these are just as important. We need to understand them better, so we can notice them properly.

LOVING

One emotion which isn't neglected in modern society is love. We hear about love all the time, through the mass of romantic images in the media. But how far does the public image of 'love' actually reflect the reality? What is really involved in the experience of love, and what is the difference in the love between a couple who have been married for 30 years, and the emotion felt by two starry-eyed teenagers. Are there different kinds of loving?

It seems that there are. A number of psychologists have investigated different kinds of love and have concluded that we often use the same word to describe some very different emotions. One of the most useful distinctions was made by Tennov (1979), who argued that love, as a long-term emotion, was actually very different from the short-term, intense infatuation which we also call love, or being 'in love'. She suggested that it would be more appropriate if we used the term limerence to describe the intense experiences, and kept the term love to refer to the attachment involved in longer-term affections and partnerships.

Limerence, according to Tennov (and as described by a vast number of writers, playwrights and musicians), is an intense, all-consuming passion, which has a very strong element of fantasy in it. The person becomes totally obsessed with their idea of their loved one and spends a great deal of time thinking about them and daydreaming. Often, these thoughts are focused around tokens of some kind, such as a letter, a lock of hair, or a photograph.

Perhaps the most distinctive feature of this emotion is that it involves a state of intense longing for the person. Because of this, Tennov argued, it is quite important that the person should be unreachable in some way – otherwise the emotion isn't likely to last very long. When two people are always together, limerence tends to die away because it is not being fed by their longing for one another.

That isn't necessarily a bad thing, of course. In many cases, the period of limerence represents an initial blissful period, which is then gradually replaced by a deeper kind of loving, which becomes a basis for a long-term partnership. But some couples find that they have relatively little in common once the period of intense limerence is over. The problem, of course, is that those experiencing limerence can't imagine it ever being over, so it is quite possible for them to make serious commitments, like marriage, while they are in this state, and then to regret it later.

The fact that limerence can be perpetuated as long as the couple are prevented from being together as much as they would like, explains why parental opposition to love affairs so often has the opposite outcome to the one which they intended. Forbidding the relationship has the effect of increasing the longing which the two people feel for one another, and so can make their attachment stronger. A more sensible course would probably be to make sure that the two people spent as much time together as possible, to see if they would still be likely to form a lasting attachment once the period of limerence is over.

Key idea

Distinguishing between love and limerence is quite important, because in everyday life we use the word 'love' to mean so many different things. Try counting all the times you hear the word during the course of a day, and see how many times the word is used with the same meaning.

▶ Dimensions of love

Sternberg (1988) accepted Tennov's idea of love and limerence and went on to look at what seems to be involved in the longer-term emotion which we also call 'love'. He surveyed 80 people between the ages of 17 and 69, asking them about the relationships which they were experiencing at the time, and ones which they had experienced in the past. From this and other data, Sternberg concluded that love seems to consist of three underlying dimensions, with different proportions of these dimensions producing different kinds of love. These dimensions are intimacy, passion, and commitment (see Table 4.3).

Table 4.3 Dimensions of love

Intimacy	How closely the two partners share in one another's lives, including communication, understanding and emotional support.
Passion	Emotions, desires and needs as well as physical passion, e.g. satisfying, nurturing, caring and personal fulfilment needs.
Commitment	A long-term commitment to building a lifelong partnership which helps to keep the couple together during difficult times.

Different combinations of these dimensions produce different kinds of love. For example, the kind of long-term companionate love which develops between two people who have been together for many years is often one which is high in intimacy and commitment, but perhaps less so on the passion dimension. Romantic love, on the other hand, tends to be high on intimacy and passion, but doesn't involve as much commitment. Sternberg referred to the kind of love which involves all three dimensions fully as consummate love.

Using his sample of 80 people of different ages, Sternberg also investigated how loving relationships changed over time and, in particular, what kinds of things became more or less important as the relationship developed. People in long-term relationships identified five things as important – that is, they believed that five things mattered more in the long term than in the short term. These are listed in Table 4.4.

Table 4.4 Important factors in long-term relationships.

Having similar values.

Being willing to change in response to the other person.

Being prepared to put up with the other person's flaws.

Having matching religious beliefs.

Having an equal intellectual level.

(Sternberg, 1988)

Interestingly, the last one in the list – having a similar intellectual level – seemed totally unimportant to those whose relationships had been going only for a few years, but was seen by people in long-lasting relationships as absolutely essential. Some things, though, became less important with time, including how interesting the other person seemed to be, and how attentively each person listened to the other. Others were judged as more important during the first few years of the relationship but then declined or mattered less as time wore on. These included physical attractiveness, the ability to make love, the ability to empathize with the partner, and expressing affection towards one another. It isn't really possible to tell, though, whether these things really became less important, or whether the couples in the long-term relationships took them so much for granted that they stopped noticing them at all.

Negative emotions

Some of our emotions, like anger or extreme fear, can be highly destructive. Since the earliest days of psychology, psychologists have been interested in these negative emotions – partly because of their social impact, and partly, as Seligman (2003) pointed out, because of a widespread social belief that underneath, people are nasty, selfish and aggressive, and that this accounts for most of society's problems. Seligman traced this idea back to the doctrine of original sin, but pointed out that actually, there is very little evidence for it. Most people would far rather be positive in their dealings with others, and the way that we become distressed when we come into conflict with other people indicates how important positive interactions are to us.

Remember this

It has been said that people who are habitually angry, irritable or worried take years from their lives, because the physical reactions accompanying negative emotions are so draining for the body.

PHYSICAL ASPECTS OF FEAR AND ANGER

We do, nevertheless, experience strong emotions, and these were the dominant focus of research into emotion throughout the twentieth century. Early psychologists were particularly interested in how the emotion that we feel connects with the physical sensations that we experience when we are frightened or angry.

Both anger and fear are very active emotions. If you are angry with someone, your muscles tense up and you become restless: some people will even stand up and pace around the room as a way of helping to control the tension. Similarly, if you are frightened your muscles become tense and you may make small involuntary movements which express that tension. The two types of tension aren't the same, of course, but they do have quite a lot in common. They are entirely different from quiescent emotions, such as depression, which involve listlessness and apathy rather than tension and activity.

In part, the tension that you feel when you are afraid is a survival response, and one shared by all mammals. In the natural world, if an animal is threatened by something so that it becomes frightened, then there are only two options. It can stay and fight, in which case it will need all the strength it can muster to win; or it can run away, in which case it will need all the strength it can muster to escape. In either case, therefore, the animal will need all its strength because holding anything back isn't much use if you end up dead. So the animal's body goes into overdrive, to give it as much energy as possible; and this is known as the 'fight or flight' response. Humans have it too.

Most of the time, we use only a small proportion of our potential strength and energy. However during the fight or flight response, the body changes the way in which it operates physically in several different ways, all of which help to release more energy to the muscles. Physical energy comes from a chemical reaction between oxygen and forms of glucose, or blood sugars. Both of these are carried in the bloodstream to the muscles where, effectively, the sugar is 'burnt' to produce energy. This process takes oxygen, so muscles that are in action need to have a continuous supply of fresh oxygenated blood if they are to work properly.

Many of the physical changes, therefore, are concerned with getting oxygen into the bloodstream. We breathe more deeply and more rapidly, increasing the oxygen supply entering the lungs. Blood pressure increases, carrying blood around the body more quickly, and extra red blood cells (which carry oxygen) are released into the bloodstream. Some other changes are concerned with getting more 'fuel' to the muscles. Stored fats are converted into blood sugars and released into the blood. The digestive system begins to work differently, ignoring long-term digestion and increasing the digestive processes for rapidly acting foods such as sugars. Saliva in the mouth changes in the same way, so that we can metabolize rapid-energy foods quickly.

Another set of changes is designed to protect us from injury as much as possible. The amount of vitamin K in the blood increases, making the blood more able to clot quickly if there is an injury. Also, if we are frightened, blood vessels near to the surface of the skin shrink, making us paler and minimizing the amount of blood we are likely to lose if we are injured. Blood supply to the internal vital organs of the body, on the other hand, increases. We also have some leftover responses designed to protect us by making us look more fearsome. In many animals, their fur stands on end as part of the fight or flight response, making them look bigger and potentially more dangerous. Humans have lost their fur, but the hairs that we have left still try to stand on end. But instead of making us look more frightening, all this actually does is give us goosepimples!

We can see, then, that the fight or flight response is a very powerful reaction, which serves an important survival function – at least, when we are faced with threats that require physical action. It isn't quite as helpful when we are faced with non-physical threats, such as anxiety about the mortgage, or a fear of failing exams. Because these threats don't require physical action, we don't have a way of using up that energy, and can quickly become stressed. We will be looking at ways of dealing with that stress in Chapter 14.

There are lesser degrees of the fight or flight response, too. When our attention is caught by something, or when we feel anxious about something, we experience the same kinds of physical changes but to a much lesser degree. The changes are strong enough to be measured, though, using sensitive detectors that will identify changes in pulse rate, heart rate, sweating, blood pressure and the like.

A machine which measures several of these changes is known as a polygraph. Some people, such as police conducting interrogations, use polygraphs as lie detectors because they can detect the slight anxiety which people feel when they tell a lie. Other machines can analyse slight changes in the voice caused by anxiety, which can sometimes be useful for detectives monitoring anonymous telephone calls.

Remember this

If lie detectors can catch the effects produced by even a single anxious thought, how many more does being continually worried produce? It's no wonder that long-term stress is so damaging.

The general name which we give to this kind of physical state is known as arousal, because it seems as though several physiological systems have been aroused at the same time.

The type of arousal which we experience in fear is slightly different from the type we experience when we are angry, but the two conditions have a great deal in common.

Back in the 1950s, a psychologist named Ax conducted a study to investigate the difference between fear and anger. Ax connected people up to an impressive-looking machine, so that they had wires and connectors all over the body. Then, when they were fully connected up, a technician came rushing into the room saying 'Hold it! There's a short circuit in the apparatus'. That was the fear condition. In the anger condition, the person was wired up and then left alone with a technician who grumbled about the study and insulted them.

Incidentally, it wouldn't be possible for a psychologist to conduct this sort of study nowadays. There are very strict rules about ethical principles which have to be observed while conducting psychological experiments. It is not permitted to cause people who are participating in the research any pain or distress (mental or physical) at all. It also isn't permitted to deceive people, except under very special circumstances and with special permission from an ethical committee, and then only as long as they are told the full truth at the earliest possible moment. However, when Ax was doing this research, these precautions didn't exist.

Ax found that there were distinct physiological differences between the kind of arousal produced by fear, and that produced by anger. These differences seemed to be the result of different hormones and brain chemicals which were involved in the two emotions. Both fear and anger involved a chemical named adrenaline (or epinephrine in the USA), but anger also involved another one, known as noradrenaline (or norepinephrine).

Adrenaline and noradrenaline are chemicals which are used by the body to stimulate a special part of the nervous system, known as the autonomic nervous system. This is a network of nerve fibres running to all the internal organs of the body. When that part of the autonomic nervous system is stimulated – a part known as the sympathetic division – the body experiences arousal. However, when the other part, known as the parasympathetic division, is stimulated, the body becomes quieter and less active. The parasympathetic division seems to be involved in quiet emotions such as depression or sadness.

So we have a number of physiological symptoms which accompany our emotions. The next question is: which comes first? If physical changes happen when we feel emotions, does that mean that our emotions are caused by these physical changes? One of the early psychologists, William James (1890), thought so. He described what happens when you trip going down the stairs and catch hold of the bannister to save yourself. During that first second, James pointed out, you simply react and do what is needed to survive. However, a couple of seconds later, your heart begins to beat faster, your hands sweat, and your breathing changes – in other words, the arousal response starts, but only after the emergency is over. It is then, James believed, that we feel the fear.

James went on to suggest that all human emotions actually come from our perceiving the physical condition that we are in. A famous quote from him is: 'We do not weep because we feel sorrow; we feel sorrow because we weep.' He believed that the brain unconsciously monitors the body for changes, and then interprets those changes according to what the situation seems to demand.

▶ Social influences

Over 60 years later, two psychologists named Schachter and Singer conducted an experiment to investigate this idea. Although it wasn't a very good experiment, because they didn't really control it very well, the experiment did give us some useful clues about how physical sensations and our own knowledge of the situation might be connected.

Schachter and Singer wanted to see what happened if people had the physical symptoms of arousal, and how they would feel in different situations. So some of their research participants were injected with adrenaline, producing the physical symptoms of arousal, while others were injected with only a neutral saline solution, which didn't have any effect. Also, they were given different 'explanations' for how they were feeling. Some of them were told accurately what was likely to happen – trembling hands, a pounding heart and feeling flushed. Others were misinformed, by being told that they might experience an itching sensation, a slight headache, or numbness. And a third group were not given any information at all, just told that the injection was mild and harmless and wouldn't have any side effects.

What happened next was that the research participants were asked to sit in a waiting room for 20 minutes, supposedly to let the injection take its full effect. Each time, there was another person in the room with them who seemed to be another participant in the study. Really, though, the person was a stooge – an actor who was pretending to be a research participant but who was really doing what the experimenters wanted.

Sometimes, during the 20-minute period, the stooge would act as if he was in a very happy mood: playing 'basketball' with pieces of paper, making paper aeroplanes, and playing with a hula hoop. Each time, he would invite the real research participant to join in, which many of them did. This was known as the 'euphoria' condition, designed to encourage the research participants to feel happy. Other people experienced a different condition. They were introduced to the stooge and given a long, personally intrusive questionnaire to fill in during the time. The stooge would begin to fill it in too, but would then become increasingly angry at how personal and insulting some of the questions were. Eventually, he would stamp out of the room in disgust. This was the 'anger' condition, designed to encourage the other people to feel angry as well.

Schachter and Singer found that, by and large, the stooge had more influence than the injection. In other words, whether they had an adrenaline injection or not, those who were in the 'euphoric' condition tended to be in quite a good mood at the end of the time, while those in the 'anger' condition tended to be irritable. The moods that we experience, their findings implied, are mainly determined by social factors – the reactions of other people around us.

Key idea

Our heritage as social animals means that we are also affected by the moods of the people around us. If we are with people who are happy and smiling, we feel happier ourselves. But people who are dejected and miserable often bring our own mood down as well.

But they also found that how intensely people experienced the emotion depended on the adrenaline – as long as they didn't know what to expect. People who had been kept ignorant or misinformed about the effects of the adrenaline showed quite strong changes in moods. But people who had been told about the real effects reacted in much the same way as people who hadn't had the adrenaline at all. In other words, they changed their mood a little, from the social influences, but not much.

The conclusion the researchers came to, therefore, was that our awareness of the situation produces the emotion that we actually feel. But our physical condition influences how strongly we feel that emotion. An aroused state contributes to the way we interpret situations, so we feel more angry, or happier, than we might otherwise. You may have found a similar effect yourself if you have been, say, running for a bus but have just missed it. Running and anxiety both raise the adrenaline levels in the bloodstream, so we can become very angry at the moment of missing the bus, even if it isn't all that important when we calm down. The arousal exaggerates the reactions that we feel.

As I said before, the study had flaws in terms of the way the conditions were controlled – and of course it involved far too much deception and manipulation for anything like that to be permitted today. However, it has given us some useful insights into emotion and how it works – in particular, by showing how our physiology interacts with our personal and social experiences.

THE YERKES–DODSON LAW

The 'fight or flight' response is an extreme state of physiological arousal. But there are less extreme forms of arousal, too. It is best to think of arousal in terms of a continuous scale, which has extreme relaxation at one end, and fight or flight at the other. In between are many different levels. A disagreement, an unpleasant interview, or even just a worrying thought are all things which can make us more aroused. Other influences, such as caffeine, exercise (while we are doing it, though not afterwards), or premenstrual tension also raise our level of arousal.

This isn't necessarily a bad thing, because a small amount of arousal is stimulating. Many people have a cup of coffee in the morning because the additional stimulation helps them to feel more alert. People do exercise for the same reason. In fact, up to a point, increased arousal helps us to do things better.

But only up to a point. If we become too aroused – say, by becoming very upset or very angry – then it can actually stop us doing things well. You might find, for instance, that you do better in an argument if you are annoyed by what the other person is saying. Your irritation helps you to find words and to argue more fluently. But if you become enraged by the other person's comments, so that your arousal level becomes too high, then you might find yourself speechless and unable to put what you want to say into words. Up to a point, the increased arousal brought on by irritation has improved your performance in the argument, but when the level of arousal goes past that point, it interferes with it.

Key idea

Arousal is cumulative, so each little stressor adds to the total load of arousal that we are carrying. That's why taking care of details and avoiding little stressors can actually help us to cope better with the big ones.

This principle is known as the Yerkes–Dodson Law of Arousal (see Figure 4.1), and it can be applied to almost every task. Being angry or upset might mean that you do the washing-up more quickly and efficiently – but if those feelings are too intense, you might break things or drop them. With a relatively simple activity such as washing-up, you can be much more aroused before you actually get to the point of breaking things, but in a complex situation, such as an argument or when doing something that you need to concentrate on, the optimal level of arousal for doing the job well is much lower. In other words, you can be put off more easily.

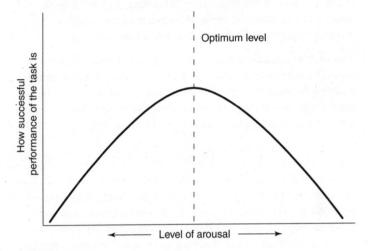

Figure 4.1 The Yerkes–Dodson Law of Arousal.

The Yerkes–Dodson Law is a useful thing to understand, because it helps us to see how stresses can pile up and eventually become more than we can deal with. If we're going in for something major, like an exam or a sporting competition, it tells us that we should manage our arousal, so that we are just worked up enough to achieve peak performance, but not so much that it prevents us from doing our best. In those situations, we can't avoid some level of anxiety – if only because it means so much to us. But we can take hold of the things that we are able to control, like preparation or transport (catch the bus before the bus you really need, so you're not stressed by traffic hold-ups), so that our total level of stress is at the optimal level.

DESCRIBING ANGER
We saw earlier how our understanding of the situation can affect our emotions. This also means that how we describe emotions can be important. So it is useful to look at how

emotions are understood in different cultures and in different languages. In the English language, for example, we tend to use the word 'anger' as a general term to describe a particular emotion. However, that can sometimes lead to confusion because there is more than one kind of anger, with different social meanings and different implications for whether we judge the angry person as being fully responsible or not.

Lutz (1991) discussed how the Ifaluk people of Micronesia have five different words for anger, and each of these describes a different kind of emotion. For example, the anger which you might feel with relatives or friends who have not fulfilled their obligations is known as *nguch*. This is regarded as a different emotion from the irritability which people feel when they have been ill, and are convalescing, which is known as *tipmochmoch*.

A third kind of emotion is the anger we experience when we feel frustrated or helpless, or trapped into doing things that we don't want to do. The Ifaluk know this emotion as *tang*, and it is entirely different from the kind of anger which builds up gradually through lots of irritating little things going wrong, which is known as *lingeringer*. Finally, there is a sort of anger which society actually encourages: the righteous anger or indignation which is to do with morality and justice, and making sure that things which happen are fair and equitable. That kind of anger is known as *song*.

When we look at these different words and their meanings, we can see that each of them reflects an emotion that Western people also feel sometimes. But the Ifaluk use different words, seeing them as quite different emotions, and so they find it easier to respond to them differently. Words might not seem to be important, but they structure and shape our understanding of the world. Having a vocabulary for different kinds of anger means that people will be much more likely to take account of the causes of that anger, and will be more prepared to treat people differently.

An Ifaluk person, for example, would be much less likely to be disturbed or upset when a convalescent person was being snappy and unreasonable, for example, because they would be aware of what was producing the emotion from the outset. We have to learn these things the hard way, because our language doesn't sensitize us to them, and we can easily become stressed or even lose friends as a result of not realizing the source of their emotion. We can learn a lot about being human from non-technological cultures like the Ifaluk, because people in such societies often have a much more sophisticated awareness of mental states than people in technological societies.

Key idea

Using a different explanation for an emotion can mean that we actually experience the emotion quite differently. The same can apply when we are trying to understand other people's reactions, too.

Positive psychology

How we describe an emotion, then, can make a lot of difference to how we understand what is going on. But what we see around us also has a direct impact on our emotional experience. The enormous emphasis on negative emotions produced by modern TV and film means that people in Western cultures often under-emphasize the positive emotions of their lives: they don't notice them, or don't think they are important. Many psychologists believe that this has produced an imbalance in modern experience, in which continually focusing on bad things adds to the amount of everyday stress that people feel. Yet those people in public life who talk about the need for more good news, or more positive TV, are often ridiculed as 'soft' or 'touchy-feelies', when actually they are only talking good sense.

Key idea

Positive psychology is a much-needed attempt to bring the balance back into psychology. Instead of concentrating on the negative sides of life, it tries to understand and promote the positive side as well. What's the point of understanding unhappiness if we can't also understand what it is to be happy?

HAPPINESS

Positive psychology is about helping people to obtain a more balanced perspective, by learning to recognize and value the positive aspects of our everyday life. Effectively, as its founder Martin Seligman (1998) says, it is about happiness. As we have seen, being happier can help us in many ways – even physically, as researchers have shown how positive and happy thoughts can stimulate the immune system and help us to recover from many of our ailments and illnesses. A better awareness of positive psychology could help us all to live life more easily.

We all have the capacity to live a positive life, but we don't all do it in the same way. Martin Seligman (2003) identified three sorts of desirable life: the pleasant life, the good life, and the meaningful life. A pleasant life is one in which the person is aware of, and enjoys, positive emotions about the past, present and future. Table 4.5 describes some of these emotions. A good life, in Seligman's terms, involves using your strengths and virtues to obtain gratification in the main areas of your life. And a meaningful life is the use of your strengths and virtues in the service of something much larger than you are.

Table 4.5 Time perspectives in positive emotions.

Emotions directed towards the past	e.g. contentment, serenity, satisfaction, pride.
Emotions directed towards the present	e.g. pleasures: bodily ones like enjoyable sights or feelings; higher pleasures such as mirth, fun, bliss and thrills; and gratifications, such as activities which we like doing and find absorbing.
Emotions directed towards the future	e.g. optimism, hope, confidence, trust and faith.

As with any psychological classification, most people will have a combination of these different types of life, and everyone goes through periods when they experience loss, grief, or other negative experiences. What Seligman is talking about is the dominant emphasis of our lives, not the details. If we generally hold on to an optimistic outlook, and adopt positive coping strategies to deal with our stresses, we can all learn to be happier and healthier as a result. As we will see in Chapter 15, there can even be positive aspects to recovering from serious life-disasters, depending on how we go about dealing with them.

Some critics have argued that happiness spoils people, making them depraved or selfish. Veenhoven (2003) pointed out that quite the reverse is true: studies of the consequences of happiness show that it fosters altruism and sociability, as well as activity, initiative, and of course, health. There is no evidence in psychological research for any negative effects of happiness.

LEARNED OPTIMISM

In his early career, Martin Seligman investigated a phenomenon known as learned helplessness. He showed that repeatedly experiencing unpleasant stimuli or events, without being able to do anything about it, produced a state of apathy and hopelessness which was so strong that people (or animals) wouldn't do anything to help themselves even when they could. It's a kind of 'victim mentality', which prevents people from taking positive action, and traps them in bad situations.

Key idea

Learned optimism is the opposite of learned helplessness. Instead of feeling that things are bound to be unpleasant and we can't do anything about them, we can learn to hope for the best and see the good side. That would help all of us to live longer.

As Seligman continued his research, he found that it was possible for people to overcome these thought habits, and to learn more positive, optimistic ways of thinking. One way, for example, was for therapists to work with people to develop a positive attributional style. Seeing things as specific rather than global, temporary rather than permanent, and controllable rather than uncontrollable leads to a far more positive way of appraising situations. It gives people a positive sense of agency – that they are actively in control of their own lives, and able to make their own choices. And this is a much more psychologically healthy way of thinking.

The importance of positive thinking has been known for a long time. One method used by therapists is called the Pollyanna technique, after the title character in a children's book published in 1913. It involves looking for something good – no matter how small – to come out of every event or disaster. That doesn't mean we have to ignore or belittle the problems, of course, but it means that we need to see things more realistically – that even apparently awful events can sometimes have positive side effects. Most importantly, it trains people in a constructive way of thinking, which doesn't just focus always on the worst side of things. That sort of pessimism is very bad for people, because it increases their overall stress levels. But Seligman showed how optimism is a much more positive state of mind, and how we can learn to become more optimistic with the right therapy or self-training. Essentially, he showed people how to replace learned helplessness with learned optimism, and have a more positive life as a result.

Key idea

Research has shown that people who take a positive outlook recover better from cancers and other illnesses than people who are depressed or anxious. That tells us a lot about the power of positive thinking, and why we should all try to achieve it.

MINDFULNESS

Mindfulness is another approach which has become popular in positive psychology as a valuable addition to everyday life. Mindfulness is all about focusing on the present moment, and achieving a mental state which accepts and acknowledges bodily sensations, thoughts and feelings. It needs some practice, and some people find it helpful to join mindfulness groups or classes to get started, but it is a way of creating a bit of mental 'space' which gives us relief from the pressure of constantly distracting thoughts and anxieties.

Mindfulness isn't a new idea. It developed from a combination of Buddhist meditational traditions and the work of the Gestalt therapists of the 1960s and 1970s, who developed a number of therapeutic techniques which also encouraged people to focus on the immediate moment. Other related practices, such as yoga and meditation, have been shown to have the same kinds of benefits, but they often require considerable training and self-discipline. Mindfulness, on the other hand, is something which can be learned by anyone, even children, and has been shown to have general health benefits as well as psychological ones.

The idea of mindfulness is that we spend a period of time each day being fully aware of the present moment. That isn't always as easy as it sounds, because we need to learn how to control or shut off the distracting thoughts or ideas which continually pop into our minds. One of the ways we can do this is by labelling them: recognizing a recurrent thought as an example of anxiety or recognizing an idea as being unhelpful, and putting them aside. Another way is to think of them as buses that we don't want to catch, going past a bus stop where we are sitting. The aim is to focus our thinking on our immediate surroundings and feelings to the exclusion of everything else. It takes practice, but it is worth it.

It has therapeutic benefits too. Branstrom, Duncan and Moskowitz (2011) conducted a large-scale population study looking at the relationship between mindfulness and psychological functioning. They found that mindfulness was strongly related to well-being and people's own perceptions of being healthy. They also found that it seems to act as a buffer in dealing with stress, and recommended that mindfulness training should be offered to people who were experiencing stress, as a way of coping with it. This idea has been supported by many health organizations, and mindfulness is also recommended by the National Institute for Health and Care Exellence (NICE) as a way of preventing depression. As a result there are therapeutic approaches, such as mindful cognitive behaviour therapy (MCBT), which incorporate mindfulness training with other therapeutic techniques, and there are also a number of free online courses offered by various health organizations, which help people to learn how to incorporate a period of mindfulness as a regular part of their everyday lives.

We can see, then, that the psychological study of emotions can give us a great many insights into this aspect of our lives. Studying fear and anger raises interesting questions about how our experiences relate to the physical states that we are feeling. The psychological study of anxiety and stress has allowed us to identify a number of positive ways to cope with stress and other problems. More importantly, we have many more positive emotions than we sometimes realize, and these may be associated with quite small events as well as quite large ones. We can see from the research into positive psychology how happiness and other positive emotions represent a rich part of human experience, which we should recognize much more clearly than we sometimes do.

Focus points

Social factors mean that we often fail to notice positive emotions.

Long-term love is different from limerence, which is the obsessive form of romantic love.

The 'fight or flight' response is extreme arousal producing a short-term increase in energy through various bodily changes.

Emotions can be affected by social and cognitive factors, and the words we use to describe them may also affect how we deal with them.

The Yerkes–Dodson Law suggests that arousal can improve performance up to a point, but after that will hinder it.

Positive psychology is concerned with the pursuit of happiness and other positive emotions. Mindfulness can help people to reduce everyday stresses and anxieties.

Learned optimism is psychologically healthier than pessimism or learned helplessness.

5

Consciousness and the brain

In this chapter you will learn:

- ► *to identify biological rhythms that affect us psychologically*
- ► *about cycles of sleep, dreaming and wakefulness*
- ► *about the different effects that psychoactive drugs can have on the mind.*

In this chapter we will be looking at how our brains influence our experiences – and in particular, at how we experience different states of consciousness. Our brains are physical structures, consisting of a network of nerve fibres and connections. They work using a combination of electrical and chemical messages: brain chemicals (known as neurotransmitters) stimulate brain cells (known as neurones), to produce electrical impulses. Those impulses travel along the neurones, causing more neurotransmitters to be released and make contact with the next brain cells. This stimulates those brain cells to fire in their turn, and so messages are passed around.

This is all very well, but as millions of neurones make connections in our brains, they produce consciousness. Consciousness is something that we often take for granted: we are generally aware of being conscious; we worry if someone becomes unconscious and many people believe that it is consciousness that separates us from animals. But it is difficult to define. We know, for instance, that we have different states of consciousness. Sometimes we feel wide-awake and alert; sometimes we feel pensive and dreamy; sometimes we feel drowsy and tired; and sometimes our consciousness has been affected by drugs. These are all different states of consciousness, and that is what we are looking at in this chapter.

Biological rhythms

Our state of consciousness changes all the time. We may be in a good mood and then something happens which puts us in a bad one. We may feel sleepy, but then an alarming experience brings us fully alert. We may be relaxed, but the sight of someone we really want to talk to can rouse us to an unexpected level of energy. All of these are changes in consciousness. Sometimes, we change our state of consciousness deliberately by using a drug, such as alcohol or caffeine. We will be looking at how these work later in this chapter. But a lot of the time our state of consciousness changes simply because of biological rhythms.

There are many biological rhythms in nature: daily rhythms, lunar rhythms, seasonal rhythms. Plants and animals all respond to these: birds begin courtship rituals when the lengthening days signal that it is spring; some plants open up during the day and close at night, and so on. And human beings, too, respond to natural rhythms. Poets and dramatists have long commented on the way that spring often results in young people thinking of love and romance. I am not aware of any psychological evidence which would either prove or disprove that, but psychologists have shown that we respond, physically, to increasing day length.

Many people experience a form of depression during the long winter months, which clears up completely when spring and summer come. Seasonal affective disorder, as this kind of depression is called, has a great deal to do with a lack of natural daylight. After all, for many people who work indoors, in factories or offices, it is possible to pass several months in the winter only seeing natural daylight at weekends. It is dark when we go out to work or college, and dark again when we return home.

Special lamps which mimic daylight have been very successful in treating seasonal affective disorder. The person spends a period of each day exposing their face to the light produced by these lamps, and that stimulates hormones and neurotransmitters in the body and brain which help to reduce the depression.

But how can day length have such a strong effect? The answer lies in a small gland in the brain, known as the pineal gland. This gland is situated deep in the brain, in a place which is roughly behind the centre of the forehead. The ancient Greeks regarded it as the location of the soul and, in other religions too, this place often has a mystical significance. As far as psychology is concerned, we have recently become aware that the pineal gland changes its activity in direct response to day length. When our skin is exposed to light of the correct wavelengths, the pineal gland stimulates the body to produce chemicals which lift our moods and make us feel more energetic.

CIRCADIAN RHYTHMS

We have other rhythms which are connected with the 24-hour cycle of the day. These are known as circadian rhythms, and they actually influence a great deal of our day-to-day experience. Through the course of the 24-hour cycle, we experience a regular increase and decrease of activity in several physiological systems, including body temperature, blood pressure, pulse rate, blood sugar level and hormone levels. Our moods, alertness, concentration, skills and abilities also vary according to this cycle.

Remember this

We are more affected by biological rhythms than we realize. That's why so many motorway accidents happen in the early hours of the morning, even though there is very little traffic.

For example, between the hours of two and six in the morning, our blood sugar levels are low, our body temperature is low, and so is our blood pressure. If we are awake, we generally experience quite a subdued mood unless we are in very stimulating social surroundings. If we are trying to do a demanding task of some kind, we are much more likely to make mistakes. This isn't just from tiredness, because as soon as morning comes, we begin to feel better and more alert, and our performance improves. So between two and six o'clock in the morning isn't a good time to do complex tasks. On the other hand, the period between the hours of eleven in the morning and about three o'clock in the afternoon has been shown to be the best time for classroom learning. Before and after those hours, school pupils work best with individualized tasks, but classwork has been shown to be much better during those hours – as long as they fit with the prevailing culture, of course.

SIESTAS

As we progress through an ordinary day (not one where we have stayed up all night!) we find that there are certain 'low' points, where it is easy to become sleepy and to take a nap. Our biological rhythms are set to bring sleep twice a day: at night, of course, but also in the early afternoon. In hot climates, a siesta is usually an accepted cultural practice: everyone dozes or sleeps for a couple of hours in the middle of the day, and then wakes up to resume work once the hottest time is over. Even in colder climates, where a siesta is not the standard practice, many older people take a nap after lunch if they have the opportunity, while others find they are inclined to daydream at that time.

There are other changes which occur during the course of the day. For example, psychologists have shown that the time between about four and six in the evening is the best time for exercise – the body gains more benefit from exercise at that time than from the same amount of exercise at other times of the day. Many people experience a slight 'dip' around about 6 p.m., and then find that their energy levels gradually rise for the rest of the evening, until they drop again when it is time to go to bed. Figure 5.1 shows the highs and lows of body temperature rhythms during a 24-hour period, and psychological alertness often follows a similar cycle.

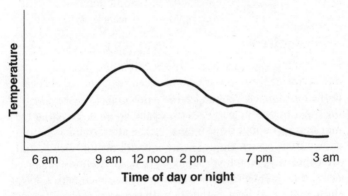

Figure 5.1 Body temperature throughout the 24-hour cycle.

What keeps these cycles going? They are partly habit, in the sense that our bodies do adapt to our usual practices. But they go deeper than that. Our bodies go through these rhythms even if we are in completely artificial situations, because these cycles have been part of us from infancy. But without external stimuli, they can drift: when psychologists asked people to live in a deep cave for a few months, they drifted into a 25-hour cycle. There are certain physical cues which help the body to keep them in time with the 24-hour clock. These cues are known as zeitgebers – external signals, like external activity or noise levels, which stimulate these rhythms. And natural daylight is the strongest zeitgeber of them all.

SHIFT WORK AND JET LAG

Sometimes, our body rhythms are disrupted so that we have to be alert at different times of the day or night. There are two common reasons for this: shift work and international travel. When we are doing shift work, we have to adjust our bodies to a different 24-hour rhythm, sleeping at different times of the day, and being awake at times when we would normally be asleep. When we are travelling across time zones, we also have to adjust to a different rhythm of activity.

Both cases produce the same type of problem, which we call jet lag when it is brought about by travel. Although people can adapt to working at odd times, in that they are not aware of being particularly stressed, human performance is always influenced by circadian rhythms. Nobody works as efficiently as they would do at their optimal times of day, and at its worst, it can produce irritability, poor performance at work, and poor decision-making.

There are some ways in which the damaging effects of shift work can be minimized. For example, it seems to be easier for people to move forwards in time, rather than backwards. So a shift-work cycle which progresses through the 24-hour period, with someone going from a night shift to an early one, then from an early shift to a late one, and then on to nights again, is much easier for people to adjust to than a shift cycle in which someone goes from an afternoon shift to an early morning one. It's a simple thing, but it can lead to a measurable decrease in industrial accidents or errors at work.

Remember this

Even people who think they are 'night owls' still have their most alert period during the day. But if you have been used to a siesta, it can be very difficult to stay alert in the afternoon.

In international travel, too, shifting the 24-hour system forwards (for example, by staying awake for a longer period than you might do normally) can be helpful in minimizing jet lag and becoming adapted to the new time. Without that, it can take anything up to ten days to get fully adapted to a new cycle. As a result, politicians or business people who need to make flying visits to countries on the other side of the world sometimes cope by sticking rigidly to their 'home' timetables for meals and sleeping, and fitting their meetings in between, rather than trying to make the transition to new times and then having to re-adjust a day or so later.

Sleep and dreaming

One of our main cycles of consciousness, of course, is our sleep–wake cycle. For many years, psychologists regarded sleeping as a time when nothing much happens, except for the occasional dream. But in the late 1930s, psychologists began to use electro-encephalograms (EEGs), which are measures of the electrical activity of the brain recorded by electrodes attached at various places on the scalp. When they recorded brain activity during sleeping, they found that the brain is extremely active while we are asleep, even though the body seems to be quiet.

During a normal night, we pass through several different phases of brain activity, which are shown in Figure 5.2. The lightest form of sleep, level 1, involves very rapid and irregular activity of the brain, with very low voltages. Level 2 sleep still shows rapid and irregular activity, but with greater changes in the voltage becoming apparent from the peaks and troughs on the chart. Also during this level of sleep, patterns known as spindles begin to appear, which are very rapid, changeable bursts of activity. By level 3, the frequency of the electrical activity has become a little slower, and the peaks and troughs (the amplitude) on the graphs are higher, meaning that the changes in voltage have become larger than they were in the first and second levels. This trend continues with level 4, which shows very large changes in voltage, and a much slower rate of change.

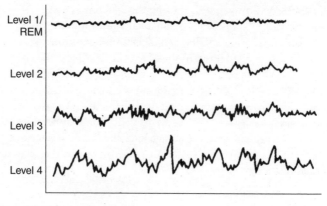

Figure 5.2 EEG traces during sleep.

These patterns of sleep, like so many other aspects of consciousness, happen in regular cycles through the night, as Figure 5.3 shows. A complete cycle, from level 1 to level 4 and back again, usually takes about an hour and a half. For the most part, too, these levels of sleep reflect how deeply asleep we feel. It is much harder to wake someone up from level 4 sleep than it is if they are in level 2. The exception to this, though, is level 1, which is a bit special because it's the part of our sleep when we dream.

Key idea

REM sleep is sometimes called paradoxical sleep, because our brain waves imply that we are only lightly asleep, yet we can be really hard to wake up, as if we were in a much deeper sleep state.

In level 1 sleep, our eyes are continually making very quick movements. For this reason, level 1 sleep is often called REM sleep, with REM being short for 'rapid eye movements'. If people are woken up from this sort of sleep, they report dreaming. We all dream four or five times during the course of an average night, although some people remember dreaming while others don't. That seems to depend on what point in our sleep cycle we are in when we wake up.

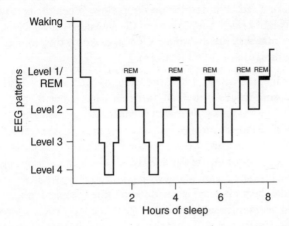

Figure 5.3 Cycles of sleep.

DREAMING

Although we seem to be 'switched off' while we are asleep and dreaming, we aren't totally unaware of our surroundings. Dement and Wolpert (1958) sprinkled people lightly with water while they were in REM sleep. Then, a little later, they woke them up and asked what they had been dreaming about. Some people had dreamed about being under waterfalls, some about swimming, and some about being out in the rain. Most of them dreamed about water in some way. In other words, they had managed to incorporate the outside stimulation of the water into their dreams.

In fact, we may have far more control over our dreams than we realize. Most of us have occasionally had dreams in which we knew we were dreaming, but the dream carried on anyway. These are known as lucid dreams. Recently, psychologists have discovered that it is possible to learn how to make a dream into a lucid dream, and then for the person having the dream to control what happens.

For this to work, people need to know when they have begun to dream. In psychological sleep-research laboratories, this is done by giving dreamers a pre-arranged signal. The signal won't be enough to wake them up, just enough for them to become aware that it is happening, like a tiny electrical tickle to the wrist, or a red light flashing on the eyelids. When the person begins REM sleep, they are given the signal, so they become aware that they are dreaming. Once they know this, they can make things happen in the dream.

According to Hearne (1981) the secret of controlling a lucid dream successfully is to make sure that what happens is believable – as far as the dream is concerned. For example, if you wanted to dream about a particular person, you couldn't just make them appear from nowhere. But you could dream that there was a door nearby, and that the person came in through it. Some people dream about flying, and so they would be able to make themselves fly, in the dream. Other people don't, so it would be impractical for them to try it in a lucid dream. Green and McCreery (1994) found that training in lucid dreams can be used therapeutically, for example, in counteracting nightmares.

Remember this

Many insomniacs actually do sleep for quite long periods during the night, but during that time, they dream that they are lying awake. So when the morning comes, they believe that they haven't slept at all.

▶ Functions of dreaming

But what is dreaming for? In the early days of psychology, psychoanalysts, led by Sigmund Freud, believed that dreams come from the unconscious mind telling us about our innermost secret wishes and desires. These are disguised by the brain, using symbols to stand for the real meaning. The books about dream interpretation that you sometimes see on railway and airport bookstalls are following this idea, but need to be taken with a pinch of salt. Most psychologists do not believe that dream symbolism is quite as extreme as Freud maintained, and people's experiences are so individual that it is doubtful whether the universal symbols which he claimed to have identified are as relevant in our diversified and fragmented modern world.

A few medical researchers believe that dreams come from random brain activity, which happens as nerve cells restore and reorganize themselves while we are asleep. The experience of the dream is simply imposed by our mind, as it tries to make sense of these haphazard bursts of nerve cell activity – in the same way that we can sometimes 'see' castles or animals in cloud shapes. According to this view, then, dreaming is just an accidental by-product of the physiological activity of the brain, and has no real significance.

The psychological evidence, though suggests that there is a psychological function to dreaming as well as a physiological one. Dreaming plays an important part in how we organize our psychological experience. Throughout each day, we are bombarded with a massive amount of sensory information and experiences. At some time, the mind needs to make sense of it all: to store information in its proper place so that it connects with similar things that we know; to identify patterns in our experiences, and to filter through things that have happened to us to identify particularly meaningful events. It does this while we are dreaming.

Key idea

Everyone dreams, even people who insist that they don't. We only remember our dreams if we wake up from them. If we wake up from another point in the sleep cycle, it feels as though we haven't been dreaming at all.

This explains, too, why sleeping on a problem is so often helpful. Before we go to bed, we may be perplexed, upset, or completely at a loss as to how to deal with something. But when we wake up, it often all seems clear. This is because we have been working on the problem unconsciously while we sleep. The brain activity which takes place while we dream has allowed us to knit loose ends together, and to put things, mentally, into their proper place. So when we wake up it is much easier to decide what to do.

Drugs and consciousness

As human beings, we don't just experience those different states of consciousness which are involved in passing through a regular day and night. We also deliberately change our consciousness by using drugs. Every human society uses some drugs to change people's state of awareness in some way. In our society, the main drugs are alcohol, nicotine and caffeine, while in Peru chewing coca leaves (which produce cocaine) is an everyday activity, and in some Middle Eastern countries smoking hasheesh or opium is legal while alcohol is banned. Drugs which influence our state of consciousness are known as psychoactive drugs.

CAFFEINE

Caffeine is a very common drug in Western society, but it is a very strong one. All psychoactive drugs affect the nervous system in some way, but they have different effects by influencing different parts of it. For example, in the last chapter we looked at the state of arousal, and the ways in which anger or similar emotions can affect how the body works. The drug caffeine, which we take in coffee, cola and energy boost drinks acts on the autonomic nervous system to produce a state of arousal in the body. It also acts on the reticular formation of the brain, as a stimulant. So it isn't surprising that it helps people to wake up in the morning! It also isn't surprising that, while a little caffeine may pep you up, too much of it can make you irritable and edgy.

Caffeine is also physically addictive, and many people who give it up find that they can experience unpleasant withdrawal symptoms, including blinding headaches, nausea and stomach upsets. This addiction comes as a surprise to many people, because caffeine is so readily accepted in society that people assume it must be innocuous. However, being addictive doesn't necessarily mean that it is damaging – most people live perfectly healthy lives with a daily dose of caffeine, with no problem that we can detect arising from that. The main problem with caffeine is that when people take it in large amounts, it can interfere with decision-making, because people are edgy and overreact to information and events; it can also add seriously to day-to-day stress. So reducing your caffeine intake is a very constructive thing to do if you are feeling under pressure.

Key idea

Caffeine is a much more powerful drug than many people realize. By stimulating the autonomic nervous system, it raises our state of arousal and strong doses can make us anxious and jittery. Many people find their sleep improves if they restrict their caffeine intake to mornings only.

ALCOHOL

Alcohol works in almost entirely the opposite way – as a sedative which calms down the autonomic nervous system and relaxes the muscles. In small doses, the influence of alcohol can often seem quite stimulating, because it relaxes the everyday tension that most of us feel and allows us to feel more at ease with other people. So we find it easy to talk and to join in with what is going on. It isn't really a stimulant drug, in a physical sense, but in small doses it can be a sociable drug.

In large quantities, the soporific effect of alcohol becomes much more apparent. People who are very drunk often slur their words, or even fall asleep under the influence, and it is a common observation that even though they are more likely to have accidents, they are less likely to hurt themselves if they fall over because their muscles are so much more relaxed. Heavy drinking is a serious social problem, though, partly because of the way that alcohol use reduces social inhibitions, with the result that people can become extremely aggressive and even violent. Most cases of domestic abuse are alcohol-related.

Other problems with alcohol come from its amnesiac effects. Alcohol can severely interfere with memory, which is why people often drink too much when they have problems. Once in a while that might not matter, but as a regular thing it can cause a lot of damage. That damage is made worse by not eating, because the toxins from the alcohol don't burn off in the same way. So people who drink heavily over a period of years and don't eat properly can lose their ability to store new memories altogether, which is much more serious. That condition is known as Korsakoff's syndrome and it can be very disturbing. Sacks (1985) described the case of a 60-year-old man with

Korsakoff's syndrome who could only remember his life up to his mid-20s. When he looked in a mirror he became extremely upset because he didn't recognize the old man he had become. Since he couldn't remember anything from day to day, his distress was just as strong every time.

The other psychological effect which alcohol has is to impair our ability to make a balanced judgement. People who have been drinking – even quite small amounts – make far more mistakes on physical co-ordination tasks than people who haven't. But, possibly because they feel relaxed by the drug, they usually shrug off these mistakes, or don't even notice them at all. This is why so many people believe that they can drive well even if they have been drinking. It's not that they really can, it's that they don't notice any of their mistakes, so they think they are driving safely when actually they are quite dangerous.

Key idea

Alcohol in moderation appears to be relatively harmless, and sometimes even beneficial. Problems arise when people don't drink in moderation – heavy drinking can cause serious damage, not only to health but also to families and relationships.

NICOTINE

Smoking is becoming less common in modern society, but it is still a common addiction. People who smoke believe that nicotine helps them to relax. But what it really does is to make their muscles more sluggish, so that they are harder to move. It also damps down the activity of the autonomic nervous system, so that they are less likely to become aroused. In the same way that alcohol can give us the illusion of being stimulated when the opposite is the case, so nicotine gives us the illusion of being relaxed when really we are just feeling more inert and inactive.

To understand how this happens, we need to take a look at how our nerve cells work. When we want to move – say, to lift an arm – the brain sends a small electrical message along our nerve cells (which are very long and stretched out) to the muscles. When the message reaches the end of the nerve cell, it causes a special chemical, called a neurotransmitter, to spill out of the ends of the nerve cell. The neurotransmitter spills out right by a special receptor site on the muscle, and the molecules of the neurotransmitter fit into the receptor site like a key fitting into a lock. That tells the muscle to contract, and if it happens with enough receptor sites, then the whole muscle will move, and the arm will be lifted.

What nicotine does is to nip into the receptor site and block out the real neurotransmitter. Nicotine molecules have nearly the same shape, so they can be picked up at the receptor site very easily. But they don't pass the message on, as the real chemical would have done. This means that only about half of the message from the brain actually gets through. The person can still lift their arm, but not as easily – it takes more effort. So they feel more sluggish, and interpret that as being relaxed.

This, of course, explains why people often feel fidgety when they are first giving up smoking. The brain has become so used to the nicotine that it sends really strong messages to produce each movement. But if there is no nicotine in the system, the whole message gets through and the muscles respond really easily, which can make people feel as if they have too much energy.

Because a similar thing happens in the autonomic nervous system, they also feel their emotions much more freely. People often comment on how they become more irritable when they have stopped smoking, and that is true. But what they often don't notice is that they also become happier, or more easily pleased. In fact, all of their emotions become more intense, not just the negative ones.

MORPHINE AND HEROIN
It is difficult to be quite so precise about the actions of some of the illegal drugs which people use to change their state of consciousness, mainly because, for obvious reasons, there has been less research into them. Nevertheless, we understand the effects of some of them fairly well. For example, we know that the highly addictive narcotic drugs such as heroin and

morphine work because they have a chemical structure which is very similar to the naturally occurring painkillers made by the body itself.

If you are doing something very demanding, it is possible to ignore injury or hurt while you are actually doing it – indeed, sometimes you might not even notice it at all. In both war and peacetime, there have been many instances of people who have been completely unaware of serious wounds or injuries while they struggled to save someone else's life. In a situation like that, the brain suppresses our own pain until the emergency is over. It does this by releasing special brain chemicals, called endorphins and enkephalins, which deaden feeling and sensation in the body.

Morphine and heroin both have very similar chemical structures. So they can slip into the receptor sites in the brain which are normally reserved for endorphins and enkephalins, producing similar results. People who take these drugs report that they make them feel euphoric, not quite in touch with reality, and good because there is no physical discomfort or fatigue. But the problem is, of course, that when the drug wears off it feels very unpleasant, and that means that it is extremely easy to become both physically and mentally addicted to these drugs. When that happens, the person loses contact with the other important values in their life, and concentrates only on the experience of the drug. What began as a pleasant 'high' becomes a psychological necessity. Also, because the person has become addicted to the drug, they also become habituated to it. That means that they need an increasing dose to get the same effect, and what used to be a 'high' is reduced to being just a relief from stress.

Endorphins and enkephalins are also released through vigorous exercise, so that is a much better way of getting the same sort of 'high' naturally, without the damaging effects. When people talk about 'feeling good' after a strenuous physical workout, they are talking about much the same effect that taking these illegal drugs produces, but they have managed to get it in a much safer and more natural way. And it doesn't have the unpleasant after-effects when it wears off, either.

Key idea

People who take morphine or heroin are really just trying to get the same high that they would get naturally from vigorous and sustained exercise. So go running instead – it's cheaper and won't turn you into a thief or burglar as you struggle to get the money for your next fix!

Both morphine and heroin are sometimes used medically because they are such powerful painkillers. This means that medical researchers have been able to investigate how they work in some detail. Marijuana, too, is increasingly recognized as having medical value, and in some countries, such as Canada, it is legal for medical use.

MARIJUANA

Marijuana, or cannabis, was widely used as a tranquillizer in the nineteenth century, and for over 2,000 years in the Far East. It acts as a mild depressant, damping down the actions of the autonomic nervous system and producing muscular relaxation. Perhaps because of this, some users report a sense of time passing very slowly, and an increased sensitivity to sensory stimulation such as music or art.

Recently, a great deal of debate has focused on the harmful effects of this drug. Many long-term users insist that limited use of the drug is effectively harmless, and there are no documented cases of people dying from an overdose. It has been associated with some heart problems, but that is generally considered to be an effect of the tobacco which it is often mixed with, rather than from the drug itself. It has been shown to be effective in relieving chronic pain, has been used to stimulate appetite in some anorexics, and also appears to help multiple sclerosis sufferers.

In temporary use, it can affect learning and the storage of new memories, although it doesn't do the same long-term damage as alcohol, and there is some evidence that long-term use may produce depression, partly as a result of the inertia which long-term use can generate. However, these are relatively mild outcomes. What complicates the issue, though, is that there are some extremely strong strains of the drug, cultivated over the decades while it has been illegal, which are almost hallucinogenic. These are believed to put vulnerable people at risk of severe depression and at times even psychotic problems such as schizophrenia.

Marijuana works chemically in the brain in a way which is similar to heroin and morphine, but it affects very different receptors. There are natural brain chemicals, such as anandamide, which have much the same effect in the brain as THC (tetrahydrocannabinol, the active ingredient of marijuana). We have specific receptors for anandamide in brain cells, and THC is taken up in the brain by fitting into those receptors. It does so very easily, and research suggests that its 'high' comes because it stimulates the receptors more than would happen naturally.

Most of the social debate about marijuana is about its illegality. Anti-legalization campaigners point to the harm done by the extreme forms of the drug, while legalization campaigners argue that if it were legal, different forms could be regulated and users would be better educated about which forms of the drug to use. They also argue that its illegality supports gang cultures and loses considerable tax revenues for the government. The debate has continued ever since the drug was first made illegal, and shows little sign of being resolved just at present.

Key idea

Legal drugs (caffeine, alcohol and nicotine) can be as damaging to people's lives as illegal ones. Many people argue that much of the harm caused by illegal drugs such as marijuana happens just because they are illegal, so their purity and dosage can't be properly controlled.

ECSTASY (MDMA)

We saw earlier how the brain chemicals known as neurotransmitters are used to pass information from one nerve cell to another or from a nerve cell to a muscle fibre. There are several different chemicals which act in this way, and some researchers have been able to trace 'pathways' of nerve cells in the brain which use a particular chemical. Some psychoactive drugs have their effects by acting directly on these pathways, and one of these is the drug MDMA, which is also known as ecstasy or just 'E'.

MDMA (which is short for 3, 4 methlyenedioxymethamphetamine) is a prosocial drug. In other words, it makes people feel social and pleasant towards one another, as opposed to aggressive and irritable. It also enhances awareness of music and colour. MDMA was first discovered in 1914, and was used in marriage guidance counselling, to ease the tensions between people so that they could talk over their problems more effectively. In the 1970s, however, it became popular as a recreational drug, and has now been made illegal.

MDMA appears to work by acting directly on a particular neurotransmitter pathway in the brain. This pathway involves nerve cells which use the chemical serotonin. Normally, when a neurotransmitter chemical is spilled out by the nerve cell, it only remains around for a few seconds, because it is then recycled by the cell that it came from. But MDMA prevents this recycling, so the spilled serotonin stays where it is, and continues to work on the next nerve cell. It does this all through the serotonin pathways of the brain, and this seems to be what produces such a strong effect on the person's moods.

There is little evidence that MDMA use in itself is physically or mentally damaging, although as with all drugs, long-term heavy use can cause some damage to the brain. As a prosocial drug it doesn't produce the problems of aggression associated with alcohol or amphetamine use, but using it unwisely can put people at risk from physical harm. Dehydration, for example is a real problem, and is made worse by combining the drug with alcohol – partly because alcohol also dehydrates the body, and partly because the use of MDMA can lower the user's awareness of how much alcohol they have been drinking. The deaths that have resulted from MDMA have originated from this problem.

AMPHETAMINES

The stimulant drugs known as amphetamines or 'speed' also sometimes appear to have a prosocial effect, at least in small doses, but they are much more dangerous than MDMA. People taking light doses sometimes find that they can talk to others more easily, and seem to be in a better mood – although often they may feel slightly edgy or tense. Amphetamines were widely used during the Second World War as a way of maintaining concentration. But in large or regular doses, amphetamines can lead to severe mental illness – a disorder which is known as amphetamine psychosis. This involves a distortion of reality, with the person becoming extremely paranoid and disturbed. Since amphetamines are also highly addictive drugs, it is all too easy for people who enjoy the effects which they have in small doses to slip into taking larger and larger amounts, often with tragic results.

Where MDMA increases the level of the neurotransmitter serotonin in the brain, amphetamines work by increasing the level of two other brain chemicals, known as dopamine and noradrenaline. We know that the dopamine pathways in the brain are associated with willpower, or motivation. Parkinson's disease comes from a shortage of dopamine in the brain, and it leaves people unable to make deliberate actions. Noradrenaline is associated with active and aroused states of the body, such as anger.

Combining these two chemicals seems to produce amphetamine's effects. In the short term, it increases motivation and arousal, so people find it easy to be sociable even if they are tired. But in the long term, and in high doses, it makes people more likely to become agitated and suspicious. This is made worse, too, by the fact that amphetamines act as appetite suppressants, so people who take them frequently usually suffer physical debilitation as a result.

LSD
Another well-known psychoactive drug is known as LSD, or sometimes just 'acid'. LSD, which is short for lysergic acid diethylamide, is a hallucinogen, and taking it gives people some very unusual psychological effects. It can produce distortions of reality, so that sounds and colours become extremely exaggerated. People who take it can also experience hallucinations, seeing things which are not actually there.

Sometimes, these experiences can become extremely disturbing, and possibly cause long-term psychological distress. Leary (1965), in research conducted while the drug was still legal, stressed that LSD should not be taken casually, but only when what he called 'set and setting' were right. Set refers to the person's mental state, since fears or anxieties can produce disturbing effects; setting refers to the physical situation, which needs to be relaxed and friendly, since being in a strange or threatening place can also bring about disturbing experiences.

Like MDMA, LSD involves the serotonin pathways of the brain, but it doesn't work in the same way. The molecules of LSD are a very similar shape to the molecules of serotonin, so they can fit into serotonin receptor sites. They produce their effects by mimicking the effect of the drug, but the chemical isn't identical. So where the normal effects of serotonin seem to be to produce a sociable, highly aware mood, the effects of LSD in serotonin receptors seems to be to produce a kind of hyper-awareness, which can easily turn into hallucination.

COCAINE

Cocaine has been used medically for a long time, because of its ability to numb physical sensations. Even before it was identified by Western medical professionals, it was used for this purpose by the people of the high Andes, in South America, who still chew coca leaves to help their bodies to cope with the rarefied atmosphere and other problems of living at such heights.

It has also been used recreationally. Cocaine was a popular recreational drug during the Victorian era, for some users producing an effect of relaxation and happiness. It does this because it prevents the neurotransmitters normally associated with positive and pleasant sensations from being reabsorbed after they have been released. As a result, they build up in the brain, and its reward pathways become over-stimulated. Because of the way it works, it is highly addictive: people can become dependent on it very quickly. And chronic use of cocaine has been linked with strokes, heart attacks, and infections of the blood. There are extra complications because it is an illegal drug, and those who sell it often mix it with other powders which can produce damaging effects.

In the last part of the twentieth century, a new version of cocaine appeared on the illegal market, which was known as crack cocaine. Crack has been chemically adjusted so that it can be smoked. This produces an immediate feeling of euphoria because it rapidly increases levels of one particular neurotransmitter, dopamine, in the brain. But it only does so for a few minutes: after that, the brain's dopamine levels reduce sharply, leaving the person feeling down and depressed. As a result, the person craves another 'hit' of the drug, and they can quickly become addicted.

Crack cocaine carries all of the harmful health risks of conventional cocaine, but because the crack sold on the streets is usually mixed with other drugs, like amphetamines and caffeine (which makes it much cheaper), it stimulates aggressive and paranoid sensations in ways which are not characteristic of ordinary cocaine. As a result, it has become associated with high levels of violent crime as well as with personal damage to its users.

This discussion of how drugs work may have been a little bit technical at times, but it shows us how closely consciousness and the chemicals in the brain are linked. We can change the chemical balance in the brain, and we do, each time we have an alcoholic drink or a cup of coffee – or even a glass of milk, which contains mild, naturally occurring morphine-like substances (which is why it can help us to feel calmer). Both natural and synthetic drugs can change our moods, our state of awareness, and our perceptions of reality.

Key idea

The long-term heavy use of any psychoactive drug will inevitably produce dependency, damage memory, and harm our general well-being. The body's normal repair mechanisms can't work properly when they are continually being interfered with.

ADDICTION

I have mentioned addiction several times during this discussion. We use the word addiction quite generally, but in medical terms it has a very specific meaning, which is that the body has become so used to the drug that it doesn't function properly without it. This is very common with some drugs, such as heroin, and it means that people who are trying to withdraw from it experience very unpleasant physical withdrawal symptoms as the body learns to cope.

For the most part, though, when we talk about addiction we really mean dependence. There are two aspects to dependence. Physical dependence is when the person has become so used to the drug that they need to use more and more of it to get the same effect. Psychological dependence is when the person has become so used to adjusting their consciousness by means of the drug that they find it unnerving and difficult to cope without it. Both are powerful mechanisms: psychological dependence is just as influential in how people tackle a drug problem as physical dependence.

Recovery from addiction is not a simple process. It is often described as a spiral, because people seem to go in circles but actually get a little bit further each time. Someone trying to get over a powerful addiction will begin by preparing mentally – making up their mind to try it, and will then give it a go. Sometimes, this is successful; at other times, they lapse back into their former addiction. But the experience of trying once makes them more familiar with the process, and the next time they try they can often manage for longer without the drug. These cycles carry on, until eventually the person is able to give it up altogether. So while it looks to family members or outsiders as if they haven't managed anything, addicts themselves may have come quite a long way in challenging their problem.

Some forms of addiction or dependence may not be particularly harmful. But others are extremely damaging, and can harm both the person using the drug and the society that they are living in. The question of illegality is important, because being on the wrong side of the law can lead people into real social problems – for instance, through contact with gang cultures. The other question is whether taking the drug interferes with that person's ability to live a happy and healthy life. As we saw at the beginning of this section, every human society has adjusted consciousness by use of drugs in some way: what matters is that how it happens is sustainable and not damaging.

Consciousness, then, is not always constant. It can be influenced in different ways, and it varies through the day or while we are sleeping. Understanding how consciousness is constantly changing and what affects it can help us to help ourselves – for example, by doing the most intensive work when we are best suited for it; or using legal drugs such as caffeine or alcohol in ways that will help to optimize our lives rather than damage them.

Focus points

Human beings, like other animals, experience biological rhythms. Seasonal Affective Disorder comes from lack of natural daylight in winter, and can be treated with special lamps.

Circadian rhythms are 24-hour cycles which affect energy and alertness in the body; shift work or long-haul travel produce jet lag and can increase accidents.

Dreaming helps us to sort out the information we receive when awake. We cycle through different levels of sleep during the night.

In addition to illegal drugs such as heroin and marijuana, there are common legal drugs which alter consciousness such as caffeine, alcohol and nicotine.

Most psychoactive drugs work by changing the normal balance of neurotransmitters in the brain.

Addiction is the physiological condition where the body cannot function without a particular drug; drug dependency may be physical or psychological.

6

Motivation

In this chapter you will learn:

- ▶ *to identify at least two ways in which human beings can be motivated*
- ▶ *three examples of 'defence mechanisms'*
- ▶ *how social motivation can help reduce racism.*

In this chapter, we will be looking at motivation – why we do what we do, and why we bother to do anything at all. If we want to understand human beings, we need to look at what makes people 'tick' – what moves us to act, or at least to action. And, as with every other aspect of psychology, there isn't a single simple answer to this question. Human motives are complex, ranging from simple physiological ones to complex issues of social respect and identity. We always have more than one reason for doing things, and it is worth trying to sort out the different kinds of motives which contribute to our actions.

Key idea

Motivation is so multi-faceted that it is almost impossible to document all of the factors involved in why people do even quite simple things. How many reasons can you think of for reading this book right now?

Physical and behavioural motives

Sometimes what we do is motivated by very basic needs: if you go to the kitchen and fetch a glass of water, it's a fair bet that you do it because you are thirsty. The level of fluid in your body has dropped below its ideal level, and this sets off a complex range of physiological mechanisms in the body. Messages about your fluid level are passed from your body to a particular part of the brain, known as the hypothalamus. This sends messages to the cerebral cortex, which is the part of the brain that you think with, so you realize that you feel thirsty and go to get a drink of water. Your physical state has triggered off behaviour which will lead you to be able to change that state.

HOMEOSTASIS

Psychologists investigating such physiological motives have found that these mechanisms are all concerned with getting the right balance in the body. As long as everything is at the right kind of level, we don't feel the motivation. But if something becomes imbalanced, for instance, if our blood sugar level gets too low or if we don't have a high enough level of fluid in the body, then we take action to put it right. This is known as maintaining homeostasis – maintaining the appropriate balance in the body so that we can function well, physically.

Of course, maintaining homeostasis also means that the brain has to have some idea of what the appropriate balance is, so that it can be maintained. Psychologists researching into hunger have found that the body has a kind of set weight, which it seems to try to maintain. In studies with animals, they found that the animals would eat until they had consumed enough food to reach their set weight, and then stop eating. Even if they were put on a restricted diet for a while, so they lost weight, as soon as the restrictions were off they would eat enough to return to the set weight.

It seems likely that human beings, too, have this kind of body mechanism, which might explain why so many people have problems with dieting. They are trying to achieve a weight that is lower than the physiological set weight which their body functioning is based on. So even if they diet and get their weight down for a short while, they find it very difficult to maintain that weight.

Physiological motivation, though, doesn't really have all that much to do with how we act in other ways. Even eating and drinking, in human beings, are affected by other kinds of motives: dieting, for instance, has as much to do with social approval as it does with physiological needs, and people often drink to be sociable rather than because they are actually thirsty. So we need to look at other levels of explanation as well, if we are really to understand human motivation.

BEHAVIOURAL MOTIVES

Sometimes, what we do comes about as much because of habit as anything else. Habits are behaviours or feelings that are associated with particular settings or situations. We learn how to act in certain places, or with certain people, and these come back to us if we find ourselves in that situation again. At such times, we can surprise ourselves with how we react.

It is interesting, for example, how powerfully an examination room can affect us, even if we are not actually taking the exam. Exam rooms are something we usually only encounter at school, and under quite tense conditions. People are usually worried and anxious when they go into an exam room to take an exam. Because we don't usually have anything to do with exam rooms at other times, those feelings of worry and anxiety often come flooding back if we go into one – even years later. So we act nervously, and not like our usual selves at all.

What has happened here is that the behaviours and feelings associated with a particular situation have been brought back, simply by being in that situation again. You might habitually buy a certain brand of trainers, simply because that is the kind you have bought in the past, in that particular shop. Sometimes we do this even though we meant to try something else, purely because the association of that particular action with that particular situation is so strong.

The same thing can happen, too, with interpersonal relationships. For example, if you meet someone that you haven't seen for a while, you can find yourself slipping back into ways of behaving with them that aren't typical of the way that you behave with other people. As a child, I used to argue continually and very vehemently with my cousin and, even now, when I am with my cousin we tend to do the same thing – though I don't argue in that way with anyone else. Being with that person brings back old habits, and it is sometimes hard to break out of them.

Habits can be broken, though – we're not stuck with them forever. For instance, teachers who invigilate exams as part of their job don't feel anxious when they go into these rooms – at least not once they have had a couple of years' experience. You can deliberately decide to try a new brand of trainers, and remember to choose them when you are in the shop. And even my cousin and I are gradually learning to communicate more reasonably with one another! Breaking a habit involves replacing the actions or feelings which are triggered off by that situation, with some other actions or feelings. It is hard at first, but the more often you succeed, the weaker the original habit becomes. We will be looking at this more closely when we look at association learning, in Chapter 8.

Key idea

We don't find it hard to change our habits when our situations change. So a good start for getting rid of a bad habit is identifying the particular situations which trigger it off, and changing them. If there are lots of those situations, change them one at a time.

Cognitive motives

The way that we think is another thing that sometimes motivates us into action. Cognitive motives are motives which come from our thoughts, beliefs and ideas. They are about how we understand what is happening to us. How we understand a situation can make all the difference to what we decide to do about it.

PERSONAL CONSTRUCTS

Each of us has had our own personal experiences, and we have learned from them. In particular, we have learned about other people. We have formed our own personal theories about what other people are like from the way that people have interacted with us in the past. These theories are called personal constructs and we use them when we meet new people.

Personal constructs take the form of a two-ended classification, such as 'kind – cruel' or 'hot-tempered – calm', or 'interesting – dull'. Table 6.1 gives an interesting exercise which you might like to try out. If you do it, it will help you discover some of your own main constructs. As a general rule, we tend to use about eight or ten main personal constructs most often, but we have several less important ones as well. Whenever we meet someone new, we weigh them up on the basis of our own personal construct system. Then we use those judgements to decide whether we like them or not.

All this is a bit like saying that our decisions about whether we like new people or not depend on whether they remind us of someone else that we once knew. And that's true, to some extent. But the new person doesn't have to be exactly like the person that we knew before – they just may have one or two qualities in common, which we can recognize as being similar. Using personal constructs, we can see how people vary, and compare their similarities and differences.

Table 6.1 Exploring personal constructs.

This is an exercise which you can do to find out the main personal constructs that you use. Begin by naming eight people who are important in your life:

A...   E...

B...   F...

C...   G...

D...   H...

Then think about these people in groups of three at a time. You will be able to think of a way that two of them are similar, and different from the other one. Write these down in the form given below:

(A, B, C) .... and .... are ...., but .... is ....

(D, E, F) .... and .... are ...., but .... is ....

(A, F, G) .... and .... are ...., but .... is ....

(B, D, H) .... and .... are ...., but .... is ....

(C, E, G) .... and .... are ...., but .... is ....

(H, B, F) .... and .... are ...., but .... is ....

(A, E, H) .... and .... are ...., but .... is ....

(D, G, C) .... and .... are ...., but .... is ....

The words you have used to describe the similarities and differences indicate the personal constructs that you habitually use. Try comparing your results with those of a friend.

▶ Individual explanations

Since each of us has led a different life, our experiences of other people have varied, and our personal constructs are also unique. They represent our own distinctive way of looking at the world, and that can be entirely different from someone else's. Two people could meet a third person for the first time and come to very different conclusions, even though they were together and had the same objective experience. One, for example, might see the new person as being friendly and outgoing, whereas the other might see them as ingratiating and manipulative. Just because we are in the same situation doesn't mean that we see things the same way.

And that, of course, can motivate our behaviour. If we see someone as manipulative and ingratiating, we behave very differently towards them than we would if we saw them as friendly and outgoing. If we used the first type of personal construct, we would be likely to avoid them, and be suspicious of any approach that they made towards us. If we used the second, we would be likely to be welcoming and to treat them as a friend.

▶ Social expectations

That sort of thing can become circular, of course. As we saw in Chapter 2, the expectations other people have of us can influence our behaviour quite a lot. They can even become self-fulfilling prophecies, so that we live up to what people expect of us. If you have a set of personal constructs which mean that you treat new people as if they were not really friendly but had some ulterior motive for pretending to be so, then they will react to how you are behaving towards them, and avoid you. You would take that as 'proof' that they weren't really being friendly, not realizing that it was your own behaviour which had produced that effect.

A self-fulfilling set of personal constructs such as this can easily mean that someone becomes very isolated from other people, and deeply unhappy. It is good to be cautious, of course, but it is not good to suspect everyone you meet, automatically. Many psychologists use personal construct theory to help people whose belief systems have become stuck like this. They use techniques that will help people to develop a new set of personal constructs, which will be more helpful to them in the long run.

DEFENCE MECHANISMS

There are other ways, too, that our minds can motivate us. Many psychologists are deeply sceptical about the ideas of Sigmund Freud, the psychoanalyst who developed a theory about the unconscious mind during the last century. But Freud did identify some important mental processes which the mind uses to protect itself against threats. These are called defence mechanisms. Other psychologists have found the idea of defence mechanisms useful, even when they don't share Freud's other views about other aspects of the workings of the human mind.

▶ Denial

Defence mechanisms are unconscious, but they can be very powerful. They are all to do with how we protect our own self-image. For example, if we are faced with an awkward or uncomfortable fact about ourselves, our first impulse may be simply to deny that it is true. Sometimes, we will be able to get beyond that first impulse and see that the idea does, perhaps, have some justification. At other times, though, the implications of the idea may be too much for us to cope with. So we stick to our denial, even though it may be quite irrational, simply because we are protecting ourselves from having to rethink all our beliefs and ideas. In this situation, denial is acting as a defence mechanism, protecting us from a threat to how we see ourselves.

▶ Repression

There are other kinds of defence mechanisms, too. One of them is repression. We often repress memories which are personally distressing, or which would seriously challenge our beliefs about ourselves. When a memory is repressed, we forget it – but it is different from normal forgetting because we become very agitated or upset if something comes close to reminding us of it again. The mind has repressed that particular memory or knowledge because it is too emotionally demanding to cope with.

▶ Reaction-formation

Sometimes, something can be repressed so hard that it turns into its opposite. For example, if someone has a very strong desire or need which they feel is wrong and needs to be suppressed, they may try very hard never to let it come to their awareness (remember that a defence mechanism is unconscious – we don't know we are doing it unless someone else intervenes and shows us what is happening). Because their unconscious mind is trying so hard, they become very hostile to any hint of that particular desire or need in other people, and react aggressively to it. This is known as a reaction-formation.

The classic example of a reaction-formation, of course, is homophobia. Most people, whether they are homosexual or heterosexual, are unaffected by other people's sexual choices. But some people become very upset and agitated when they encounter any mention of homosexuality. These people can end up reacting quite irrationally – and sometimes very aggressively – towards homosexuals. We refer to these people as homophobic. Their homophobia often comes from their own unconscious homosexual desires, which have been repressed so hard that they have become a reaction-formation.

SELF-EFFICACY AND LEARNED HELPLESSNESS

Another way that our cognitions can motivate us to action has to do with our self-efficacy beliefs. These are our beliefs about how effective we are at doing things – how capable, or how skilled, we are. They are very important, because they affect how hard we try. Bandura (1989) showed how it is generally a good thing if people have high self-efficacy beliefs because it makes them more self-confident, and more likely to succeed. It's even a good thing to have higher self-efficacy beliefs than the evidence would really warrant – in other words, to believe that you are better at things than you actually are – because that way, you will take on more challenges and improve your abilities as you deal with them!

In one study which Bandura described, a psychologist looked at how having high or low self-efficacy beliefs affected children's work in school. The children in the study had different abilities: some were good at maths while others weren't very good at it, but they also had different self-efficacy beliefs. Some of the children believed that they would be able to do it if they made an effort, while others believed that they wouldn't be successful no matter how much they tried.

The psychologist found that the children with high self-efficacy beliefs did much better than the other children, regardless of their level of ability. In other words, even if they really weren't very good at maths, children with high self-efficacy beliefs did better. They solved more maths problems in the time that they were given, they spotted where they had gone wrong more quickly, and they were more prepared to go over problems which they had got wrong. The children with low self-efficacy beliefs, on the other hand, would make a single try at the maths problems, and then give up.

Key idea

Believing in your own capabilities is an important part of positive thinking. It's actually better to overestimate your abilities than to underestimate them, because that means you will try harder, and so will be more likely to succeed.

It's not hard to see why having high self-efficacy beliefs helps you to do well. Obviously, if you are prepared to put effort into learning, and to keep trying and learning from your mistakes, then you will eventually get somewhere – even if you are working at something that doesn't come easily to you. Many psychologists nowadays believe that bringing up children (and training adults) to believe in their own ability to take effective action is one of the most important things of all.

▶ Learned helplessness

There's another side to this, as well. Some people go through a series of demoralizing or unpleasant experiences, which they can't do anything about, and then they just give up trying altogether. So when they are in a situation which they could actually change if they made an effort, they don't bother. This is known as learned helplessness – they have learned to be passive and helpless, rather than trying to influence what happens to them (see Chapter 4).

Learned helplessness has a lot to do with why people suffer from depression. When people are living for a long time in demoralizing situations which they can't do much about, they often slip into a 'victim mentality' which encourages them to feel helpless and passive. They develop an attributional style, or a way of thinking, which suggests that things happen because of global, large-scale reasons which are always likely to be there, and can't be controlled. So whenever they encounter a new problem, they see it in this way and don't realize when it is actually something they could do something about.

Key idea

The problem with learned helplessness is that it stops us from recognizing when we really can make a difference. We become discouraged, and think it's not worth trying any more. But circumstances are always changing, and taking action may make a lot of difference at a different time.

It is important for us to feel that we have some control over what happens to us. To feel that you are helpless is very stressful, which just makes things worse. So one way that psychologists try to help these people is to set up situations which will help them to raise their self-efficacy beliefs, such as encouraging them to tackle an entirely new activity, or to trying a different approach in dealing with a problem. By doing this competently, the person comes to realize that they can be effective – that they can actually do something about their situation.

We can see, then, that self-efficacy beliefs are closely linked to the idea of locus of control. This is all about whether you believe that you can control what happens to you (an internal locus of control) or whether you see the things that happen as being nothing you can influence (an external locus of control). We will be looking at this again in Chapter 14, but essentially, it is all about seeing yourself as an active agent in your own life – someone who can be at least partly in control of what happens, and who can take effective action when it is necessary. If we want to understand human motivation, we need to understand how these beliefs affect us, because they can make all the difference to whether someone takes action and tries to influence what is happening to them, or not.

Social motivation

What we do is motivated by social influences as well as cognitive ones. We are surrounded by other people, and how they see us can be a powerful influence on whether we do something or not.

We are also influenced by shared social understandings and, as we have already seen, by the expectations which people have of us. So a great deal of our motivation is social in its origins.

SOCIAL RESPECT

One of the most important social motives of all is for respect from other people. We all feel a deep need to avoid looking foolish, and sometimes, if we feel that we have made ourselves look stupid in front of the wrong people, even the memory of it can continue to embarrass us for a long time.

Harré (1979) identified the need for social respect as a fundamental social motive. A great deal of what we do, Harré argued, is aimed to ensure that people will take us seriously, or will at least notice us, and acknowledge us as worthwhile people. We hate it if other people just dismiss us or, worse still, ignore our existence. Rogelberg *et al.* (2013) showed that being late for things is seen by many as a sign of disrespect. They looked at how people felt when someone was late for a meeting, and showed that it was seen as acceptable if the person had a valid excuse, such as snowfall or traffic. Without it, though, the people waiting saw it as a message that their own time or personal concerns were unimportant and disrespected by the latecomer.

We can see how deeply rooted the need for respect is by looking at children in a playground, when there is an adult present. Most of the children will be clamouring for attention in some way, looking to 'show off' something that they can do. Although this is often dismissed as attention seeking, it is really a way of looking for social respect. A child who has learned to stand on her hands, or to do a long jump, wants an adult to acknowledge that skill and to say 'well done'. Quite rightly, children want to be noticed for their achievements.

Key idea

The way that we hate to look stupid in front of other people – and the lengths we will go to avoid it – shows just how important social respect is as a motivator for human beings.

Adults need that kind of acknowledgement too. Most of us work better if our efforts are recognized by other people – especially on those occasions when we have made a special effort. We like to know that we have been noticed. In fact, being ignored is one of the worst things that can happen to us – we feel it as a deep social insult – and we can go to great lengths to get over it by proving that those people are less important than we are, or by making sure that they are forced to acknowledge us on a future occasion. This need for social respect is quite often the motivation underpinning human ambition and achievement – although not always.

▶ Unconditional respect for persons

Lalljee (2009) argued that recognizing other people's integrity as autonomous human beings is fundamental to positive social interaction. People can vary in how much they show what Lalljee and his colleagues called 'unconditional respect for persons', but it is a strong factor in intergroup relations. In a series of studies, Lalljee showed that people who scored highly on measures of unconditional social respect also tended to promote positive action towards other social groups. They were able to avoid over-reacting when faced with sudden events such as terrorist actions or social displacement, and so act in ways which were more likely to lead to resolution of conflicts. So respect has strong political as well as social and psychological implications.

The need for social respect can work in our own minds, as well. Because we are aware of how our behaviour is likely to come across to other people, we need to make sure that our own behaviour appears reasonable, even to ourselves. One consequence of this is that we don't like to appear inconsistent. Yet each of us acts differently when we are with different people, so sometimes we can get into difficulties when we are trying to balance the two.

The musical *Grease*, for instance, was based entirely around this problem. A young couple meet during the holidays, as individuals, and fall in love, but when they meet again at school, the boy is with his friends and feels he has to appear casual and uncaring, which hurts the girl. Even though he is still in love with the girl, to show it would be inconsistent with his public image, and might lose him social respect. It is the way the two of them resolve this dilemma which forms the plot of the musical.

COGNITIVE DISSONANCE

Sometimes we resolve dilemmas of this kind by changing our attitudes or beliefs. In a famous study conducted in 1956, Festinger, Riecken and Schachter joined in with a religious cult who believed that their city – and the rest of the world – was about to be destroyed by a great flood. On a special day, the cult members sold all their possessions and spent the night praying, on a hill outside of the city. Festinger, Riecken and Schachter were there too. They interviewed the cult members and found that they believed that the flood would happen, and only they would be saved.

The psychologists wanted to know what the cult members would say when the world didn't come to an end at the appointed time. So the next day, when no flood had materialized, they interviewed as many cult members as they could. Interestingly, they found that the cult members had adapted their beliefs, so that they didn't have to face up to the fact that their actions had been a waste of time. They now believed that it was the fact that they had spent the night praying which had actually saved the world. The flood would have come as scheduled, but God had listened to them and repented at the last minute. So instead of feeling stupid about what they had done, they believed that their actions had made everything all right.

Festinger, Riecken and Schachter interpreted this in terms of what they called cognitive dissonance. We all like to believe that we are consistent, and not irrational. So if things happen which could make us appear irrational, we change our beliefs to make it seem as if we were simply doing the right thing after all. Festinger believed that cognitive dissonance is one of the main reasons why people change their beliefs: we don't like to seem foolish to anyone, not even ourselves.

Key idea

We often mislead ourselves in everyday things as well as in unusual situations, because we don't want to experience the cognitive dissonance that will come from acknowledging that we have been wrong.

Festinger gave some less dramatic examples of cognitive dissonance, as well. In one study, people were asked to do an extremely boring task for a long time. Then they were asked to go out and tell someone who was waiting outside that the task was interesting. They were paid either $1 or $20 for doing this. At the end of the study, the psychologists asked the research participants to describe how interesting the task had really been. They found that the people who had been paid $20 to do the experiment said what they expected – that the task was really boring. However, the people who had been paid only $1 said that, actually, they had found it moderately interesting.

Nobody in their right mind could really have found the task interesting. Part of it involved giving each of 48 pegs in a pegboard a quarter-turn, one after the other, for half an hour! But what seemed to have happened was that the research participants needed to justify why they had lied to the person in the waiting room. It was OK for those who had been paid $20, because they could say they did it for the money. But being paid only $1 wasn't enough, so they needed a better reason for their lying. As a result, they convinced themselves that the task hadn't really been all that bad.

Cognitive dissonance is a much more powerful motivator of human behaviour than we realize. In some ways, it is another aspect of our need for respect, in that we need to avoid looking silly, even to ourselves. So avoiding cognitive dissonance, and seeming to be consistent in our beliefs and actions is an important motivator which can lead people to cling on to unrealistic beliefs or behaviours even when they are actually quite damaging.

AGGRESSION AND SCAPEGOATING

Sometimes, one of the ways that we avoid cognitive dissonance is by blaming other people for what happens to us. This is known as scapegoating, and is a significant mechanism which underlies social aggression such as racism. Scapegoating seems to be a mechanism which can bring out the very worst in human nature. As things get difficult people become frustrated and angry, and take that anger out on the nearest clearly identifiable target.

▶ Racism and economic recession

It is noticeable, for example, that violent racist incidents increase when the economy is in recession. Recent events in Europe are an example of this, as was the massive increase of racism in Germany and elsewhere during the 1930s' depression – an increase which made the concentration camps possible. In the United States, too, Hovland and Sears (1940) showed that the number of lynchings of black people in the Southern States was closely linked to the price of cotton. The lower the price, the higher the number of lynchings.

The key to understanding this side of human nature lies in looking at where all that aggression comes from. For the most part, people tend to live co-operatively with one another. As we saw in Chapter 3, our first social impulse is to go along with other people, not to confront them aggressively. But sometimes, human beings show that they are capable of brutal inhumanity towards one another. How does that happen?

▶ Frustration and aggression

There have been a number of studies showing how aggressive behaviour in human beings is particularly likely when we feel frustrated or helpless. This idea was first put forward by Dollard and others in 1939, although at the time they phrased it in a rather limited way. They suggested that people would always react aggressively if they were frustrated in achieving their personal goals. Nowadays, we recognize that people react differently – not everyone becomes aggressive in such situations. However, for the most part, being prevented from doing something that we feel we should be able to do (even if it is only getting on with our own lives in peace) is something which makes us very tense. And some people express that tension in aggression and violent action. Some people have argued that this can also be an explanation for road rage, although psychological research tends to suggest that it has more to do with a combination of aggressive personality traits, stress, and the mental rehearsal of irritation.

There does seem to be some relevance, though, when it comes to social groups. But why should that tension become displaced onto ethnic minorities? The reason for this lies in two other important motivators for human behaviour. As we saw earlier, it is stressful for a human being to feel that they are helpless. Yet economic recessions are something that few of us can do anything about: we all feel helpless as we hear about jobs disappearing and companies collapsing. Even when we are personally threatened by these situations, there is little that we can do. So a social belief that a particular group is causing the problems means that the frustration and anger people feel in those situations becomes, wrongly and unfairly, channelled towards that group.

SOCIAL REPRESENTATIONS

One very striking characteristic of human beings is that we look for – and sometimes even make up – explanations for what is happening to us. Some people seek those explanations in ideas such as luck, or mystical concepts like astrology, while some look for them, as we are doing here, by turning to the human sciences, looking at the social beliefs and explanations which are shared by the people around them. These explanations are known as social representations, and they are an important key to understanding how economic frustration becomes displaced onto the people who are usually suffering from it the most.

Social representations, as we saw in Chapter 2, are shared beliefs which are held by groups of people in society. Each of us adopts our own set of social representations, through talking with other people, picking ideas up from the mass media, and fitting these into our own personal construct system. They give us ways of explaining what is happening in our everyday experience. In some ways, they are a bit like the personal constructs which we looked at earlier in this chapter, but social representations are shared by other people too.

Key idea

When people encounter difficulties, they look for explanations for them, and this is where social representations can become very powerful. Even if they don't really make sense, people tend to accept the explanations that 'everyone' believes.

Among racists, a common social representation is the idea that they are somehow in competition with members of ethnic minorities for the benefits of society, like jobs or housing. So when those benefits become fewer, they blame the members of the ethnic groups because they think they are taking an unfair share of what is available. (In fact, it is generally the members of ethnic minority groups who suffer most economic deprivation in these situations, but racists are not noted for logical thinking.) While most people put the blame where it belongs – with the government or economic forces – racists blame ethnic minority groups, and may express their own personal frustration through violent action towards them.

SOCIAL IDENTIFICATION

Why should these people seize on members of a particular group, rather than on particular individuals? The answer to this question lies in the mechanism of social identification, which we looked at in Chapter 2. As we saw there, it is a very basic tendency for human beings to see the world in terms of 'them' and 'us' groups. We are aware of the social groups and categories that we belong to, and we are also aware of other groups in society.

Key idea

Everyone has a social group or social category of some kind (people like us) which is important to them. Most people have many more than one. This is because belonging to social groups has been a really important part of human evolution, so it's deeply embedded in our psychology.

▶ Stereotyping

Because we tend to know the people in our own groups best, and we only see members of other groups from the outside, we notice differences between people in our own group more than differences between others. So it is very easy for us to slip into the idea that 'we' are all different, whereas 'they' are all the same. One of the first steps in breaking down any sort of social prejudice is to recognize that any group of people is made up of individuals, with their own different ideas and opinions – that 'they' are not, in fact, all the same.

These are psychological tendencies that all people have to some extent. We all tend to stereotype groups of people if we don't know them that well. The stereotyping isn't necessarily about ethnic groups: we can stereotype businessmen, doctors, schoolteachers, Americans or any other group of people you can think of. It is partly a way of making sense of the mass of information that we have to deal with, but it can be dangerous when it leads people to ignore individual differences and start to treat other people as if they were all the same – that is, not really human.

▶ Social comparison

Another aspect of social identity theory is that we tend to make comparisons with people in groups which are close to us socially and economically, because that helps us to feel good about belonging to our own group. Racists who engage in violent action tend to be relatively less educated and to undertake unskilled work when they are employed. So, rather than place the blame for their unemployment on those in charge of the economy, who are socially very distant from them, they prefer to blame people who are in a similar economic position, but belong to a different social group.

We can see, then, how asking why violent racism often rises at times of economic recession reveals a number of motivating mechanisms in human behaviour. One of these is that frustration and discomfort often produce aggressive reactions in people, partly as a way of getting rid of the tension produced by feeling helpless. Another is the tendency to use shared beliefs, or social representations, as a way of explaining what is happening. And a third is to seize on a visible group who represent a clearly identifiable target, who are close by, and who are in a weaker position, both economically and socially.

Key idea

Racism and scapegoating tend to increase at times of economic depression, as people blame minority groups for high levels of unemployment. At its extreme, this can even lead to genocide, as it did during Hitler's period of power in Germany.

COUNTERACTING RACISM

One thing which has become apparent, though, is that this kind of consequence to economic recession doesn't seem to be inevitable. In a population which is highly sensitized to issues of racism and multiculturalism, the efforts of racists to stir people up into violent action are much less effective. As people become more aware of individual differences within different ethnic groups, and of how political and economic factors influence recessions, they become less likely to produce such simplistic, and tragic, responses. We have a long way to go, but understanding the psychological mechanisms which underlie the phenomenon can give us some useful hints as to which direction we should take.

We know that human beings can act in some astoundingly vicious ways. But it is important to keep this in perspective. Most of our everyday interactions are actually positive, but we find the negative ones so disturbing that they can overshadow all the others. Even one unpleasant encounter can spoil the whole day – and this, actually, shows us how far it is from what we expect. We notice the unpleasant things a lot more than the pleasant ones, because they are not usual, and stand out in our experiences. But if we go through a day consciously noticing pleasant interactions with other people as well, it is remarkable how many of them there are, even on what seems to be a very bad day.

For the most part, people tend to co-operate with one another, rather than compete – in fact, some psychologists believe that this is the baseline for human interaction, and that it takes some kind of disruption, like frustration or illness, before people begin to interact in more unpleasant ways. There are individual differences, of course, and there are also questions of social learning, as we model our behaviour on other people around us, including characters on TV and in films. But still, in their everyday lives, most people are not aggressive most of the time.

Motivational levels

One of the most famous psychological theories of human motivation was put forward by Maslow, in 1954. Maslow was trying to understand why it is that people never seem to be satisfied with what they've got. We may be dissatisfied with our situation, and want something more, but if we get what we want, then it doesn't take long before we want something else.

MASLOW'S HIERARCHY OF NEEDS

Maslow suggested that it is useful to think of human motivation in terms of a hierarchy of needs (Figure 6.1). We have some needs which are absolutely basic – our physiological survival needs – and if these are not satisfied, they will motivate our behaviour almost completely. Our actions will be aimed towards getting food, drink, shelter from the elements, and so on, and we will have little time for anything else. But once those needs are satisfied, a different layer in the hierarchy begins to become important. It becomes important to us that we should feel safe and secure. Once that has been achieved, according to Maslow, social needs become paramount, and what we do will be geared towards fulfilling our need to belong with other people and to be accepted. Each time one level of needs is satisfied, the next level becomes important as a motivator.

At the top of the hierarchy, Maslow argued, is self-actualization – realizing our talents and abilities to the full. We have met this idea before, when we looked at Carl Rogers's work, in Chapter 2. But Rogers regarded self-actualization as a fundamental human need, whereas Maslow saw it as an ultimate achievement, managed by only a relatively few remarkable people. For Rogers, it is an ongoing process in our personal development, whereas for Maslow, it is a goal to be reached.

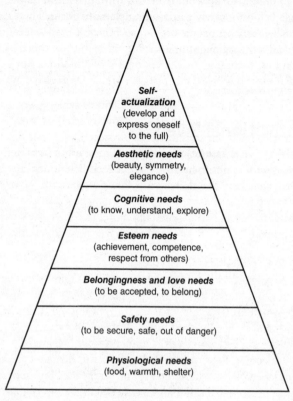

Figure 6.1 Maslow's hierarchy of needs.

The difference between how the two psychologists saw self-actualization also points up one of the weaknesses in Maslow's theory. It may be OK as a general tendency, but there are lots of examples of people acting in ways which are quite different from what Maslow's theory would predict. The 'higher' needs are often extremely important to people – so much so that whether their basic needs have been satisfied sometimes doesn't come into it.

The classic example, of course, is the dedicated poet or artist, who denies security and sometimes even goes hungry in the quest to fulfil needs for beauty or symmetry. Another example is the person who gives up the safety and security of a salaried job to do voluntary work overseas, or to take on something which is less regularly paid, but much more challenging. It may not be what most people do, but such people are less rare than Maslow's theory might predict.

Another great weakness in Maslow's way of looking at motivation is that it is very specific to Western cultures. It assumes that people are motivated by a need for individual achievement, and that things like social needs are somehow optional, at least by comparison with the satisfaction of physical ones. While this may partly represent American beliefs, or those of other parts of the Western world, it isn't by any means a good description of what human beings are like elsewhere.

For example, in many parts of the world, the kind of upward ambition and striving represented by Maslow's approach simply doesn't apply. To take one example: in Balinese culture people see their identity as firmly located within their village's community, and the idea of accumulating personal wealth is an alien one. If someone does come into money, it is usually spent on a particularly elaborate funeral celebration, or something equally transient. While Balinese people would like to be less poor than they are, the idea of achieving this through personal ambition and saving up personal wealth is not one which comes naturally to members of that particular culture.

There are other ways in which Balinese culture is different from many others. For example, the idea of 'art' as a separate entity doesn't exist. Although Balinese culture is full of what we would call art, in dance, carving, weaving and many other ways, there is no separate word for 'art' in the Balinese language. It is simply a part of day-to-day living. So seeing it as a separate set of motives, which we adopt once other needs are satisfied simply can't explain what is going on.

Key idea
The idea that basic needs have to be satisfied before 'higher' needs doesn't really hold water. Quite apart from dramatic examples like starving poets, there are many times when even ordinary people put supposedly 'higher' needs before 'basic' ones.

LEVELS OF EXPLANATION

This is only one example, but there are many others. It is perhaps more useful if we are trying to understand human motivation, to take an approach which looks at it in terms of levels of explanation (see Chapter 1) rather than trying to explain it as a hierarchy of needs.

We all operate on different levels at the same time. We may do something because it is approved of by our social group, but also because we personally want to do it and because we believe it will be good for us. Some of our motives are conscious and deliberate, while others are unconscious and we aren't even aware of them at the time. And most of the things that we do are stimulated by several motives, rather than just one at a time.

By looking at the many different kinds of motives which people have for their behaviour, we can identify some of the influences which might be producing that behaviour at a given time. It isn't a particularly simple way of explaining things, but then human beings aren't all that simple, either. It does, though, allow us to recognize the complexity of human life, and in that way, seems to be more useful in explaining why human beings act as they do rather than going for simplistic explanations which only look at one level of experience at a time.

Focus points

The study of motivation is about finding out why people do things.

Habits are strongly learned behaviours which can act as motives, but can be changed by deliberate action or relearning.

Cognitive motives come from our personal understandings and intentions, and sometimes from unconscious self-protective mechanisms.

Motivation is increased when people believe their actions can be effective.

Social respect and group identification are powerful motivators. They can lead to vicious behaviour, but can also produce peaceful co-operation.

Although Maslow suggested that motivation can be explained as a hierarchy of needs, with basic ones needing to be satisfied before higher ones become important, modern research suggests that different levels of motives act simultaneously.

7

Cognition

In this chapter you will learn:

► *the difference between System 1 and System 2 thinking*

► *about the Gestalt principles of perception*

► *why information you are interested in is easier to remember than information that doesn't interest you.*

This chapter is all about cognition – about how we think, how we take in new information, and how we remember. In other words, it is about how the mind works. Psychology began as the study of the mind, so the study of cognition goes back to its very earliest history, when psychologists explored memory, perception and other aspects of cognition. But psychology's emphasis changed during the first half of the twentieth century as a result of the influence of behaviourism. The behaviourists thought that studying the mind was impossible, since we can't see it, or analyse it directly. So although some psychologists did continue to study the mind, they had only a limited influence on psychology until the last few decades of the twentieth century.

From the 1950s onwards though, psychologists began to develop ways of studying the mind in a more objective manner. They found that it was possible to do controlled experiments which would show how the mind was working. Doing this, they identified some surprising things about how we think and remember. Most of all, they discovered that the human mind is not just a passive recording and analysing machine. It has its own influence on what we perceive and remember, and on how we think.

Thinking

The first thing that comes to mind when we think of cognitive activity is thinking itself. We all know what thinking is, but when we try to define it, it is not that easy. Thinking can include anything from daydreaming and imagining to trying to work out problems or make sensible decisions. In this chapter we will begin by looking at problem-solving, before going on to look at two systems of thinking identified by psychologists.

Key idea

Thinking is something that we all take for granted, but actually it's an amazingly complicated thing – particularly the way that one thought leads to another. Psychologists haven't even begun to explore the subtleties of that yet.

PROBLEM-SOLVING

In the 1960s and 1970s, a number of psychologists investigated how human beings go about solving problems. They found that, often, we don't seem to do it particularly logically. There are a number of mental 'traps' that we fall into very easily. One of the most important of these is when we have expectations about what we are likely to find, and these expectations affect what we do. Expectations can mean that we develop what is known as a mental set, which is a state of being especially ready to think in certain ways.

▶ Mental set

There are lots of examples of mental set because it is such a powerful cognitive mechanism. One of the first demonstrations was by Luchins, in 1932, who asked people to solve problems involving water jars which could hold different amounts of water. People were asked to work out how they would get an exact amount of water by pouring water from one jar into another. The first few problems could be solved by pouring water from large to small jars in a particular order and, as people worked through the problems, they got used to this way of doing things. Then Luchins gave them problems with a much simpler solution. Because they had become used to the other way of doing it, though, they didn't see the easy answer at all. Instead, they solved the problem using the method they had been using before, which was much more complicated than it need have been.

What had happened was that they had developed a mental set – a readiness to see one particular way of solving the problem – which meant that they simply didn't see the other possibilities. The mental set in Luchins's study was developed by their experience with other examples of the problem, but sometimes, we draw on our existing mental sets rather than creating one specially. The nine-dot problem shown in Figure 7.1 is only hard because of the assumptions and expectations we have of such problems.

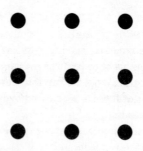

Figure 7.1 The nine-dot problem.

Join the dots without taking your pen off the paper or going over the same line twice.

▶ Lateral thinking

Sometimes, we can train our thinking so that it deliberately avoids being influenced by previous expectations and assumptions. In the 1960s, Edward de Bono developed a technique known as lateral thinking, in which people consciously learned to try to solve problems by thinking 'outside the box' – in other words, by ignoring the usual approaches and going at the problem from an entirely different angle. Someone faced with the problem of being unable to get into their car, for example, because the key had snapped or the lock was frozen, would normally try to work out how to get into it by resolving the immediate problem. But a lateral thinker might ask whether it was actually necessary to get into the car at all right now? Could the journey be avoided, or its purpose achieved in some other way? Lateral solutions aren't always the right ones, of course, but being able to think laterally helps to increase the range of options that we see as available to us, and can often help to overcome tricky problems.

A group-based form of lateral thinking is also useful when people are looking for new ideas. It is known as brainstorming, and when it is done properly its first stage is for people to produce as many ideas as they possibly can, with nobody dismissing anything as impractical or unrealistic. After that, there is a second, separate stage where the ideas are evaluated. Having an open ideas session first can sometimes generate ideas which seem completely unrealistic at first sight, but actually prove to be workable and positive when they have been looked at thoroughly.

Key idea

Brainstorming has become a common term for any type of ideas session, but true brainstorming has to be based on the principle that anything at all is acceptable in the first stage. Discussing whether an idea is practical as soon as someone says it is not real brainstorming, and reduces the effectiveness of the exercise.

▶ Groupthink

Groupthink is another major discovery from psychologists exploring different aspects of thinking – although unfortunately, our understanding of what it is and how it happens doesn't seem to stop politicians and others from doing it. Essentially, groupthink happens when a group of people have become so certain that their own way of seeing the world is right, that they ignore or dismiss any information which contradicts their ideas. This can lead, and has led, to absolutely disastrous decisions at times. The launch of space shuttle Challenger against technical advice resulted in it blowing up in mid-air, killing not only its usual crew but also the USA's first space-travelling civilian, setting back the space programme for several decades. The invasion of the Bay of Pigs in Cuba was a disaster for the US military. And the economic decisions made by the UK government during the 2008/9 credit crunch were disastrous for the UK economy. These are just a few of many examples of groupthink in the real world.

The symptoms of groupthink were documented by Janis in the 1970s. They include a sense of invulnerability, in that the group feels secure and unlikely to be seriously threatened; self-censorship as people who disagree or have doubts keep them to themselves rather than risk the scorn of others; rejecting undesirable information by stereotyping those who provide it or treating it as unacceptable; and most importantly, maintaining an illusion of unanimity, because everyone is conforming to the majority view. Many psychologists see this as one of the best ways to diagnose groupthink. If everyone appears to agree with everyone else, then that's a sure sign that either someone is hiding something, or that the group needs some fresh viewpoints.

Key idea

Groupthink is one of the most dangerous traps in our decision-making. It's particularly likely because it taps into deep social identification mechanisms – everyone likes to feel part of a group – and our avoidance of conflict. But consensus without any conflict at all almost always means that other viewpoints are being ignored, and the consequences of groupthink can be disastrous.

SYSTEM 1 AND SYSTEM 2 THINKING

Set, groupthink and other errors in problem-solving happen because of our habitual ways of thinking and interacting with others. Kahnemann (2011) discussed how psychologists have identified two entirely different forms of thinking, which we all use all the time. System 1 is our normal way of thinking. It is automatic, and doesn't involve any cognitive effort on our part. It's the kind of thinking we do, for example, if we decide we like someone who smiles at us, or read a simple sentence, or calculate $2 + 2 = 4$. Kahnemann argued that most of our thinking is System 1 thinking of this type. It's very fast, doesn't involve checks for accuracy, and often just feels like intuition.

System 1 thinking is easily influenced by priming and mental set. If we have just encountered things to do with food, for example, or if we are feeling hungry, we may be more likely to see a half-finished word as something to do with food. Kahnemann gives the example of SO_P. In normal circumstances, we might be just as likely to read it as soap, but the word you probably thought of when you saw it was more likely to have been soup. That's because the sentence before primed you to think of food or eating. Mental set, as we have seen, is a state of readiness to see certain things rather than others: our personal experiences and interests, our physical state and what is happening around us can all contribute to mental sets, and will influence our System 1 thinking.

System 1 thinking is very comfortable. It is easy, familiar thinking, and feels true and effortless. We are also more likely to engage in System 1 thinking when we are in a good mood, and for some people, it may be linked with creativity. But it can also easily lead us into errors. In Chapter 15 we will be looking at consumer decision-making, and at some of the common errors we make, which arise directly from System 1 thinking.

System 2 thinking, on the other hand, involves a lot more cognitive effort. It is more cautious, less impulsive, and is all about reasoning things out. In another of Kahnemann's examples, he talks about walking along a footpath with a companion. You can easily keep up an ordinary conversation – that's System 1 thinking – but if you asked your companion to calculate a sum like 17×27, they would almost certainly stop walking while they worked it out. The sum would be using up all of their mental energy in System 2 thinking, and there wouldn't be any left for System 1, which in this case is the minimal attention we need to keep on walking.

System 2 thinking needs our conscious attention. But it is also lazy: Kahnemann argues that we will easily slip into familiar ways of solving problems if it seems appropriate, and our logical calculations can be easily misled in this way. It is also closely linked with self-control – we are less likely to keep up our levels of self-control (like sticking to a diet) if we are engaging in a lot of System 2 thinking than we are when we are doing things which come easily to us. This might be because self-control takes up mental energy, and so does System 2 thinking.

Using up mental energy isn't just a metaphor. Gailliot and Baumeister (2007) showed that we really do take up more glucose (which is the fuel for our energy) when we are engaging in System 2 thinking. It is both cognitively and physically demanding, which is why people who have a working day involving hours of intense concentration can be as tired at the end of it as if they had been doing strenuous exercise.

That doesn't mean that System 2 thinking is unpleasant. It can even be experienced as a joyful or fulfilling state. People who engage in prolonged bouts of concentrated thinking sometimes experience what Czikszentmihalyi (2011) called 'flow' – a state of effortless concentration, which is so deep that people forget everything else, including time and problems, as they immerse themselves in the challenge. Many people get a similar, though less extreme, positive experience from mental challenges such as quiz shows and puzzles. But it is a very different type of thinking from System 1.

Key idea

Most of our everyday thinking is System 1, because most parts of our day-to-day lives are habitual, and don't really need much attention. How often during an ordinary day do you use System 2?

These are only a few aspects of thinking, of course. In a book this size we can't give a full account of the many insights which have been made by psychologists working in this area, but they do give us some of an idea of what the psychology of thinking includes.

Perception

Perception is another aspect of our cognitive activity. It is all about interpreting the information that the mind receives from the outside world, and working out what it means. So the psychological study of perception involves looking at how the mind acts on the information it receives through the senses, to give us our perceptual experience.

Most psychological research into perception has concentrated on visual perception because vision is the most important sense for human beings. But there are other kinds of perception too. We make sense out of what we hear, what we touch, what we smell and what we taste. Party games which involve touching different objects while blindfolded show us how strongly we interpret what we receive through our sense of touch. Sometimes, a particular smell can bring back a whole flood of memories. And we saw in Chapter 4 how the way we interpret our physical state can influence the emotions that we feel. So perception really involves all of our senses, even though it is vision that we know most about.

ORGANIZING PERCEPTION

Our perception, like other aspects of our cognition, is strongly influenced by our evolutionary history, and is structured in a way that helps us to survive. This is particularly true of how we organize our visual perception: it is all based on the needs of the active human being in dealing with the world. Seeing objects, animals and other things in the world is important, and so is being able to detect movement. So one of the first things we need to explain when we are looking at visual perception is how we can distinguish things, rather than simply seeing a whole mass of disconnected colours and patches of light and dark.

The retina of our eyes, which receives the information from the outside world, is simply composed of an array of light-sensitive cells, so what we actually receive is a bit like the dots which make up the TV screen. But automatically, it seems, we organize our perception so that we perceive whole objects and shapes, set against backgrounds. We do this by applying a set of perceptual 'rules' to what we are seeing. These rules tell us how to group different bits of information together into whole units. They are known as the Gestalt principles of perception, after the Gestalt psychologists who discovered them during the first half of the twentieth century. There are four of them altogether, and together they show how our perceptual system automatically tries to make complete, meaningful units out of the information which it receives.

▶ Principles of perception

The first Gestalt principle is the principle of similarity. In the absence of any other cues, we group together items or stimuli which are like one another (as shown in Figure 7.2a). The second principle, though, overrides the first one. It is known as the principle of proximity, and is the way that we tend to group things together if they are close to one another, even if they aren't very similar (see Figure 7.2b).

The principle of closure, the third of the Gestalt principles, overrides the other two (Figure 7.2c). If a group of stimuli hint at a closed or complete figure, the mind automatically groups them together and fills in the gaps. This tendency is so strong that if people are asked to draw an incomplete figure that they have seen, they will often fill in the gaps automatically, because they didn't notice that they were there. And the fourth principle is that we tend to look for figures which have good Gestalt, or whole, complete shapes, rather than figures which seem to be 'bitty' or disconnected. Together, the Gestalt principles of perception mean that we can organize the information we receive through our eyes into meaningful units – objects against backgrounds.

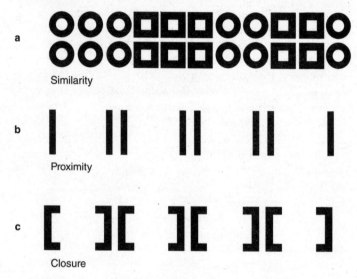

a Similarity

b Proximity

c Closure

Figure 7.2 Three Gestalt principles of perception.

Key idea

Films, cartoons and neon signs all apply the Gestalt principles of perception to fool us into seeing movement instead of disconnected dots or shapes.

▶ Brain cells and perception

There is some suggestion, too, that our tendency to see objects and shapes against backgrounds – which is known as figure–ground perception – may be hard-wired into our nervous system. In the late 1970s, Hubel and Wiesel showed that there are special cells in the visual cortex (the part of the brain which interprets visual information) and in the thalamus (the part of the brain which channels information from the eyes to the visual cortex) which help us to identify patterns and shapes.

One type of cell, known as a simple cell, fires when it detects a single type of stimulus, such as a line at a particular angle in a particular part of our vision. A second type of cell, known as a complex cell, receives information from lots of simple cells, so that type of cell fires when it detects a line at that particular angle anywhere in our vision. And a third type of cell, known as a hypercomplex cell, receives information from lots of different complex cells. These cells fire when they detect simple shapes, such as a triangle or a square.

Although we are only just beginning to understand how visual cells in the brain combine information, what we do know suggests that seeing shapes and objects may be something that our cells do automatically, from the way that they are connected up. The psychologists Marr and Nisihara (1982) showed how connecting information about edges and surfaces, detected by simple and complex cells, and then applying computational rules like the Gestalt principles of perception, allows us to identify whole, real objects like people, trees or animals. The process is complicated, involving several stages, including one where the image detected is almost like a stick figure. But by the time the image is completed, we can make sense of it as a three-dimensional object.

Marr's computational approach tells us something about how we perceive the physical world, as does work by other psychologists, notably Gibson, who analysed how we interpret movement and textures. In many ways, our visual world is made up of figures against backgrounds, and it is also shaped by movement and change. This means that a system which computes edges and objects, and looks at how our visual impressions change as we move around in our worlds, is ideal for the basic survival needs of most animals.

In the modern world, though, the things we are looking at are often more complex than that, and have special meanings. When we are making sense of these, we use our schemas and our existing knowledge, as well as processing the physical images that we receive through our eyes.

PERCEPTUAL SET

Just as our experience gives us mental sets which influence how we think when we are solving problems, so expectation or mood, or other social influences, can give us perceptual sets, which influence what we perceive. In one famous study, Bruner and Minturn (1955) showed people sets of letters or numbers. Each time they saw a letter or a number, they were asked to say what it was out loud. Then they were shown an ambiguous figure, which could be seen as either the figure 13 or the letter B. People who had previously been looking at letters said that it was a 'B', while people who had previously seen numbers said that it was a 13. Their prior experience had given them a perceptual set, which had affected their perception.

▶ First impressions

Perceptual sets can be set up in other ways, too. In one study, researchers asked people to watch as a student tried to solve a set of difficult multiple-choice problems. Each time, the student got 15 out of the 30 problems right. However, when some people watched, most of the correct answers came near the beginning, so that their first impression was that the student was very good at them. Other people saw the student get more wrong answers at the beginning, and more correct ones towards the end. When they were asked to estimate how many questions the student had got right in the end, the two groups of people made entirely different estimates. Those who had seen more correct answers at the beginning estimated that the student had got around 20 out of the 30 questions right, compared to estimates of only 12 out of 30 by those who had seen more wrong answers at the beginning. So our perception can be influenced quite powerfully by first impressions –

something you need to bear in mind if you are going for an interview, or into another situation where first impressions might be influential.

▶ Motivation and perception

Perception can also be influenced by our physical or motivational state. Back in the 1950s, Gilchrist and Nesburg asked people to look at pictures and to rate how bright they were. Some pictures were of neutral stimuli, such as landscapes, while others were of food and drink. If the research participants had gone without food or drink for four hours or more, they saw pictures of food and drink as brighter than the other pictures. Their motivational state – hunger – had affected how they perceived the pictures.

THE PERCEPTUAL CYCLE

All this sounds as though we only see what we want or expect to see. That's partly true, but it isn't the whole story. We can also be surprised by what we see, so it's obvious that our expectations don't entirely determine our perception. Neisser (1976) described perception as taking place in a continuously active cycle. We begin with schemas that we use to make sense of the world. Those schemas help us to anticipate what we are likely to encounter, so Neisser referred to them as anticipatory schemas.

Our schemas direct what sorts of things we notice as we explore the perceptual world. We don't take in everything around us – if we did, we would soon become overloaded. We wouldn't know when to take notice of the shadow of a leaf, or the texture of the tarmac on a road, or anything else. So what we do is sample the relevant information. If we want to cross the road, we notice the speed of the car that is approaching, the width of the road and other bits of information which might be relevant to what we want to do, and we ignore the rest. We sample the perceptual world through our perceptual exploration and that exploration in turn has been shaped by our anticipatory schemas (Figure 7.3).

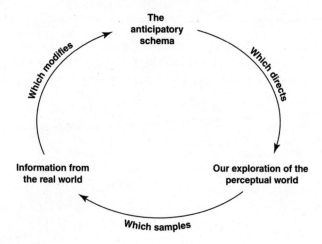

Figure 7.3 Neisser's perceptual cycle.

Once we have sampled that information, it feeds back to the anticipatory schema, and modifies it. You may be about to step into the road because your anticipatory schema has to do with being on the other side, but your perceptual exploration leads you to focus on approaching cars, and the information available tells you that there is one coming up fast. So you modify your anticipatory schema, waiting until the car has gone past. The modified schema in turn directs a new set of perceptual exploration (looking further down the road to see how many more cars are coming), and so on.

In Neisser's model, then, perception is a continuous, active cycle, not just a passive snapshot of what is there. What we anticipate or expect to happen affects what we perceive, but what is actually there affects what we anticipate. So our expectations are continually changing and adjusting themselves as we take in new information and revise our schemas accordingly.

Key idea

The perceptual cycle shows us how active our everyday perception is. It's unconscious, but we are continually registering information, comparing it with what we expect, and adjusting what we expect accordingly.

Memory

Memory, too, is an active mental process rather than a simple tape-recording of what has happened. In many ways, this is quite a hard concept to grasp, because we always feel as though we are remembering exactly what happened. But it's true, nonetheless. The trouble, though, is that we don't often have a separate, objective record of what actually did happen, so we can't compare our memories with the real thing.

ACTIVE REMEMBERING

There are a few occasions when we do have some objective evidence to compare it with, though. Have you ever been to see a film twice, with a gap of several years in between? If you have, you will often find that some of your favourite scenes in the film don't happen exactly the way that you remember them. Even though you felt you remembered them word for word, they turn out to be different when you actually see them again.

It's the same with our other memories, too. Very often, we think that we are remembering a conversation word for word, but really we are remembering a slightly different version of it. The great psychologist Ulrich Neisser showed how this can happen in an analysis of some of the evidence given during the Watergate trials in the USA, which eventually resulted in the impeachment of President Nixon.

▶ John Deane's memory

One of the important witnesses in these trials was John Deane, a man who was considered by many to have an astoundingly accurate memory. During the trials, he related a number of very specific conversations which had taken place between the President and other people in the White House. Deane was convinced – as were the other people involved – that he had recounted them accurately. However, later on in the trials, a number of tape-recordings of the same conversations were discovered. So in this case, it was possible for Neisser to compare the testimony given by John Deane, including his word-for-word descriptions of conversations, with an objective record of what had actually been said.

The results were fascinating. In almost every conversation, John Deane's recollection of the words that had actually been said was wrong. Different words were used, topics were mentioned in a different order, and sometimes particularly memorable phrases hadn't actually been said at all. And yet, even though the details were all wrong, the actual meaning of what had gone on was perfectly correct. Deane didn't remember the details as accurately as he thought he did, but he did remember accurately what had really happened. It was the social meaning of the events which he remembered, and his knowledge of what it all meant that influenced his recall of the details.

▶ Stories and schemas

This reflects a very powerful feature of our memory, which has been known to psychologists for a very long time. Bartlett, in 1932, showed how when people are asked to remember a story, they make sense of the story in their own way. We fit new information into our existing thought structures – into the schemas that we use for understanding the world. This often means that we unconsciously adjust the information so that it will fit.

Bartlett found this out by telling people a story which wasn't the sort of story that they were used to hearing. He used a Native American legend, called 'War of the Ghosts'. This story tends to be confusing to European and white American listeners, because it includes the involvement of the spirit world, in ways that seem illogical to Westerners. When people wrote down what they remembered of the story, Bartlett found that they made systematic changes as they tried to make sense out of it. The more often the story was reproduced, the more it changed until eventually it was nothing like its original.

Bartlett identified seven types of changes, which are listed in Table 7.1. These changes can be detected when we are remembering other types of information, too, and that can sometimes be very important. A lot of courtroom evidence, for example, is based on the idea that people can remember things accurately. So we need to be aware that someone's memory of what happened is likely to have been influenced by their own expectations and social assumptions, no matter how accurate they try to be, or believe they are being.

Table 7.1 How memories change.

Changes in importance	People tend to focus on one part of the story and see that as most important, even if it isn't really.
Changes to the emotional impact	People adjust the story so that it fits with their own reactions and emotions.
Drifting	The more often the story is told, the more its meaning gradually changes.
Shortening	The story becomes shorter and less detailed, as things which the person doesn't understand are left out.
Coherence	Bits are added to the story, or its sequence is changed around, so that it seems to make better sense.
Conventionality	Well-known ideas and themes are introduced, so that the story becomes more like other stories which are known in that culture.
Losing names and numbers	These get lost as the story is repeated, or sometimes change into more familiar forms.

Key idea

Our memory is much more active than we realize. We change and adjust our memories all the time, so they fit in with our expectations and our understanding of the world. But we don't have any idea that we are doing this, so it always feels completely factual.

▶ Words and memory

Memories can be influenced by all sorts of subtle factors. In a study described by Loftus and Loftus in 1975, people were shown a film of a traffic accident. They were then asked questions about it. Among the questions was one about the speed of the cars, and this was phrased very carefully. Half of the people were asked 'How fast were the cars going when they hit one another?' while the other half were asked 'How fast were the cars going when they smashed into one another?' All the other questions were the same.

A week later, the same people were asked to remember the film they had seen. Among other things, they were asked whether there had been any broken glass in the film. There hadn't been any, and those who had been asked about the cars hitting one another remembered that. But those who had been asked about the cars smashing into one another distinctly remembered broken glass strewn around the road, and were surprised to find that it wasn't there when they saw the film again. The words which were used when they were asked about the accident had directly influenced what they remembered – to the point of introducing details which hadn't been there originally.

This is an important finding, particularly for people who have to ask questions to witnesses for court. People can pick up subtle hints and suggestions from the words that are used, and are often entirely unaware that they are doing it. In some American states, the police experimented with helping witnesses to remember what happened by using hypnosis, because they believed it would help people to recall events. But when people are hypnotized, they are even more easily influenced, and they are also trying very hard to be co-operative. Because of this, they often adjust their memories without knowing it, to fit what they think the questioner wants to know.

It is now generally accepted that the use of hypnotism on witnesses in police investigations is pretty well equivalent to tampering with the evidence. Memory doesn't work like a tape-recording. It can be changed and adjusted even some time after the event, without the person even knowing. And once that has happened, there is no way at all of telling the difference between a constructed memory and a 'real' one.

CODING MEMORIES

Memories may be affected by social influences, but this doesn't mean that everything we remember is wrong. And we do store a tremendous amount of information, which means that we have to have a way of retaining it in the mind, and bringing it back to awareness again when we need it. So a part of the research into the psychology of memory has been concerned with studying representation – how information is represented in the brain, as it is stored.

▶ Modes of representation

The kinds of memories that we are most aware of using in everyday life generally involve one of four different modes of representation. One of these is when information is stored in complete meaningful units, such as concepts and schemas, which have been built up from our social and life experience. The other three are interesting because they show us how memory develops as we grow older, and also because of the implications that they have for studying and using our memory for tests or exams.

When an infant is first born it has a lot to learn, and a great deal of that learning has to do with the body. A baby needs to learn how to move its arms, legs, eyes and head when it wants to, and it needs to make sense of the different sensations and feelings it experiences. Since actions and feelings are the central part of the child's interaction with its world, its memories tend to be stored as impressions of actions – as 'muscle memories'. This is known as enactive representation.

It is possible to see babies using this enactive representation as they repeat actions that have produced an effect – such as moving a hand as if they were hitting a rattle, even though the rattle isn't there. You, too, are likely to have some memories stored using enactive representation. Imagine the feel of a fairground waltzer or a rollercoaster, and the chances are you will get an impression of how it felt in the muscles of your body. That's enactive representation. Adults can use it too, but they have other ways of storing information as well.

One of the other ways is known as iconic representation. This involves storing information as images, like pictures, or images of sounds. Iconic representation first develops as the young child's world begins to expand, and they encounter some kinds of information which can't really be stored using muscle memories. When you are reading a book, for instance, or watching TV, the muscle actions which you use are much the same. But the information you are receiving can be quite different. So the brain needs to develop additional ways of storing information.

Children use iconic imagery a great deal. They often remember what things looked like very clearly, and sometimes even photographically. About one in ten children has eidetic imagery – visual memories that are so clear they are almost photographic. But this usually disappears with puberty, and the number of adults with eidetic memory is estimated to be less than one in 10,000.

One of the reasons why it seems to disappear is because iconic memory is much less flexible and adaptable than other ways of remembering. Bruner and Kenney (1966) showed that children who used iconic imagery could remember a particular pattern of glasses, arranged on a grid in ascending size and order (Figure 7.4) quite accurately. But if they were asked to describe what the grid would look like if the order was reversed, they couldn't do it. Their memory was limited to what the original grid had looked like.

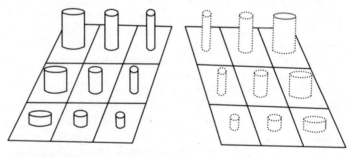

Figure 7.4 Bruner and Kenney's experiment.

Children who used symbolic representation, though, could do it easily. Symbolic representation involves remembering things by using symbols to represent the information in the mind. We actually learn this from a very early age – numbers, for instance, are symbols, and we use those to remember many different kinds of information. As we approach adulthood, symbolic representation becomes more important because it is so much more flexible and adaptable than iconic imagery. It also lets us remember abstract information, which can't be visualized very easily.

So by the time we are approaching adulthood, we have a number of ways of remembering which are available to us. We can use enactive representation, iconic representation, symbolic representation, and schemas, as well as some more specific modes which we don't have space to look at here. We draw on each of these as we need to, because each of them works best when remembering different types of information.

Key idea

All our memories are linked with other ones, in some way. So one bit of information can be a cue which helps you to remember quite a lot of others.

WHAT MAKES A GOOD MEMORY?

There are times when the type of representation which we choose to use makes a great deal of difference to whether we remember things or not. You may have wondered what makes a good memory and why some people seem to have good memories while others don't. A very large part of that answer is to do with how we go about storing the information in the first place.

Whenever we store information, we process it in some way. At the very least, we are changing it from an external stimulus in the outside world to an internal, mental form and, sometimes, we change it a great deal more than that. We might, for instance, change something from a verbal form (words) into a visual form, such as a diagram or a picture. Or we might hear someone say something and store it in terms of the meaning of what they have said – linking it with other things which have similar meanings, and so on. All this is mental processing of the information.

▶ Levels of processing

What is particularly interesting is that the amount of processing we carry out affects how well we remember things. People who have bad memories – or who think they have – are people who tend to try to remember things passively, accepting the information but not trying to process it mentally.

People who have good memories are people who process the information that they receive. They think about it, work out what it means and examine how it links with other things that they already know. By the time they've done that, they know it, and can remember it.

In fact, all of us have extremely good memories – for things that we are interested in! Even someone who thinks they have a bad memory has no problem remembering their social life, and what has been happening lately among their friends – because they are interested in it. But usually they find it difficult to remember schoolwork and other information because they aren't all that interested in it, and so they don't process it much.

And this, of course, becomes circular, because schoolwork can only become interesting when you do think about it and link it with other things that you have learned. People who are 'good at school' do this automatically. People who aren't are generally people who haven't learned the trick of making themselves interested. It can change, though – a lot of people learn how to make themselves interested by following up details and thinking about implications. When they do this, they find that the subject is much more interesting than they thought it was.

▶ Interest and motivation

Being interested in something can make a dramatic difference to how well you remember it. In one classic study, Morris *et al.* (1981) asked people to remember a list of words and numbers – a single number attached to each word – which was read out to them. They had two groups of people participating in their study. One group was not particularly interested in what they were doing, but tried to remember the list anyway. The other group was really, deeply interested in it. When they were tested to see how many items from the list they could remember, the interested group remembered far more than the disinterested group.

The reason why they were so interested was because they were very keen football supporters, and this was Saturday afternoon.

They had agreed to come along to the researcher's laboratory, and were hearing the results of that day's matches read out on the radio. So as they listened, they were thinking about each result, about how it fitted into the overall picture, and what difference it would make to that team's league position. In other words, they were processing the information. The others, who were not particularly keen on football, just listened and tried to remember, but they didn't process the information as much, which is why they didn't remember as well.

The researchers made sure that the two groups were just as good at remembering things by giving them another set of scores to remember, which had been made up. In this case, the football supporters were just as bad at remembering as the others. It was because they knew that the first ones were real results that they put the effort into processing the information.

So, if you want to try to improve your memory, there's the answer. Don't just try to remember things passively: process them. Change the form of the information in some way: use iconic imagery to change it into pictures, or change it into symbolic form. Fit it into your schemas and concepts, by working out what it means and why it matters. You'll be surprised how much you can remember when you do that.

Key idea

Everybody has a good memory – for things that they are interested in. Even people who say they have lousy memories have no difficulty remembering what is happening in their social lives. So the real trick in successful revision is to get the good side of your memory to connect with the other stuff.

In this chapter, we have taken a brief look at some aspects of cognitive psychology. There is much more which could be said: psychologists have been studying memory for over 100 years now and we know a great deal about it. But in a book like this, all we can really do is look at some of the psychological findings which are most helpful for understanding human beings in their everyday lives. Our evolutionary history, too, has left influences on our cognitive processes, and we will look at some of these in the next chapter.

Focus points

Cognition is mental activity, such as thinking, perception or memory.

Human problem-solving is strongly influenced by expectations and assumptions. Mental set is a state of readiness or preparedness for particular mental activities.

Groupthink can result in disastrous decisions as the decision-makers fail to take other information or opinions into account.

We have two systems for thinking. System 1 is intuitive, automatic and impulsive, and we use it most of the time, while System 2 is cautious, disbelieving and takes mental effort in reasoning things out.

Perception is how we organize and interpret sensory information. The perceptual cycle shows how we can still notice new things even though our anticipations direct what we pay attention to.

Memory is an active process – we fit our memories to our knowledge and expectations. Memories can be stored as images, actions, words or symbols, and can be improved by processing information more effectively.

Evolution, genetics and learning

In this chapter you will learn:

▶ *about the evolutionary process of natural selection*

▶ *how evolution can encourage learning*

▶ *how scanning methods can show us how the brain works.*

As we've seen, there are many different approaches to understanding people. So far we have looked at how social, cultural, developmental, physiological and cognitive influences contribute to what it means to be human. Each of these levels of analysis helps us to understand a bit more about human beings. But there is another level of explanation which is also important in psychology, and that is the biological level: the level of explanation which says that since human beings are animals, evolutionarily and physically speaking, then understanding what we have in common with other animals will also help us to understand ourselves.

By understanding evolution, we can see how the human brain has come to be organized in the way that it is, how human genetics have evolved over time to develop us into the human animals that we are, and how our physiological make-up allows us to adapt to so many different environments. Human beings have learned to live in almost all parts of the world, under wildly different physical conditions. That learning is only possible because we have evolved such a large amount of flexibility and adaptability in both our brains and our immune systems. Looking at how brains and learning capacities have developed in other animals can help us to understand more about how we have come to be like we are.

But we also need to be cautious when we are trying to generalize from other animals to human beings, because of the very diverse ways that other animals have evolved. Animal learning and animal biology are closely tied in with the types of environments in which each animal has evolved. Behaviour, habits, learning, and even physiology all vary, and many of them are completely different for other animals than they are for human beings.

Nature often uses the same materials, but in very different ways. Some studies of animal physiology, for example, have shown that the same brain chemical, in apparently the same part of the brain, can produce completely different behaviours in rats and cats – behaviours as different as sleeping and aggression. Animal social organization varies widely, sometimes even in the same species – for example, plains baboons have a much more rigid social hierarchy than forest baboons, which are more relaxed and 'egalitarian' in their relationships with one another. So we should be very careful in making our comparisons.

Key idea

Studying animals in their natural contexts can give us insights into our own behaviour as well as theirs. But we have to remember that the natural context for humans is other humans, which is why we can survive in so many different physical environments.

Learning has its natural contexts too. In the first half of the twentieth century psychologists studied association learning in the laboratory, investigating how animals can learn new behaviours and complex tasks by applying different kinds of reinforcements or rewards. This is the kind of training we use to teach tricks to pets, or to train performing animals – although there has always been a certain amount of debate as to whether the animals are really responding mechanically or whether they are simply going along with the trainer because they enjoy it! In the second half of the twentieth century, though, comparative psychologists became much more interested in investigating animal behaviour in the natural environment. This is known as ethology, and many psychologists see this approach as much more useful, as well as kinder to the animals concerned.

Animal learning is closely tied up with its species' evolutionary history. So we will begin this chapter by looking at how evolution happens, since that gives us the basis for understanding why animals are different from one another, and also why human beings are different from other animals. As part of that, we will be looking briefly at genetics, and how we inherit characteristics from our ancestors – even if we have not been brought up by our biological parents. We will go on to look at human and animal learning a little more closely before taking a brief look at how the human brain has evolved and can be studied.

Evolution

Comparative psychology is firmly based on the idea that all animals, including human beings, have evolved from primitive common ancestors. The theory of evolution, as put forward by Charles Darwin in 1859, proposes that animal species have changed and developed over time, as they become better suited to their environments. Evolution happens as the species adapts to the demands of the environment that it lives in. It is slow, because it happens through tiny changes in genetics, which are passed on from parent to offspring. We will be looking in more detail at the genetic basis of evolution later in this chapter. For now, though, we will look at evolutionary processes in general.

NATURAL SELECTION AND ADAPTATION

Individuals are a combination of biological inheritance and environmental experiences. It isn't an 'either-or' process – either genetics or environment – as some early psychologists used to believe. Both genetics and the environment work together, each making it possible for the other to have its influence. Humans, for example, learn from their environments all the time. But without the human brain, which has developed as a result of genetic factors, that learning would be totally impossible. And without its earlier environment and pressures, the human brain would not have taken that particular form in the first place.

Key idea

There will always be small genetic variations, but most of them just remain as individual differences. They only produce species change if they give some kind of advantage. But if the environment changes, previously unimportant variations can sometimes become helpful and that's when species change is likely to happen.

Any organism, whether it is a plant or an animal, exists in the world and needs to survive in it. This means that it needs to obtain enough nutrients and living space or other conditions it needs to keep it alive. It also needs to have some way of combining reproductive cells with another member of the same species, if it is to reproduce by sexual means. And in doing all this, it will often be in competition with other animals or plants, which are also trying to survive.

▶ Survival of the fittest

So anything which helps an organism to get an advantage over the competition will be useful. Slight physical changes produced by genetic mutations, can sometimes give an organism just the edge it needs. If a mutation helps the animal to become better adapted to its environment, it will be more likely to survive than other members of its species. And, because it is a little bit healthier, it will also be more likely to reproduce successfully, so its beneficial mutation can be passed on to future generations.

One of the 'classic' examples of evolution is that of the finches on the Galapagos Islands. When Darwin reached these islands, on the voyage made by the famous ship HMS *Beagle*, each island had a slightly different kind of finch living on it. However, when he examined the different finches, it was apparent that, at some time in the past, they had all developed from just one species of finch which had originally colonized all the islands. Because each island presented a slightly different environment, though, natural selection meant that the birds had gradually adapted to their particular island. In the process, they had become different from the finches on the other islands.

Imagine, for example, an island in which the main source of food was seeds, with thick, strong shells. If a finch inherited the genes for a slightly thicker, stronger beak – perhaps as the result of a genetic mutation – then it would have an edge over the other birds on the island. It would be able to get to its food more easily, using less energy than the others. So it would be likely to become strong and healthy. When it mated, some of its offspring would also inherit the gene for a thick strong beak and they, too, would become stronger and healthier than the others.

Then if something happened which made the food supply scarce – perhaps a drought, or some other natural change – these would be the birds which survived. They would be less likely to die of starvation because they were healthier and better fed in the first place. And they would be more likely to be able to get at particularly tough seeds which the other birds couldn't manage, so they could make the most of whatever was available. As a result, more of them would survive the drought or famine than the ones with smaller beaks. In the end, over thousands of years, it would be their descendants which occupied the island.

On an island where the main food supply was insects which hid under stones or tree bark, a thick strong beak wouldn't be much help. Adaptation to that particular environment would benefit birds with thinner, longer beaks which could poke into crevices. They would be the ones who would become better fed and stronger, and so they would be more likely to survive the hard seasons. Natural selection is all about the survival of the fittest – and 'fittest' means best adapted to its environment.

HUMAN EVOLUTION

This continuous process of adaptation and development has produced a vast diversity of living organisms, ranging from plants and yeasts to mammals and birds. Each species has evolved its different characteristics through natural selection, and when we look at different species, we can sometimes use those comparisons to detect part of their evolution, or of the evolution of some particular structure or ability. For example, Figure 8.1 tells us something about the evolution of the largest part of our brain, the cerebrum, and how it has developed in different animals.

Human beings are primates, which is a group of animals that also includes monkeys, lemurs and apes. Primates have a number of distinctive characteristics, but the one which is being

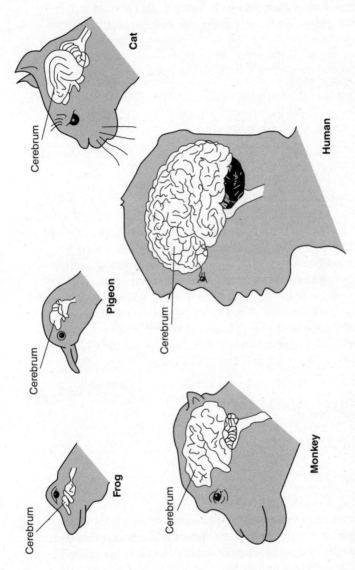

Cat

Human

Pigeon

Monkey

Frog

Cerebrum

Cerebrum

Cerebrum

Cerebrum

Cerebrum

Figure 8.1 Evolutionary development of the cerebrum.

illustrated in Figure 8.1 is the large cerebrum. Having a large brain helps an animal to learn and therefore to adapt to new environments quickly. As we can see, the human cerebrum is particularly large, which may give us the key to the way that human beings seem to be able to adapt to so many different environments.

Although it's quite common, it's a mistake to think of evolution as a straight-line development leading up to the human being. Human evolution is only one out of many different branches of evolution. There are lots of different groups of animals, each of which has adapted to its environment in different ways. We often think of a shark's brain as being primitive, for instance: it isn't really up to much in the way of learning or intelligence. But a shark is superbly adapted to its environment and in many ways represents a triumph of evolution. It would be hard to design a more efficient and better-adapted animal to fill the ecological role which the shark plays. In a sense, every animal which is alive today is the outcome of a battle for survival which has been going on for millions of years, so none of them can really be regarded as either inferior or 'better' than others.

The most important part of the whole evolutionary process is the fact that the animal is able to pass its genes on to its offspring. For the most part, natural selection favours an animal that can make sure that its offspring will survive. A species might do this, as frogs do, by having hundreds of offspring, so that at least a few will avoid being eaten by predators and grow up to become mature frogs. Alternatively, members of a species might have just one or two young, but nurture them carefully until they are old enough to look after themselves.

When we actually look at what plants and animals do, we find a tremendous range of different behaviours and options. The principle of biodiversity means that there are examples of almost every different kind of activity that we could think of, somewhere in the animal kingdom. In many species, for instance, it is the fathers which rear the young rather than the mothers – after all, they too have invested their genes in their offspring. In some species, males hold territories; in others, females do. The more we look, the less there seems to be general rules about what is an optimal strategy for survival.

▶ Sociobiology

Sometimes, even, we find that an animal helps its genes to survive by laying down its own life. The sociobiologist E. O. Wilson (1975), from his studies of ants, showed how it was often an evolutionary advantage for a single animal to die to protect its relatives, since they too shared the same genes. Moreover, it was also sometimes an advantage for an individual animal not to have offspring directly, but instead to devote its life to taking care of siblings or cousins, which again shared the same genes. In this way, ultimately, that animal's own genes would survive and be perpetuated.

Wilson used this argument to explain how ant societies, and similar insect communities in which very few individuals reproduce directly, could have evolved. In these societies, altruism, or self-sacrificing behaviour could sometimes become an evolutionary advantage. Survival of the fittest didn't necessarily mean the biggest and strongest, but the one which was best able to make sure that its genes were perpetuated.

Remember this

We need to be very careful about making wild comparisons between insects and human beings. Every animal species is different, and it really only makes sense to compare humans with their closer relatives – mammals and, specifically, social primates. Our evolution has taken a very different direction from that of ants.

▶ Evolutionary psychology

Wilson, and also Dawkins (1976), then went on to draw a number of parallels between the sociobiological processes which he had observed in ant societies, and things which happened in human societies. This way of thinking eventually became the basis for a school of thought in evolutionary psychology, which is extremely controversial. Although almost all psychologists accept the idea of human evolution, the argument that what human beings do – in terms of things like aggression, prejudice, mate attraction and other such phenomena – is a direct outcome of our evolutionary history is nowhere near as widely accepted.

This is partly because the theory of sociobiology was based on creatures which are very different from human beings. Ant societies are highly structured, but not in the same way as human societies and the species as a whole invests much less in a single individual than do mammals. Human beings use a rather more direct method: by caring for their children, teaching them, and helping them to survive to maturity. So simplistic parallels between what human beings do and what animal societies do are very misleading. They may appear attractive on the surface, but don't really stand up to scientific scrutiny because they don't take into account the amount of individual learning which happens as each person develops. Nor do they take into account other types of animal behaviour – the massive behavioural diversity that we see when we look at different species, which produces a huge range of behaviours and possibilities.

The main objection to the sociobiological version of evolution as applied to human beings isn't really the ideas themselves, but some evolutionary psychologists' claim that human behaviour is determined by the same biological mechanisms as very different animals. Our evolution has certainly influenced our development, but it has done so by making us supremely adaptable. We have a generalized body-form which can do a wide range of things; we have a large brain capable of storing lots of information and learning lots of skills; and we are even born at an earlier stage in our development than other animals, to allow for this large brain which continues growing after birth. Given such a capacity for adaptation and learning, it isn't very likely that we would inherit fixed behaviour patterns, determined by biological mechanisms. Also, human behaviours appropriate for survival vary too much from one period of history to another and from one environment to another, to make biological determination practical.

What human beings do needs to be understood on a number of different levels, including cultural, social and interpersonal ones.

We are influenced by our evolution – indeed, our evolution as social animals has shaped us more than we realize, in that it has made us so very prepared to learn from one another and to organize and identify with social groups. But what we learn is different in each generation and each culture, and as human beings we are as much determined by our cultural as our evolutionary history.

Key idea

Scientists who talk about modern trends in human evolution often underestimate how many generations of consistent environmental pressure it would take to change humans physically. Humans are a long-lived species; even the Roman invasion of Britain was only about 40 grandfathers ago, which isn't enough time for evolutionary change. Demands change with society, and the physical characteristics needed for survival in medieval times were very different from physical characteristics aiding survival now.

COEVOLUTION

Evolution isn't just a one-way process. Animals don't just adapt to their environments, they also change those environments, simply by living in them. Even an amoeba, which has only one body cell, secretes chemicals into the water that it swims in, and so changes that water. And more complex animals often exert quite a strong influence over their environments, so that the environments also evolve with the animals.

This process is known as coevolution and it is something which is often overlooked when people talk about evolutionary processes. The usual assumption is that the relationship between animals and their environment is just a one-way thing; that animals use their environment to live in, but don't really affect it, except to use up its resources. But that isn't really the case, and a number of large-scale ecological problems have arisen from this rather simplistic view of the world.

When the first white settlers arrived on the American prairies, for instance, they found it teeming with buffalo, as well as the small animals known as prairie dogs. When they exterminated the buffalo and introduced cattle, they also systematically wiped out the prairie dogs. Since these ate grass, they reasoned, they would be in competition with the cattle. More recently – and almost too late because the prairie dog was nearly extinct – biologists have found that the prairie dogs' activities didn't use up the grass at all. Rather, they enriched it, so that it grew more lushly and provided more foodstuffs for the buffalo and everything else.

Similarly, Trevor (1992) reported on a 30-year-old experiment in Tsavo National Park, in Kenya. In other national parks, the elephant population was culled when it seemed to be growing too large for the park's resources, but in Tsavo they decided to let nature take its course and see what would happen if the elephants were allowed to multiply unrestrictedly. Although this led to some heartbreaking scenes in the short term, by producing a country virtually stripped of vegetation and the deaths of a large number of elephants through starvation, in the longer term the country became richer and more lushly vegetated than before. The elephants' activities had spread the vegetation more widely, they had scraped out new waterholes during the drought, and all the other species had benefited too, over the 30-year period.

These examples of coevolution show how animals and their environments interact – and there are similar examples with human societies, too. For many thousands of years, for example, Native Australians managed the Australian bush using fire. Every few years an area of land would be burned, renewing the vegetation and enhancing the environment. Both plants and animals adapted to this management, so the environment changed, as well. Australian plants burn easily, but their seeds and roots are well protected, and they regenerate from fire very quickly indeed.

In some sanctuaries in Australia which have been set up by white people, and protected from fire for many decades, the native plants often develop serious diseases. They haven't evolved resistance to plant disease, as European and American plants have, because they didn't need it. Under the Native Australians' management, regular fires wiped out the diseased plants and sterilized the soils so that the new plants grew up more healthily than before. Preventing fire has led to more ecological problems than allowing it.

Coevolution, then, is a significant part of the evolutionary process. Animals have evolved in order to be well adapted to their environments, but environments also adapt to their animals (or their management by people). And sometimes, animals shape their environments so that they will fit their needs better. It is this two-way relationship which we need to bear in mind when we are looking at what the study of animals can tell us about animal or human psychological processes.

Genetic mechanisms

We saw earlier that evolution is determined by the genes we inherit from our parents. Natural selection – the basis of evolution – works by 'shaping' the set of genes that we inherited from our parents. Each of us is unique, and the same applies in other species too. The genes tell the body what characteristics to develop. But how well that development happens depends on the environment. We all have cells for storing fat, for example, but we can only become fat in an environment where food is plentiful. In recent years we have come to understand a great deal more about how genetic change happens.

Inside the nucleus of each of our body's cells, there is a complex substance known as DNA (deoxyribonucleic acid, to give it its full name). Nuclear DNA (the DNA found in the cell's nucleus, as opposed to mitochondrial DNA which we will look at later) is made up of long strands of molecules. These have two strands running side by side, arranged so that the molecules are linked together in pairs, a bit like a zip fastener. The strands are twisted so that they form a spiral-like shape known as a helix. Because there are two strands, the end result is a double helix – like a very twisted ladder (Figure 8.2).

Evolution works because there are often small errors in copying the DNA when the special reproductive cells are made, and these result in the new individual becoming different in some way. These differences are known as genetic mutations.

Large-scale genetic mutations are quite rare, although they do happen occasionally, but they are not normally passed on to the next generation because such individuals are often sterile. Most of the time, mutations are just tiny changes in the DNA, which may only make a tiny difference to the individual's development.

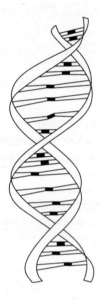

Figure 8.2 A double helix.

GENES AND CHROMOSOMES

There are four kinds of DNA molecules, and they make different combinations all the way along each double helix. Together, they spell out what is known as the genetic code – a tremendously complicated set of information, which gives instructions to the cells in the body so that they develop in certain ways. As a result of these complex instructions, we grow specialized liver cells, heart cells, hair cells, skin cells, and all the other different types of cells which make up a body. Sections of DNA – known as genes – also give instructions about when different types of cells should develop, and whereabouts in the body they should be. So we also develop differently from one another – colour of hair, face shape and all the little physical things which make us individual.

DNA codes for similarity – what makes us all human, or makes a dog a dog – but it also codes for individuality. The strands of DNA in our cell nuclei are grouped together into larger units, known as chromosomes, which are also arranged in pairs. For the most part, each pair of chromosomes is very similar. The genes on each chromosome have matching genes, known as alleles, on the other one. The exception is a pair of chromosomes known as the X and Y chromosomes: the Y chromosome is much shorter so it doesn't have a full matching set. These are the chromosomes which determine gender – that is, whether we will end up male or female. Females have two X chromosomes, while males have one X and one Y chromosome.

When we, or any other living things, reproduce ourselves sexually – that is, by combining sperm from one parent with ova from another – we do it by producing special cells which only have half of the chromosomes: one from each pair. They combine with similar half-sets of chromosomes from the other parent to form a full set, which can then develop into a new individual. So the new individual inherits some characteristics from each of its parents, but that mixture is slightly different every time.

MITOCHONDRIAL DNA

It used to be thought that the genes and chromosomes in the cell nucleus were the only sources of DNA – and therefore the only set of instructions which the body uses to develop. But we now know that there is also DNA in another part of the cell – in the mitochondria, which are small structures in the cell body which have a number of different functions. One of these functions is to give instructions about the body's development, starting as a foetus develops in the womb and continuing throughout our growth and development. So it isn't just the DNA which we inherit through sexual reproduction which matters in our development. The DNA which we acquire from our biological mothers during the gestation period also has quite a strong influence in how we become like we are.

This observation has been useful in tracing a great deal of the human evolutionary story, and is also used to trace individual people's genetic heritages. But it challenges quite a lot of assumptions. It used to be thought, for example, that we could grow an identical copy of an animal just by using the DNA from the cell nucleus – a process known as cloning. But experiments with cloning, such as the famous one that produced Dolly the sheep, have shown that the new animal also absorbs mitochondrial DNA from the host mother – that is, from the animal which provides the womb for the cloned embryo to develop in. Although the clone is almost identical to its genetic parent, it isn't completely so because of the difference in mitochondrial DNA.

Key idea

The old science-fiction idea of growing hundreds of identical clones has been challenged as we realize how important mitochondrial DNA is to development. The clone's 'parent' and the host both contribute DNA, so two clones could only be really identical if they grew in the same womb at the same time, like identical twins.

GENOTYPE AND PHENOTYPE

The genetic code, as we've seen, provides instructions for how the body should develop. But that doesn't mean that the body automatically develops that way. From the moment that the embryo begins to develop – in other words, from the moment of conception – there is a continual interaction between the two types of DNA and the environment in which the individual is developing. Factors such as the amount of oxygen or nutrients available, the presence of stress hormones or drugs, and the amount of activity of the mother all have an influence on the embryo's development in the womb or the egg. These environmental factors continue and become even more important as the individual continues to develop.

So inheriting genetic characteristics from our ancestors is only part of the story. How we develop them depends on our experiences, and how they affect us. Someone who has a restricted diet when they are young, for example, may not develop the full height and bone size that they might have had with a richer diet. The total set of genetic characteristics that we inherit is known as the genotype – but nobody ever sees a genotype in real life. What we actually see, in any animal, plant or human being, is the phenotype – what has actually developed as a result of the interaction between the genes and the environment.

That's an important thing to know, because it tells us that genetic influences are not fixed and inevitable. Genetic influences work alongside environmental influences, and they predispose us towards certain types of development. But the environment can make a tremendous difference. Take heart disease, for instance. Some people have inherited a genetic tendency towards heart disease, which means that with certain kinds of environmental stressors, they are likely to develop it. But if they know that they carry the gene, then they can develop a lifestyle which will help them to avoid the illness – by keeping to a healthy diet, taking regular exercise, and so on. Having a genetic tendency to something doesn't make it inevitable. It just means we are more vulnerable and so we need to take precautions.

GENE THERAPY

As a result of the human genome project – a massive scientific research initiative designed to map the whole human genome – scientists have developed a much better understanding of what is involved in human genetics. This has helped us to understand how many genetic disorders work and, as we have seen, that understanding can make all the difference to someone with a genetic 'vulnerability' to a disorder. It has also helped scientists to develop better treatments for a number of problems. Knowing that a particular genetic disorder comes from the body failing to produce enough of a particular chemical, for example, means that we can often correct the problem by making sure that the person gets that chemical in other ways – through injections or other medical treatments.

Research into stem cells – cells located in the bone marrow and other areas of the body – shows that even when we are adults, we still have some of the 'all-purpose' cells which we had when we were younger. These cells contain the full genetic code, but haven't yet become specialized, so they can develop in different ways in different parts of the body. Some very successful therapies have been developed which allow people to regrow parts of their own organs which have become damaged, as a result of stimulation with stem cells.

Key idea

Stem cell therapy could conceivably do away with the need for organ donors, as it becomes possible to regrow replacement organs from the person's own stem cells instead.

Other aspects of genetic research are more controversial. Some researchers manipulate animal genes so that those animals will grow 'spare parts' for human bodies, or produce important biochemicals for drugs to treat human disorders. Those concerned about animal rights in medical research have some doubts about whether this type of activity might produce more problems in the long run, as well as being concerned with what is happening to the experimental animals themselves. The artificial genetic modification of crops, too, is controversial, and many ecologists are concerned that introducing plant crops with, for example, genes from fish, will distort the natural environment and produce long-term problems in plant life. Foods developed in this way have been called 'Frankenstein foods', and many consumers don't want them included in their diets. But the scientific discussion is not as clear as it might be, because the debates have also been affected by the unethical behaviour of some big corporations implementing this research.

Who we are, then, is partly influenced by our genes and our evolutionary history. But that is far from being the whole story. Our genetic make-up is largely established at conception. But the environment that we live in continues to affect and shape us throughout our lives – both physically, and through learning.

Levels of learning

Learning can happen on all sorts of levels. In the next chapter, we will be looking at some of the distinctly human aspects of learning – how we learn from symbols, language and imagination, for example. But for now, we will look at some of the different levels of animal learning, ranging from learning which is tightly controlled by genetic influences, to learning which is much more flexible.

Just about all types of animal are capable of some kind of learning – even those with very primitive nervous systems. But each species is predisposed towards the types of learning which are most appropriate for the environment in which they live. So genes can facilitate learning, by making some kinds of learning easier than others.

ASSOCIATION LEARNING

Perhaps the most basic type of learning is pain avoidance. Even a flatworm, which has a very primitive, ladder-like nervous system, can learn to turn in a particular direction if turning the other way brings it into contact with a painful stimulus. That kind of learning happens at a very simple level, in the connections made directly by the nerve cells and, as you can imagine, it is an important mechanism to help the animal survive.

Pain avoidance is a kind of association learning – a simple connection between a stimulus (e.g. pain) and a response (e.g. movement). But association learning doesn't have to be based on pain. At the beginning of the twentieth century, Ivan Pavlov showed how the salivary reflex in dogs, which normally happens when they see food, could be trained so that dogs would salivate at different times. By ringing a bell every time dogs were fed, the sound came to be associated with the food and the dogs would salivate when they heard the bell.

Psychologists explored association learning in considerable depth in the early part of the twentieth century, looking at different types of stimulus, different responses, and the ways in which the two can be connected with one another. Association learning is a factor in human behaviour too – for example, many of the problems that people have in giving up smoking arise because they have formed associations between the act of smoking and particular situations or experiences. To give up, they need to learn new habits – that is, form new associations.

There are two main forms of association learning, or conditioning: classical conditioning, and operant conditioning. We will look at how they relate to human learning more closely in Chapter 9.

LEARNING FOR SURVIVAL

Some kinds of learning are closely directed by genetic mechanisms. One of the best examples is the way that we avoid foods which have made us sick. This is a useful mechanism to evolve, since in the natural world, something which makes you sick is likely to be poisonous, so learning to avoid that food helps an individual to survive. It is an example of what is known as one-trial learning – a form of learning which is so powerful that we only need one connection between the stimulus and response to make it stick. Avoiding foods that have made you sick in the past isn't confined to humans – it's something that most animals will do. Both human beings and animals can have an inherited predisposition to learn some things very quickly indeed.

Another very rapid form of learning is shown by some precocial animals soon after they are born. Precocial animals are ones which can move around very soon after birth, such as foals or lambs, ducklings and goslings. If they didn't learn quickly how to recognize their mothers and stick with them, they'd be at risk of wandering off and getting eaten by predators. So they have a very rapid form of learning, known as imprinting, whereby they develop an attachment in the first few hours after birth. With young goslings and ducklings, it seems to be mostly visual, in that they will imprint on the first large, moving object that they see, but with lambs the sense of smell and hearing seems to be more important than vision. But whatever the mechanism, it is a fast, almost irreversible form of learning which has tremendous survival value.

▶ **Preparedness in learning**

The more comparative psychologists have looked at animal learning, the more they have found that an animal is most ready to learn what it will need to survive. For example, in one study in 1966, Garcia and Koelling looked at how rats respond to different unpleasant experiences. They began by showing how the animals quickly learned to avoid salty water, if they had been given an injection to make them sick soon after drinking it. But rats who drank salty water and were then given an electric shock didn't learn to avoid the water. They didn't learn to connect the two stimuli at all, although they could learn to connect the electric shock with a light or a clicking sound.

In other words, the rats had been ready to learn some connections, but not others. They could associate shocks with lights or sounds, but not with tastes. They could associate sickness with tastes, but not other unpleasant happenings. It's easy to see, I think, how this type of learning fits with the idea of evolutionary adaptation. In real life, you would probably be able to hear or see something which was about to cause you pain, but you would taste something which was about to poison you. So it makes sense for any animal to be ready to learn those kinds of associations.

▶ Learning by instinct

Pretty well all animals, it seems, are more ready to learn some things than others. Honeybees, for instance, find it very easy to learn to recognize particular smells. If a bee is fed with food that has been scented with a distinctive smell, such as lavender, then it begins to select lavender scents, and to go to those for food even if other food is available. They make the association between smell and food very readily.

But they don't associate other stimuli with food as easily. Menzel and Erber (1978) showed that a honeybee can learn to connect flower smells and food 90 per cent of the time, after just one learning session. They take longer to learn smells which are not from flowers, and they take even longer to learn stimuli which aren't smells at all. For instance, although they will learn to go to a particular colour for food, it takes them three or four learning sessions, not just one. And it takes them five or six learning sessions to go to a particular shape. They can learn it in the end, but they are not nearly as quick to learn as they are with flower smells.

There are some stimuli, too, which bees simply will not learn at all. For instance, they don't learn to associate light with food, no matter how many learning sessions they are given. It simply doesn't form an association. Yet bees are very sensitive to light: they detect polarized light and use it in navigation. Evidently, as far as bees are concerned, foraging for food and finding your way home are two entirely unconnected skills!

What we find, then, when we look at this kind of animal learning is that it isn't simply a matter of random associations between stimuli. Evolutionary pressures have 'shaped' both animals and humans to be ready to learn certain things rather than others. We've seen a human application of this principle already, when we looked at how strongly the human infant is pre-programmed for social interaction with other people, and how readily human children learn by imitating others. Gould and Marler (1987) discussed how this evolutionary 'shaping' of the capacity to learn applies across many different species, and seems to be a fundamental feature of learning.

Key idea

Each species is really good at learning things which are directly relevant to their traditional survival. That's why human beings in general are more fascinated by social information than by abstract knowledge like maths or philosophy. Our survival depends on it.

GENERAL LEARNING

Learning, though, isn't only about linking one stimulus with a response. Some animals have inherited a predisposition for a more general kind of learning. They will explore places, or be curious about new objects. And sometimes, too, they seem to be ready to learn entirely new forms of behaviour.

Rats and monkeys, for example, will generally explore new situations and investigate strange objects that they come across – unless there is some good reason to avoid them. And this exploration, too, can be an evolutionary advantage. In one study, Blanchard, Fukanaga and Blanchard (1976) put experimental rats in a box with a cat – separating them by a clear screen. If the rats had been in the box before, and so had explored it, they crouched down and remained immobile to avoid attracting the cat's attention. But if they hadn't had a chance to explore the box, they ran around looking for a way to escape.

In other words, rats use the knowledge that they obtain from their natural tendency to explore new places, to tell them what to do in the case of a potential threat. If you know that you are in a place with no escape, then the best thing to do is to try not to attract a predator's attention. If you don't know, then the best thing to do is to try to find a way out. But it is better to know, so exploring new places is a good way of surviving.

LEARNING AND BRAIN DEVELOPMENT

As we saw in Figure 8.1, the cerebrum of the brain is much larger and more highly developed in some species than it is in others. This is the part of the brain which we use for learning and thinking, and those animals which have the largest and most highly developed cerebrum also seem to be those animals which are most able to take advantage of opportunities for learning. As far as land animals are concerned, human beings have the most highly developed cerebrum of all. And we are also capable of learning more than any other land animals.

Key idea

The reason why the human brain is so folded and grooved is because it is the surface – the top few layers of cells – which does the actual thinking and processing. The layers underneath are connections between different parts of the brain. Crumpling the surface up means you can get more of it into a small space.

A dolphin's cerebrum is even larger and more convoluted than a human being's, but we don't really know what that implies, since a dolphin's experience is so very different from ours. Almost from the first time that human beings can co-ordinate their muscles, we are manipulating objects, changing them and shaping our environments. Although dolphins play with objects, too, their experience is much more to do with living in and experiencing their environment: they don't manipulate it as much. That's very different and it's not at all clear whether we actually have any common ground for understanding dolphin intelligence.

It is apparent to anyone who works with dolphins that they are intelligent, but it is unlikely that 'intelligence' means the same thing in a dolphin as it does in a human being. We do know, though, that dolphins are very ready to learn all sorts of things, including entirely novel kinds of behaviour, and they give every sign of enjoying it. Pryor, Haag and O'Reilly (1969) trained a dolphin to perform a new type of action each day, by giving her a reward when she did something she hadn't done before. By the end of the study, the dolphin was producing many entirely new actions, including tail-walking and back flips, and some actions which were so elaborate that the researchers found it hard to describe them!

We can see, then, that when we are talking about animal learning being shaped by the demands of adaptation to the environment, we are not just talking about learning simple responses. If an environment is constantly changing, it makes evolutionary sense to be prepared for novel kinds of learning. A species which can live in different environments may need the ability to learn very different behaviours to survive. Human beings live in all kinds of conditions, from arctic wastes to tropical forests, so it would be inappropriate for us to be genetically prepared to deal with a particular physical environment. Instead, we are genetically prepared to interact with and learn from other human beings, and that's what allows us to survive.

The human brain

We are also prepared for the learning we have to do because we inherit such a large brain. If we look at how the human brain (see Figure 8.3) is structured, we can trace its evolutionary heritage from the most primitive kinds of nervous system to the complex cerebrum which we looked at earlier (Figure 8.1).

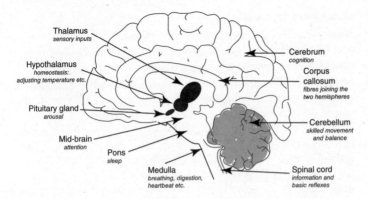

Figure 8.3 The structure of the brain.

The most basic functions are contained in the spinal cord, which reacts immediately to painful stimuli, and is also involved in the most basic kinds of association learning. Just above that, the spinal cord thickens out into two structures known as the medulla and the pons. The medulla controls automatic bodily functions, such as breathing, digestion and heartbeat, while the pons is involved in sleeping and wakeful states. So we can see the 'control' functions of the brain becoming more sophisticated as we move on from the spinal cord.

Above the pons and the medulla are the thalamus and the hypothalamus. The thalamus is involved in some basic decoding of incoming sensory information – hearing and vision, and it also channels that information on to the areas of the cerebrum where it can be fully analysed. The hypothalamus is a small structure below the thalamus, which plays an important part in keeping the body properly regulated. It will set off thirsty feelings if we become dehydrated, hunger if our blood sugar levels fall below what they should be, sweating if we become overheated, and so on.

Then, at the very back of the brain, is the cerebellum. This is a lobed, tightly wrinkled structure which has been called the 'little brain', because it co-ordinates bodily information like balance, movement and skilled actions, and a number of other processes. And then, covering everything else, is the cerebrum, which carries out learning, cognition, social recognition, and all those other functions which make us human.

STUDYING THE BRAIN

All nerve cells work by generating tiny amounts of electricity
and passing these on to one another. Neuropsychologists
study how the brain works by studying the electrical activity
of the brain. We saw in Chapter 5 how sleep researchers used
electro-encephalographs (EEGs) to monitor brain activity. These
record general changes in electrical activity. Figure 8.4 shows
an EEG chart which also shows a small seizure that the patient
experienced while the EEG was being recorded. The diagram in
the top left-hand corner shows where each electrode was placed
on the person's head, and the lines show the electrical activity
detected by the electrodes.

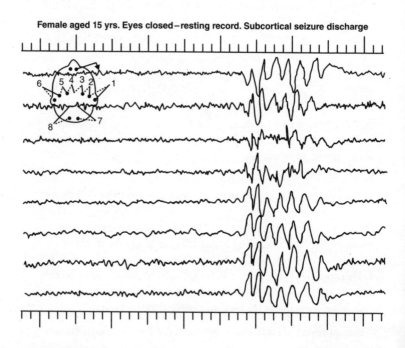

Figure 8.4 An EEG chart.

Of course, interpreting an EEG is a bit like standing outside a factory and trying to guess what they are making by listening to the noises coming through the window. However, EEGs have revealed some general patterns of brain activity. For example, when we are relaxed, an EEG trace shows large waves of electrical activity (large for the brain that is) known as alpha rhythms. We produce them just before we drift off to sleep, or when we are daydreaming or just relaxed and happy. But when we are concentrating hard, the EEG trace shows rhythms which are smaller and closer together, known as delta rhythms. Being generally awake doesn't produce detectable rhythms at all – just continuous intensive activity with no particular pattern (see Figure 8.5).

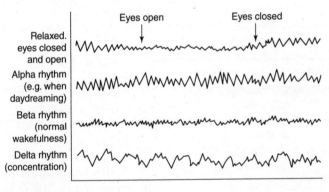

Figure 8.5 EEG traces of consciousness.

▶ Brain scans

For many decades, EEGs were the main way of studying the working brain. But they have now been replaced by modern scanning techniques, which are much more precise and have given us much better ways of looking at the brain. For example, one type of scan, known as a PET scan (short for positron emission tomography) involves looking at how much blood is being used by a particular part of the brain. Each time a nerve cell fires, it uses up some nutrients, and has to replace them from the blood supply. So PET scans identify which parts of the brain are using most blood. The blood is 'labelled' using a mildly radioactive chemical, which is detected by the scanner and shows up the neural pathways which are being used, and any blockages in blood flow.

CT scans (computed axial tomography) take a set of X-ray images of the brain and combine them to build up a three-dimensional picture. They can show areas of deformed or damaged tissue, such as blood clots or regions where the blood supply has been interrupted. But the most popular and useful form of modern scanning for psychologists is functional Magnetic Resonance Imaging (fMRI). This type of scanning works because the water molecules in brain cells have tiny magnetic fields which are influenced by the strong magnetic field of the scanner. They act slightly differently when a cell is active than when it is quiet, and this is detected by the scanner. fMRI brain scans only take a couple of seconds, so cognitive neuropsychologists – psychologists who are investigating the workings of the brain – can explore cognitive processes as well as medical disorders. For example, they might ask someone to read a word or remember a special event, and see which parts of the brain become active. Scanning techniques have helped us to learn a great deal more about the functioning of 'normal' brains, and researchers are slowly building up a picture of some of the principles of how the brain works, and which parts do what.

Human learning, then, includes association learning and the basic survival mechanisms. But it encompasses much more than that. Our heritage as adaptable social animals means that, as we saw in Chapter 2, we are engaging in social learning almost from birth: belonging to social groups is a significant motivator for human beings, and 'how to belong' is one of the most important forms of learning that we do. Our intrinsic ability to use and develop language means that we are able to pass on learning culturally, from one generation to another. And we also have a capacity for abstract thought and reasoning, resulting in the more formal kinds of learning which we will be looking at in the next chapter.

We can't deny our evolutionary heritage, because it has shaped our preparedness and our capacity for learning. But it hasn't shaped what we actually learn, nor what we do with that learning. In the next chapter, we will be looking specifically at human forms of learning, and at the human capacity we know as intelligence.

Focus points

It is useful to study animals in their natural contexts, because that can help us to understand more about human traits or abilities.

Natural selection happens when environmental circumstances favour a trait or traits, with the result that those who possess them are more likely to rear young successfully.

The principle of biodiversity means that there is no single line of 'progress' in evolution; just variations which help adaptation. Coevolution is all about how animals shape environments as well as being shaped by them.

Human beings have evolved as social primates, with an ability to adapt to widely differing environments through learning.

The cerebral cortex is the part of the brain directing most of our learning. It is larger and more folded in the more 'intelligent' animals, such as dolphins and humans.

Brain scanning techniques allow neuropsychologists to study the working brain, as well as detecting medical abnormalities.

9

Learning and intelligence

In this chapter you will learn:

▶ *to identify at least five different ways in which we can learn*

▶ *about the possible uses of intelligence testing*

▶ *why it is misleading to talk about 'intelligence' as an ability.*

Human beings learn all the time. Indeed, the amount that we can learn seems to be one of the main things which distinguishes us from other animals. Not the fact that we can learn at all – as we've seen, other animals can also learn, and those which are closest to us in evolutionary terms can learn a tremendous amount. But human beings seem to have a greater, and slightly different, capacity for learning than any of these other animals.

Forms of learning

So how, exactly, do we go about doing that learning? As we've seen, human beings are complex and operate on a number of different levels. Learning, too, can take place on several different levels. As human beings, we have several different kinds of learning available to us, and each kind is appropriate for different aspects of our experience. In this chapter, we will look at several different aspects of how people learn, before going on to look at how modern psychologists see the general abilities and knowledge which we think of as intelligence.

Key idea

Humans, as highly adaptable animals, have lots of different ways of learning. We've inherited the primitive mechanisms of early animals, the more sophisticated ones of higher animals, and also our own social and cultural ones. It's having all these different learning abilities together that makes us so special.

As we saw in the last chapter, one of the most basic forms of learning, and one which is shared by other animals too, is known as association learning. Association learning is sometimes called conditioning, on the grounds that it is all about producing a particular response under particular conditions. It isn't really a 'thinking' type of learning at all. Instead, it is where we have learned to make an automatic response to some outside event or stimulus. This response is controlled by the lower parts of the brain, and sometimes directly by the spinal cord, rather than by the cerebral cortex, which is the part of the brain concerned with thinking and decisions.

CLASSICAL CONDITIONING

There are two main types of conditioning, known as classical conditioning and operant conditioning. Classical conditioning, as studied by Ivan Pavlov, is the purest form of association learning and also seems to be the most primitive kind of learning of all. Pavlov studied dogs, and showed that their salivary reflex, which they produced automatically when they received food, could be conditioned to take place when they heard a bell or a buzzer.

But classical conditioning works in human beings, too. One of the best examples of this was a study conducted by Menzies, in 1937, concerning the reflex which we call vasoconstriction. This is something which the body does automatically when it is cold. In order to retain heat, the blood vessels near the surface of the skin shrink, while those in the middle of the body enlarge. This is why your skin will go paler when you are cold. It is an automatic reflex and one which we can't control deliberately.

Menzies asked research participants to plunge their arms into a bucket of ice-cold water, and each time they did so, a buzzer sounded. As you might expect, the cold water produced vasoconstriction. What was even more interesting, though, was that after a few trials, the vasoconstriction was also produced when the people heard the buzzer. It had become conditioned to the sound of the buzzer.

We can see, then, that classical conditioning can work even on responses which we don't consciously control. Vasoconstriction is an autonomic response – in other words, it is controlled by the autonomic nervous system. As we saw in Chapter 4, many of our emotional reactions are also controlled by the autonomic nervous system, and this may be why we sometimes find that emotional reactions can be triggered off suddenly by an unexpected event or situation.

Key idea

Classical conditioning is the most basic form of learning, and can be done by almost all animals. It doesn't need a complex brain, just a primitive nervous system, but it helps any animal to avoid pain or immediate danger.

▶ **Treating phobias**

Certain phobias – extreme fears which interfere with a person going about their ordinary life – seem to have a lot to do with classical conditioning. They are often formed by a learned connection between the object and a fear response in the past. Many people become frightened of spiders or wasps, for instance, because as small children they see adults responding in a frightened kind of way, which also frightens the child.

One difference, though, between animal and human learning is the way that human beings use imagination. Phobias are often kept alive and strengthened by the person imagining the feared object, and frightening themselves at the thought. Each time someone does this, they are strengthening the association between fear and the object, not physically, but in the mind. So conditioning in people isn't always exactly the same thing as conditioning in animals.

Conditioning can also be used to break a phobia, if it is deliberately used to make new associations with the object. One method for doing this is called systematic desensitization. In this method, the person gradually learns to relax in the presence of the object. They begin with something very indirect and non-threatening, like, say, a picture of the object, and learn to relax while looking at it. Once they can do this, they move to a slightly closer stimulus, like a realistic photograph of the object, and learn to relax again. Since you can't relax and feel frightened at the same time, what this method does is to replace the conditioned fear response with a learned relaxation response and, by doing this, the phobia disappears.

Another approach is much more direct. As we saw in Chapter 4, the fear response is all about getting as much energy available as possible. So it is very demanding of the body's resources, and hard for us to keep it up for long. After a while, the physiological fear reaction dies away and we calm down, even if we are still in the presence of the thing that we are frightened of. So another approach to treating phobias, known as implosion therapy, is simply for the person to be placed in a room with the thing that they are frightened of until the fear subsides. It may sound unpleasant, but it works – and it is much quicker than desensitization methods!

OPERANT CONDITIONING

The other main type of association learning is known as operant conditioning. In this type of conditioning, we learn something because it is immediately followed by a pleasant effect. That pleasant effect is sometimes a direct reward. For example, a squirrel will learn to climb a washing-line pole to reach a bird-feeding tray and gain the food. Sometimes, though, the pleasant effect comes from the removal of something unpleasant. An animal might learn to press a lever in order to avoid receiving an electric shock, or a schoolgirl might do her homework purely in order to avoid getting into trouble the next day.

▶ Reinforcement

These two types of pleasant effect are both known as reinforcement – because they reinforce, or strengthen, the behaviour that we have learned. The kind where we receive a reward is called positive reinforcement, whereas the kind where we escape from, or avoid, something unpleasant is known as negative reinforcement. Both positive and negative reinforcement have to happen immediately after the particular action which is being learned. Conditioning doesn't work if they happen later – if we do learn from delayed rewards, it is a different type of learning.

Sometimes people confuse negative reinforcement and punishment, but the two are really quite different. Both positive and negative reinforcement are about training a person or animal to do something – they encourage a particular kind of behaviour. But punishment is about stopping the person or animal from doing something, not about encouraging them to do something else. It's a bit confusing, because the threat of punishment can sometimes act as negative reinforcement, but the punishment itself never does.

The psychologist who became known as the 'father' of operant conditioning, B. F. Skinner, insisted that punishment was a very bad way of training children – or animals, for that matter – because all it did was to try to stop them from doing something, but it didn't give them any idea of what they ought to be doing instead. Skinner believed it was better to train children using operant conditioning, because that way they were rewarded for doing the right thing, and so encouraged to act correctly.

Key idea

Operant conditioning, in its essence, is learning by the effects of actions: whether their effects are pleasant or not. Most animals can do this, but some are better at it than others.

▶ Behaviour shaping

Operant conditioning has been used in a number of different ways, including training severely autistic children to talk by rewarding them with pieces of fruit for making noises, and then words.

Many of these methods used the principle of behaviour shaping, which allows us to use operant conditioning to produce entirely new types of actions. In behaviour shaping, a new action is trained by gradually changing what needs to be done to earn the reward.

For example, at the beginning of training, if an autistic child who is normally silent makes a noise, that would be enough to earn a reward. After a while, the child makes noises more often. Once the child is making noises, the psychologist or parent rewards them only when they make noises which sound a little like words. Once they have learned that, then they are rewarded only for making proper words. Eventually, the rewards 'shape' the child's behaviour until it is saying proper words, even though at first it was unable to speak.

Of course, we don't have to produce a reward every time. In fact, learning is generally stronger if the reward comes only now and again. This is known as partial reinforcement. People who play fruit machines are a classic example of how human behaviour can be manipulated by partial reinforcement: they will often play for hours (if they can afford it), only receiving a reward now and again. Computer games don't give money rewards, but they do give a strong sense of achievement when we get a bit further each time. Their programs are carefully calculated to make sure that we get enough rewards to continue playing with the machine.

▶ Conditioning and society

In 1972, Skinner went on to argue that society as a whole should develop systematic ways of conditioning people into behaving appropriately. People are always conditioned by the reinforcements around them, he argued, but these reinforcements act in a random, haphazard manner. If society were to take control of these reinforcements, it would be better than the random, unplanned approach, because then people would be trained to meet society's needs, and wouldn't act in antisocial ways.

As you might imagine, this caused a considerable amount of debate. The real core of the argument was that Skinner, along with many of the other behaviourists, believed that all human learning and personality came from conditioning. His book was called *Beyond Freedom and Dignity*, because he was arguing there was no such thing as 'freedom' or 'dignity' – they were just an illusion, and all human behaviour was really shaped by conditioning. Even language, Skinner argued, was only 'verbal behaviour', and had developed simply through conditioning and association.

Other psychologists, as well as people from other professions, disagreed. They argued that people do have free will and are able to make real choices. Skinner's reductionist argument was claiming that everything could be reduced to stimulus-response learning. But there are other ways that human beings learn and interact as well: being human does include responding to conditioning, but it is much more than that. There are other levels of learning, and as adaptable social animals, we do a great deal of learning directly from other people.

SOCIAL LEARNING AND ADAPTATION

From its very earliest days, a young infant is learning to handle its world. At first, that consists mainly of learning to control its body movements, and to make sense of the information which it is receiving through its senses. But as we saw in Chapter 2, human infants are predisposed to react most strongly to other people, and learning from others is an important part of how the infant continues to develop. Its knowledge of its world, and its competence in handling it become more sophisticated and continue to develop throughout childhood. This applies to the infant's social world just as much as it does to the physical world. The young child's sociability means that human beings are a major factor in the child's early learning.

Key idea

Early learning for all young animals, including humans, is all about becoming competent in dealing with the demands of their particular world. So the learning that they can do in infancy is shaped to what they need to survive.

This links with another very fundamental ability which the human infant has – that of adaptation. A human infant is able to adapt to a tremendous range of physical environments, child-rearing practices and diet. As long as it has a good quality of social interaction, and adequate physical care, an infant is able to adapt and develop. And as a result of this, human beings are found living successfully in nearly every part of the world.

▶ Transactions and contingencies

What enables the infant to adapt so well is its ability to learn. Infants are strongly predisposed to learn – indeed, that is what the large human brain is all about. Some scientists believe that the reason our babies are so helpless by comparison with other animals is because they are born prematurely, to allow the brain to continue growing outside the womb. It wouldn't be possible for the brain to reach a comparable level of maturity to other animals before birth, because that would make the brain much too large for the birth process.

Whatever the reason, part of an infant's predisposition to learn involves responding very strongly to certain types of events, such as transactions. Transactions are social exchanges between people, and babies are particularly fascinated by activities which allow them to create exchanges with people, such as turn-taking games or being talked to and responding in some way. Stratton (1983) discussed how transactions are a very important way that the young infant learns about its social world, and acquires the basis for social interaction in later life.

Another very special mechanism of learning for the infant is learning about contingencies. Contingencies are events which happen as a result of a particular action or activity. For example, making a car move along a road is contingent on starting the engine; winning the jackpot on a fruit machine is contingent on putting in money and pulling the handle. Just as infants are particularly interested in other people, so they are also particularly responsive to contingencies. If they can make something happen by, say, hitting it, they will do so over and over again.

This is the reason why babies like rattles and other things they can do to produce a noise. When the baby discovers that waving its hand around causes a rattle to make a sound, it explores that effect and continues to practise it over and over again. In this way, it gradually gains control over the situation. Infants become fascinated when they find that they can do something which makes something else happen, and this is the basis for many infant toys – and also games that they play with adults. Their interest also means that they will continue to try to master the skill. So human beings are strongly predisposed to learn from contingencies: it is an important basis for skill learning.

▶ Discrepancy

Infants also become very interested when things are different from what they expect. Not if everything is totally new, of course – then they are simply bewildered. But moderate amounts of discrepancy between what they expect and what actually happens is something that fascinates infants, and this, too, is the foundation for further learning. Learning about the world also involves learning what to expect under different circumstances. As the infant continues to develop, its environment will broaden and so will its range of experiences. We all learn most when the results of something are not quite the same as they have been in the past.

Of course, it is only moderate discrepancies which are helpful to the child's learning. If everything suddenly changes, then all the child's carefully acquired competence in dealing with its environment has been lost, which doesn't help it much. But some discrepancy is very good, even for relatively young children. For example, if an infant is staying with a grandparent or other relative, many aspects of its daily routine will be the same, but some will be different. Those differences allow the child to explore new contingencies and transactions and so help it to broaden its understanding of the world.

▶ Schemas

One of the reasons discrepancies are important is because they help the child to build up its store of knowledge. The child psychologist Jean Piaget argued that knowledge development in children happens through the formation of schemas – cognitive structures which store information. This isn't just information about the outside world. It also includes information about plans, intentions, and what is the right thing to do in certain situations. Adults use schemas too, and we will look at how they develop them later in this chapter.

The very first schema that an infant develops, Piaget believed, is the body schema – the idea that some parts of the world are 'me' while others are 'not-me'. This distinction, he believed, is originally enough to encompass everything that is important about the young infant's experience. But gradually, as the infant becomes more aware of its world, its experience becomes more differentiated, and its 'not-me' schema begins to expand and divide into different areas. One of the first of these is the differentiation between the physical environment and other people – we have already seen how the young infant responds differently to other people than it does to the things around it, and this suggests that it may be using different schemas.

▶ Developing competence

All of these mechanisms work together to help the young infant-then-child to develop competence in its dealings with the world. Perhaps the most important principle of child-rearing, in psychological terms, is that child development should be a continuous process of developing a sense of competence and effectiveness in dealing with the world. We have already seen how feeling helpless is stressful to human beings. Feeling competent is the opposite: when we feel that we can deal with our world adequately, we thrive, both mentally and physically.

As we saw in Chapter 6, when we feel competent and have high self-efficacy beliefs we are more likely to cope with problems, to make efforts to overcome difficulties, and to be successful in the end. So a child who has been brought up to interact competently in its world – who has experienced appropriate transactions and contingencies, and enough discrepancy to keep stimulating its interest in learning more – is a child who is better equipped to deal with the problems and disappointments which it may encounter in later life than a child who has not had those experiences.

Many of the damaging effects of the experience of refugee children, those who have suffered abuse from adults whom they trusted, and others with different traumatic experiences, originate from the sense of helplessness and total lack of control as the child's safe, secure world is torn apart. There are other sources of psychological damage in those situations as well, of course. But it takes a great deal of love, safety and help before a child – or an adult for that matter – is likely to feel secure and competent enough to begin a personal and emotional recovery.

CHILDHOOD LEARNING

In Chapter 3, we looked at how people use social scripts to help clarify and direct social interaction. Much of what children learn as they grow up involves developing those scripts – that is, broadening their understanding of what counts as appropriate behaviour in different situations. Children pick up social scripts from their families, their school experiences, and through books and TV – which is one reason for concern about the content of the TV that a child watches. We will be looking at this again in

Chapter 12. But children also learn from imitating other people, and this too is an area which has been studied by psychologists.

▶ Imitation and modelling

The most important of those psychologists was Albert Bandura. Bandura was particularly interested in how we learn by imitating others. Imitation is an important form of learning because it is a kind of shortcut. If we learned everything through operant and classical conditioning, we would have to do everything by trial and error – doing it, and seeing what the consequences are. But life is too short for that. Using imitation we can learn much more quickly.

Bandura performed a number of studies showing how people learn through imitation, and whom they are most likely to imitate. In one well-known study by Bandura and Walters, young children saw someone in a playroom with a lot of toys. The person was acting aggressively towards a bobo doll – a kind of doll which rocks backwards and forwards when it is hit. Some of the children saw the scene in real life, some saw it on film, and some saw a cartoon version. After they had seen this, they were then let into the same playroom and left to play with the toys.

After a while, the experimenters came in and removed the toys that the children were playing with. This was to make the children feel aggrieved and frustrated, so that they would be more likely to act aggressively. Then they observed how the children acted. Table 9.1 shows the average number of aggressive actions towards the bobo doll which children made during the next 20 minutes. As you can see, those children who hadn't seen anyone acting aggressively didn't make as many aggressive acts as those who had seen aggression being modelled.

Table 9.1 Aggressive acts performed towards a bobo doll.

Situation	Average number of aggressive acts
Real-life model	83
Filmed model	92
Cartoon model	99
Model playing unaggressively with toys	54

(adapted from Bandura and Walters, 1963)

When the children's actions were analysed more carefully, so that the researchers could tell which actions were specific copies of what the model had done, Bandura and Walters found that it was the real-life model which was copied most closely. In other studies, Bandura also found that children were most likely to imitate models like themselves – other children in preference to adults, people of the same gender, and so on. They were also more likely to imitate people that they admired.

Key idea

Imitation learning is more sophisticated than conditioning, because it involves whole sequences of behaviour and a certain amount of memory as well. But imitation allows us to learn what to do much more efficiently than by the trial and error involved in conditioning.

▶ Latent learning

The most important finding of all, at least as far as psychology was concerned, was that what the children had learned from the model didn't necessarily show up straight away. It remained latent, until it was needed. A child could see someone acting aggressively, and not seem to copy it at all. But later, if the child was in a situation where acting aggressively looked as though it would be useful, the child would act out the behaviour it had learned. Children store what they have learned, and only use it when the time seems right.

This is an important finding for two reasons. The first, of course, is what it suggests to us about the influence of violence on TV, and we will be looking at that a bit more closely in Chapter 12. But it is also important in terms of our general understanding of how learning happens. Skinner and the other behaviourists saw learning as an immediate change in behaviour. But Bandura showed that we can learn things even if we don't change our behaviour straight away. We can store our experience and use it later.

COGNITIVE LEARNING

In fact, Bandura wasn't the only person to have shown how we store our experience for later use. As early as 1932, Tolman had shown how experimental animals can develop cognitive maps, so that they have a mental image of what a maze looks like. Tolman gave a set of rats the opportunity to explore a complicated maze. If they were just put in the maze, they would just wander around. But then, if they were put in the maze and given a reward for getting out of it quickly, they would make their way straight to the exit point. They could use what they had learned from their explorations, but they only did so when it was worthwhile.

Human beings use cognitive maps too. Learning our way around somewhere new is often a matter of joining up apparently disconnected places until we have a mental map which makes sense to us. We organize our cognitive maps in terms of landmarks, such as special buildings that we have particularly noticed. Often, too, we have only a vague idea of the distances between these landmarks. Briggs (1971) found that we underestimate familiar distances, so they seem shorter. But we overestimate distances that we don't know very well. This is why, when you go somewhere new, distances often seem very large, but they shrink as you get to know the place.

Imitation and cognitive maps are both cognitive forms of learning, in that they involve remembering and thinking rather than just linking a stimulus with a response. There are other types of cognitive learning too. One of these is known as insight learning. In this, we learn something new by suddenly understanding its underlying principles. We might solve a maths problem, for instance, by getting a sudden insight into how we should reach the solution – why the problem is like it is.

Animals can show insight learning too. In 1925, Köhler reported a study with a number of different chimpanzees. One of them, Sultan, was particularly good at insight learning. He would be given problems to solve, such as reaching a piece of fruit hanging high above his head out of reach. A number of boxes would be scattered about in his cage. In one typical trial, Sultan dragged a box under the fruit and tried to reach it but it was still out of reach. After a few unsuccessful jumps, he would seem to give up. But then, suddenly, he would go to the other boxes and begin to pile them up until they were high enough for him to reach the fruit. He had solved the problem by getting an insight into what he needed to do.

▶ Learning sets

Some researchers argued that the chimpanzees in Köhler's study weren't actually thinking at all. Rather, they had simply learned from a lot of experience with trial and error learning. Harlow (1949) showed that monkeys could develop what he called learning sets – a readiness to solve a particular type of problem, rather than just learn a single answer. By rewarding a monkey with a raisin or a peanut each time it solved an odd-one-out problem, Harlow showed that the monkey could learn to look for the odd one, instead of just choosing the object which had hidden the reward on the last occasion.

Harlow took this as evidence that simple trial-and-error learning was all that an animal really needed to produce what seemed to be insight. But it can just as well be taken as evidence that animals, too, can develop concepts. It would be very difficult to draw a clear line between a learning set and the type of stored experience which we call a schema.

▶ Schemas

A schema is a whole set of knowledge or experience which we use in particular situations. Schemas are an important way that human beings learn. We fit new experiences into what we already know and try to make sense of them that way. Sometimes, we are successful, and the new experience fits into our existing schemas, without anything needing to change much. That learning process is known as assimilation – where an existing schema is applied to a new situation.

Sometimes, though, our new experience doesn't fit into our previous schemas very well. When this happens, the schema has to change, as it adjusts itself to the new information.

This is known as accommodation. Some psychologists and educationalists see accommodation as being the basis of all cognitive learning: we develop our understanding by extending and adjusting our existing ideas.

SKILL LEARNING

Not all types of learning are to do with absorbing new information though. A great deal of the learning that we do is concerned with learning skills – both physical skills and mental ones. And one of the main features of skill learning is that if we are skilled at doing something, we don't think about it, it just comes easily to us.

Key idea

A lot of childhood is about learning the basic physical skills so well that we don't have to think about them. It begins with essential actions like reaching out and taking hold of things, and gets progressively more sophisticated as we get older and our lives become more complicated.

Whether we think about what we are doing or not is what distinguishes experts from learners. A skilled skater doesn't think about balancing his body, but someone new to skating thinks about it all the time. A fluent reader doesn't have to look at each word in a sentence: instead, she usually looks directly only at one or two words in the middle of the sentence, and recognizes the others instantly by their shape. Someone who isn't very good at reading, though, has to read every single word. A skilled driver doesn't have to think what to do when changing gears to turn a corner, but a learner tries to remember everything at once and often gets very flustered as a result.

▶ Automatizing actions

All of these skills are different, but they all have one thing in common. That is, the individual units of the skill have become automatized. The person does them automatically, without thinking about it. Because they don't have to think about specific actions, this leaves them free to concentrate on other aspects of what they are doing – such as thinking about their complete performance in a skating exhibition, or the meaning of the story they are reading, or the best route to take.

An action which has been automatized is actually controlled by a different part of the brain than an action which we have to think about. The cerebrum is the part of the brain which we think with. It also has areas which receive information from our senses, including the body, and it has an area which is used for deliberate movement – when we consciously decide to move a particular part of the body. This area is known as the motor area and, as you can see from Figure 9.1, it is on the top of the brain, next to the sensory area which receives bodily feelings.

But the area of the brain which co-ordinates skilled movements isn't in the cerebrum at all. Instead, it is an entirely separate part of the brain, known as the cerebellum. The cerebellum is also concerned with deliberate movements, but it co-ordinates all the little actions which are involved so that they happen smoothly. If you decide to take a drink from a cup, for example, you don't think about reaching out, closing your fingers around the cup, and so on. All you think, if you think about it at all, is that you'd like a drink. The cerebellum co-ordinates all the actions needed to make that happen.

When a set of actions becomes automatized, control moves from the cerebrum to the cerebellum. A learner driver coming up to a corner has to think about the actions needed for signalling, braking, changing gear, turning the wheel and looking out for other traffic all at the same time, because these actions are all single, conscious ones being controlled by the cerebrum. We become flustered because it's a lot to think about all at once. But as we get more practised, the physical actions gradually weld themselves into a fluent unit, which is controlled by the cerebellum. This leaves the cerebrum free, so it can concentrate on looking out for other traffic, and can be alert for anything unexpected that might happen.

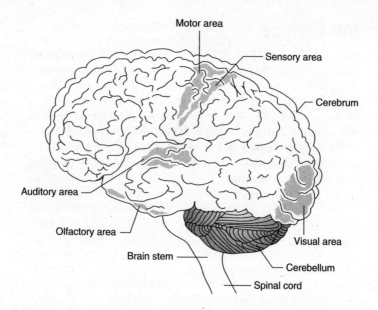

Figure 9.1 Areas of the brain.

Skills become automatized through practice. The more we do a set of actions, the more likely we are to link those actions into a complete, fluent movement that we don't have to think about. We can automatize mental abilities as well as physical actions. Reading is the main example: it only becomes automatized through lots of practice. But we can automatize other mental abilities, too, like the ability to do arithmetical calculations or to recognize patterns. With enough practice, people can acquire many different mental skills. And it is generalized mental skills which we are referring to when we talk about the human quality known as intelligence.

Key idea

All skill learning is really about practice and feedback. That applies just as much to cognitive skills, like writing essays, as it does to physical skills like playing musical instruments.

Intelligence

Intelligence is a difficult thing to define. Everyone knows what they mean when they say the word, but it is hard to pin down that meaning exactly. Perhaps the best definition anyone has been able to come up with was from the psychologist, Alice Heim, who said: 'Intelligence consists of grasping the essentials in a situation and responding appropriately to them' (Heim, 1970). It may not be a very specific definition, but it does seem to carry the general meaning which we think of when we think of intelligence.

Psychologists were studying intelligence throughout the twentieth century, although for the first 50 years that research was seriously distorted by political and social influences. These distortions occurred mainly because of some influential psychologists who believed in eugenics: the idea that people who were genetically inferior should not be allowed to reproduce, because they would weaken the species. And they measured 'inferiority' using intelligence tests, which were often very culturally biased.

It was an old-fashioned idea, stemming partly from a limited view of evolutionary theory, but mainly from the nineteenth-century belief that people inherited their abilities and characters – and also their position in society – and that these could not, and should not, be changed. But it was a vicious idea too. It formed the ideological basis of several political atrocities, including the Nazi concentration camps, restricted immigration for certain groups of people, and compulsory sterilization laws in some American states for those who did not achieve a certain IQ level.

▶ Temperament and potential

Nowadays, most psychologists take a much more positive view of the human being. We are aware that inheritance provides us with potential – for example, that each infant has a different temperament – but we are also aware that the potential is shaped and guided by our subsequent experience. A child who is born with a physically active, fidgety temperament can develop in many different ways, depending on social factors.

A lot will depend, for example, on whether the family sees that temperament as a positive thing, so that the child is encouraged to develop physically active skills and competences. If they see it as a nuisance, on the other hand, they may try to make the child learn to be quiet and restrained, which might cause some difficulties for the child and with its relationships with other people.

In other words, the same temperament can develop into very different personality traits depending on how people respond to it. Also, as we have seen, people continue to grow and develop psychologically throughout life. So to speak of genetic influence as if it were a fixed thing, setting some kind of top limit to our potential, is an idea which has become increasingly implausible as we have discovered more about the mechanisms by which people adapt and develop, throughout adulthood as well as in childhood.

Key idea

Intelligence is all to do with our ability to appraise situations and respond appropriately to them. So intelligent behaviour varies from one situation to another.

▶ Intelligence tests

Psychologists do, however, use intelligence tests sometimes. Not because they measure the limit of our intelligence (you can get better at intelligence tests if you practise them) but because they can help us to know a bit more about that person. Intelligence tests may not tell us exactly how intelligent someone is, but they do tell us how well developed certain of their skills are. Some skills – such as the ability to comprehend words quickly and accurately – are skills which we often need in modern life.

There are two kinds of intelligence tests: group tests and individual tests. Group tests are usually pencil and paper tests (nowadays generally administered by computer, though), which consist of several different problems that the person has to solve as quickly as possible. Because they are carried out in conditions a bit like an exam, it is possible for several people to be tested at once, and they are often used for selection to courses or career opportunities, such as the civil service.

Individual tests, though, involve a psychologist seeing just one person and presenting each part of the test to them separately. They consist of lots of varied tasks, each of which assesses different mental skills, and so they are often useful for helping to understand people who are having specific difficulties, perhaps with learning, or sometimes in coping with their day-to-day lives.

No psychologist nowadays would see an intelligence test, on its own, as giving enough information to make a decision about whether somebody was suitable for a job or a course. Intelligence tests, like other psychometric tests, have to be used along with interviews and records of achievement: they are not accurate enough to be the sole basis for decision-making.

THEORIES OF INTELLIGENCE

We actually use the word 'intelligent' to mean a lot of different things. Sometimes, we are talking about someone who is very quick to grasp important matters and make fast decisions. Sometimes we are talking about someone who is a 'deep thinker', and can see into problems more deeply than the rest of us. And sometimes, we are talking about someone who can be quick-witted and humorous in conversation. Each of these is an example of what we would think of as intelligence, but they are actually very different.

▶ Intelligence as multiple abilities

In modern psychology, one way of looking at intelligence is to see it as consisting of a number of different abilities. Gardner (1986) proposed that there isn't a single thing called intelligence, but that what we are actually referring to is a set of seven entirely different intelligences. The seven types of intelligence he identified are listed in Table 9.2.

Table 9.2 Gardner's seven intelligences.

Linguistic intelligence	– to do with language and how we use it.
Musical intelligence	– to do with musical appreciation as well as performing and composing music.
Mathematical–logical intelligence	– to do with calculation and logical reasoning.
Spatial intelligence	– to do with art and design, as well as finding your way around.
Bodily kinaesthetic intelligence	– to do with physical skills, like sport, dancing and other aspects of movement.
Interpersonal intelligence	– to do with interacting with people socially and sensitively.
Intrapersonal intelligence	– to do with understanding your own personal self and abilities.

Each of these intelligences, according to Gardner, is completely separate. Most people that we would call 'intelligent' have a combination of these different abilities, but some are particularly good at only one or two, and not at the others. A musical genius, for instance, will have one type of intelligence very highly developed, but might be quite ordinary in other respects. What we call an 'idiot savant' is someone who is well below average intelligence in most respects, but has one outstanding ability – such as to remember, or to calculate. Gardner's idea of separate intelligences shows how this may be possible.

One problem with Gardner's approach, though, is that it tends to treat these separate intelligences as if they just developed within the person, and have nothing to do with social influences. Although he drew much of his evidence from the biographies of high-achieving people, Gardner ignored the social influences on them. But people who achieve outstanding ability in any area have usually had at least one person who believed in them and encouraged them. Some psychologists believe that this influence may be more important than we realize.

Key idea

Modern psychologists are agreed that intelligence isn't a single thing, but a combination of lots of different abilities. But different psychologists have different ideas about which particular abilities are important.

▶ The triarchic theory of intelligence

Another way of looking at intelligence is to see it as nested very firmly within its social and cultural context. Sternberg (1986) developed what became known as the triarchic theory of intelligence. He identified three different aspects of intelligence, each of which contributes to how intelligently we interact with other people.

The first facet of intelligence is contextual intelligence. Any intelligent act or ability, Sternberg said, takes place within a context. It happens in a society and a culture, and that makes all the difference to how the act or ability is regarded. For instance, imagine someone who is particularly quick at responding to something that has been said to them. In one culture, this might be regarded as a sign of intelligence, but in another culture, it might be seen as a sign of impulsiveness and lack of thought. A slower, more thoughtful way of responding would be considered more intelligent. So one part of intelligence is to do with how the person responds to the demands and expectations of their culture.

The second facet of intelligence which Sternberg identified is experiential intelligence. In the last chapter, we saw how experiences and expectations affect the way that we think, perceive and remember. We also learn from our experiences, and all this forms a significant part of our intelligence. Experience can influence intelligence in two ways: firstly, because of the automatized skills which we have developed and, secondly, because of the way that it helps us to recognize the demands of a situation, and what would be the best thing to do.

The third facet of intelligence is the one which is usually assessed by intelligence tests – or at least, by modern intelligence tests. Some of the early ones were very culturally biased, assuming that anyone who was not familiar with the practices of white American or English culture was automatically mentally inferior. But modern tests are much better at assessing what Sternberg called componential intelligence. Componential intelligence consists of three parts: firstly, our ability to learn and acquire knowledge; secondly, how well we actually carry out a task, such as problem-solving or calculation; and thirdly, higher mental abilities such as our ability to plan and make decisions.

So each part of componential intelligence contributes to how well we think and process information. But how we do it is also influenced strongly by our own personal experience, and by the cultural and social setting in which we find ourselves. Intelligence isn't something which just happens in a social vacuum: it is part of social living. And different societies value different intellectual skills, which means that what we consider to be 'intelligent' behaviour also varies.

▶ **Emotional intelligence**

In 1995 Goleman argued that there was another form of intelligence which had been completely neglected by other researchers, which is all to do with maintaining positive interactions and relationships with other people. Some people are noticeably better at this than others. They show more social understanding, are more likely to spot when someone is distressed or upset, are more diplomatic in how they say things, and generally more sensitive to social demands. Goleman argued that these people have higher levels of emotional intelligence, and that this is another quality which makes a considerable difference in everyday life.

Since Goleman's first book, other psychologists too have been looking at the idea of emotional intelligence. It seems to consist of a number of different facets: a list produced by Petrides, Furnham and Frederickson (2004) is summarized in Table 9.3. Researchers have also shown that people can improve their emotional intelligence through sensitivity training and other activities, and a number of training courses have been based on these ideas. As we can see from the table, the idea of emotional intelligence also links quite closely with the positive psychology movement which we looked at in Chapter 4.

Table 9.3 Facets of emotional intelligence.

Adaptability	flexible and willing to adapt
Assertiveness	forthright and frank with people
Emotional expression	able to communicate feelings to others
Emotional management	able to influence other people's feelings
Emotional perception	clear about our own and others' feelings
Emotion regulation	capable of controlling our own emotions
Low impulsiveness	reflective, not giving in to immediate urges
Relationship skills	having fulfilling personal relationships
Self-esteem	self-confident and successful
Self-motivation	persistent in achieving goals, not giving up easily
Social competence	having good social and networking skills
Stress management	able to withstand pressure and regulate stress
Empathy	seeing things from someone else's point of view
Happiness	cheerful and satisfied with everyday living
Optimism	confident and looking on the bright side of life

(adapted from Petrides, Furnham and Frederickson, 2004)

▶ An adjective, not a noun

Inevitably, though, researchers have argued about how to measure emotional intelligence, and how it should be defined – as they do with all other aspects of intelligence. Rose, Kamin and Lewontin (1984) argue that part of the reason why people find it so difficult to define what intelligence actually is, is because it is an adjective, not a noun. It isn't a 'thing' which people have, it's more a question of how we approach things.

When we talk of someone being intelligent, what we really mean is that they are able to do something intelligently. They have done an intelligent act, or had intelligent thoughts – in other words, they have gone about things in a certain way, which is distinctive. Rose, Kamin and Lewontin question whether intelligence as a separate 'thing' actually exists at all, in the sense that it is elusive to define, means different things in different social contexts, and doesn't really help us to understand what people do or why they are like they are. Taking all the evidence into account, it is probably more useful if we think of intelligence in this way, because this means that we are much more likely to see intelligent actions in their context.

We have seen, then, that human beings can learn in some very different ways. As with all of the other aspects of psychology in this book, we have only been able to skim over some of the main areas – there are other forms of learning, too, and much more psychological research into these areas than we have been able to look at here. What is important, though, is to remember that as human beings, we don't just use one way of learning. We can learn in a number of different ways, and sometimes even on several levels at once.

Focus points

Learning is not a single skill, but takes many different forms.

Conditioning is the most basic type of learning. Classical and operant conditioning can both help change some very specific types of human behaviour.

Infants show social learning almost from birth. Their readiness to learn from transactions, contingencies and discrepancies shows how their capacity to learn from others is quite sophisticated.

Much of our learning happens at a cognitive level and doesn't immediately show in our behaviour. Information becomes organized into mental structures such as schemas, which help us to deal competently with the world.

Most childhood learning has to do with developing cognitive and physical skills, through practice and automatization.

Intelligence is difficult to define, and probably doesn't exist as a single 'thing': most modern psychologists see it as composed of many different skills.

10

Childhood and adolescence

In this chapter you will learn:

- ▶ *why 'playing' is so important for human infant development*
- ▶ *how children develop social competence*
- ▶ *the four approaches to understanding adolescence.*

In the next two chapters, we will be looking at how we develop throughout our lifespan. In this chapter, we will look at childhood and adolescence, and in the next chapter we will look at adulthood and ageing. Until about the 1980s, developmental psychology was more or less entirely child psychology, because the focus of interest was on how children develop. It was assumed that by the time people were 20 or so, their development was largely over. We know now, though, that this is completely wrong. People continue to develop throughout their lives. As ten-year-olds, we are obviously very different than we are as 20-year-olds, but we are also different at age 20 than we are at age 30, and different again at 40, and so on. So modern developmental psychology covers the whole lifespan and not just the early years of life. For various reasons, though, there has been more psychological research into childhood than any other period of life, so we will begin by looking at some of the major findings.

Childhood

During the course of this book we have already covered many different aspects of child development. In Chapter 2, we saw how the young infant is primed to be sociable, almost from the first moment that it is born. In Chapter 6, we explored the importance of self-efficacy beliefs for children's learning, and in the last chapter we saw how children learn through building up their schemas about the world around them. There are several other examples throughout this book. So, in this chapter, we will try to bring together some of the main aspects of childhood, looking in turn at the child's social development, motivational development, and skills development. But we will begin by looking at research into children's play.

PLAY

Playing is one of the main ways that children learn. Through play, they practise important skills, broaden their knowledge of the world around them and, of course, develop physically. There are several different kinds of play, and the main ones are listed in Table 10.1. We will look at each of these in turn.

Table 10.1 Types of play.

Physical play	e.g. running, jumping about, spinning, climbing
Pretend play	e.g. imagining situations, characters, scenes
Play with words	e.g. puns, rhymes, riddles
Play with objects	e.g. playing with toy cars, dolls, household objects
Social play	e.g. ring o' roses, competitive games, role-play

Key idea

The different types of children's play reflect the very complex lives we live as humans. All of them give children practice in necessary skills and understanding.

▶ Physical play

Each type of play serves its own function. Physical play, of course, helps the child to develop a strong body through exercise, and improves the child's general physical health. It also encourages the child to develop a clear body schema, so that it becomes aware of its physical capabilities and develops better co-ordination. Physical confidence isn't everything, of course, but it can be quite an important source of self-efficacy beliefs, and we have seen how important those are. Although it has often been overlooked in modern Western societies, or relegated to the limited arena of school sports, physical play sets an important psychological as well as physical foundation for later adulthood.

Physical play is sometimes a purely individual activity. Most children will simply enjoy developing the physical skills involved in swinging on a bar, or clambering around a climbing frame. Indeed, the urge to climb on things is very powerful in small children, and may represent an inherited drive to develop our physical skills to the full. Some physical play, though, is more social. Rough-and-tumble play between children, or between adults and children, is also something which children evidently enjoy a great deal, and it serves a social as well as a physical function.

▶ Pretend play

Pretend play, on the other hand, is about a different sort of learning. It allows the child to explore its world and the possibilities which it offers. It is no accident that children's pretend play usually begins by acting out simple domestic situations, because understanding its social world is important to every child. Pretend play allows the child to practise different social roles, and to develop an awareness of the wider social world.

Pretend play also encourages the child to develop its imagination, and many children do this to quite a high degree. It isn't uncommon, for example, for a child to develop an imaginary playmate who accompanies the child and becomes the focus for its exploration of the world. These imaginary playmates may be human, or they may be humanized animals, such as a lion or a horse. Although parents sometimes worry when their child begins to talk to someone who isn't there, there is no evidence at all that it is harmful. Some psychologists have even studied the number of high-achieving scientists and public figures who had imaginary playmates when younger, and have suggested that exercising the imagination in this way is actually a very positive thing for a child to do. But it is hard to obtain evidence for this idea one way or the other.

▶ Play with words

Children also enjoy playing with words. Indeed, as anyone who has heard a toddler babbling knows, they seem to enjoy playing with speech sounds before they even have words, and this urge to experiment continues throughout early childhood. Many children talk constantly to themselves as they play. This type of talking, known as egocentric speech, doesn't have much to do with communication. Its main function is to help the child to think. Vygotsky (1962) argued that when a child is using egocentric speech it is actually thinking aloud – the language is a kind of running commentary on what the child is thinking about. As the child grows older, this way of using language becomes internalized – we think it to ourselves, but don't say it out loud. That is, unless we have become too used to being on our own when we often revert to thinking out loud again. People who live alone often talk to themselves, but as with small children, this doesn't mean anything except that they are thinking about what they are doing.

Children also engage in sociable playing with words. In the late 1960s, Lorna and Peter Opie went around children's playgrounds collecting the word games which children used. They collected an enormous set of rhymes, riddles and puns, and argued that these form a verbal culture, passed on from child to child. Many of these rhymes are still current nowadays, and the popularity of these word games implies that they are an important part of how children learn to interact with one another. They also help children to develop an understanding of how subtly words can be used. It doesn't stop with young children, either – the fascination with 'double-meanings' shown by adolescents who are just learning about sex is another example of the many different ways in which people play with words.

Key idea

Playing with words, like other forms of play, doesn't stop at childhood. Most teenagers go through a stage of seeing double meanings in just about any innocent remark, and adults enjoy puns, crosswords and many other kinds of word play.

▶ Play with objects

A great deal of children's play doesn't actually involve toys at all. But some does, and even from quite a young age, an infant will play with an object, holding it, sucking it and being interested in it. Lowe (1975) discussed how play with objects becomes more sophisticated as the child grows older and its social awareness develops. Lowe's stages are presented in Table 10.2.

Table 10.2 Stages in playing with objects.

Age of child	Activity
9 months	The child will hold, wave, bang and suck objects.
12 months	The child looks at things before sucking, waving, banging them about.
15 months	Familiar objects are used as if in everyday life, e.g. 'pretend' drinking from a cup.
21 months	The child uses more than one thing together, e.g. 'feeding' a doll from a toy bowl.
24 months	The child's play with objects is becoming increasingly realistic, mirroring everyday life, e.g. driving toy cars along marked-out 'roads'.
30–36 months	The child begins to get toys to 'act' for themselves, e.g. a doll may put the other toys to bed.

Toys which attract curiosity and interest in children seem to be preferred to toys that are simple representations of objects. Corinne Hutt suggested that exploratory play is linked strongly with both mental and emotional development in children, which suggests that it is a good idea for a child to have toys which encourage it to explore and to be curious. In one set of studies, Hutt used a 'supertoy', which was a wooden box with wheels, buzzers, bells, counters, pedals and levers. Playing with different combinations of levers and pedals would produce several different outcomes – noises would sound and counters would be covered up or revealed. Children enjoyed playing with the supertoy, and would play with it for longest if it was set to maximum complexity.

Hutt also observed two- to three-year-old children playing with the supertoy, and then saw the same children four years later. Those children who had been most interested in exploring the supertoy were more confident and more social, and also had higher IQ levels than those who didn't explore it much. Nobody is suggesting from this that playing with the supertoy produced these differences, of course. But it does suggest a strong link between an inclination to explore, and later development. And this in turn suggests that toys which encourage exploration and curiosity in children are likely to be of positive benefit.

Key idea

Some of the most popular toys for young children are ones which mimic objects used by the adults around them. Sometimes, these can shape a child's preferences to such an extent that the final career the child chooses is directly related to those early favourite toys.

▶ **Social play**

Social play is another category of playing which has been studied by psychologists, although as we have seen, several of the other kinds of play can be social at times. Essentially, there are three main kinds of social play: free play, which is worked out by the children themselves as they go along; formal play, which has clearly defined rules and procedures, such as skipping games or card games; and creative play in which children develop a new game together, perhaps involving imaginary characters or entirely new rules.

Early research into children's play tended to focus on children in playgroups, and so was all to do with how children of the same ages played together. But of course most social play actually takes place between members of the same family – brothers, sisters, parents and other relatives – that is, between people of different ages. Cohen (1987) used diary methods to record the play of his two young sons within the family, and found that even from a very early age, children would initiate different favourite games with different members of the family.

Garvey (1977) showed that when pre-school children are left to play with someone of the same age, they often begin a kind of dramatic play, involving familiar scenes and stories. Younger children, for example, often play games about mothers taking care of babies; while older children are more likely to play games which reflect their growing awareness of a wider context, like doctor–nurse games or acting out fairy stories.

We can see, then, that children's play is quite varied, and can take many different forms. Through playing, children develop skills and engage in exercising both their mental and physical muscles in preparation for adult life. What is very striking, though, is how much of children's play is social in character. Even if a child is not actually interacting with other people directly, it is often rehearsing social roles or expressing its social awareness as it interacts with toys. The psychological study of play, like so many other aspects of psychology, shows us just how powerfully we are influenced by other people and our social worlds.

SOCIAL DEVELOPMENT

Children develop socially in other ways too. Young children do a great deal of watching and learning from the adults around them, and from the scenes they see portrayed on TV or in other contexts. We saw in the last chapter how important imitation and modelling are in the child's learning, and much of that focuses on the scripts and social schemas which are acted out in front of the child. Children learn about social ways of expressing emotions, ways of dealing with situations, and also different ways of interacting with others.

In the middle of the twentieth century, psychologists tended to believe that a child's developing understanding of its world occurred simply as a result of interacting with things – people or objects, it didn't matter which. The child would build up its schemas through assimilation and accommodation (see Chapter 9), and gradually become capable of formal abstract thinking as it matured. These ideas were based on the thinking of the famous Swiss psychologist, Jean Piaget. But in the last 20 years of the twentieth century, psychologists came to realize that Piaget had underestimated the power of social influences on children and, as a result, had failed to appreciate how sophisticated even a young child's thinking can become.

▶ Developing social competence

In the 1980s, a group of researchers based at Cambridge University carried out a large-scale ethological study of young children in their families. They explored how small children interact at home, and found that in this context, children are far more socially competent than they had thought. Dunn (1988) argued that the play, humour, emotions and conflicts in family life are part of the way a child learns. The child doesn't just pick up what it is supposed to do from praise or punishment – it takes part, actively, in a series of dynamic and emotional exchanges.

Some of those exchanges consist of teasing older brothers or sisters. Dunn found that children often deliberately provoke their siblings, sometimes bringing them to the point of tears. Every family is different, and some families quarrel more than others, but teasing is a very common activity among pre-school children, and one which they become more sophisticated at as they grow older. Up until the age of about two, the child tends only to tease its older or younger siblings, but from age two onwards, it is just as likely to tease its mother – often by deliberately beginning to do something forbidden while she is watching, and seeing how she reacts.

Children don't just tease though, they also comfort their siblings, and even their parents, when they are upset. Even children as young as two years old will respond to a brother or sister's distress, and try to comfort him or her by offering toys or stroking. Comforting was particularly evident among the older pre-school children in Dunn's study. By 14 months or so, younger children will also comfort their older brothers and sisters when they are upset, or their parents when they have accidents or minor upsets.

Key idea

Dealing with teasing and frustration when interacting with other children gives us the social learning that we need to deal constructively with irritating people or difficult social situations in adult life.

By and large, a child becomes fully aware of other people as independent individuals, with minds and feelings of their own, round about the age of three-and-a-half. This awareness is the basis for empathy, social responsibility and all sorts of other qualities which are such an important part of belonging to society – and we acquire it far earlier in life than researchers used to think.

Dunn identified four features of social competence which young children evidently possess and which imply that they are far more competent than people often assume. These four features are listed in Table 10.3. There is, of course, much more to the child's social cognitive development than this, but the information that researchers have gained from studying children's social competence has told us a great deal about what we can normally expect from a child, at what age.

Table 10.3 Developing social competence.

Understanding others' feelings	'Tuning in' to the moods of others, and responding to distress, amusement and other emotions.
Understanding others' goals	Developing an awareness of other people's intentions and personal plans.
Understanding social rules	What is and is not permitted, when rules will or won't apply, the idea of responsibility, and the use of excusing and justifications.
Developing a theory of mind	Understanding that other people have minds of their own and may know or not know things that the child knows.

(adapted from Dunn, 1988)

▶ Social influence

Children continue to develop throughout their childhood, and later childhood is an important period for the formation of friendships, physical and linguistic competences, and all sorts of other abilities. But that learning doesn't happen in a vacuum. It is structured by school, by parenting, and by other social interactions that the child experiences. The Russian child psychologist, Vygotsky, emphasized the importance of other people in the child's cognitive development, and argued that their influence is essential if a child is to realize its full cognitive potential.

The zone of proximal development (ZPD), according to Vygotsky, is that part of the child's potential which the child is able to achieve with structure and guidance from others. This is far greater than a child can manage on its own, as parents and teachers know intuitively. It includes abstract thinking, reasoning, problem-solving, complex language use and the development of sophisticated memorizing. All of these are cognitive abilities which are brought on and developed by the child's school and family experiences – the informal teaching which happens in families, schools and neighbourhoods is just as important for the child's cognitive development as formal teaching in school. Both of them contribute to the child's increasing ability to handle sophisticated ideas and abstract thinking as it becomes older, and they are both important in the child's socialization – that is, in the way that the child becomes able to take full part in its culture and society.

Key idea

Vygotsky showed how children need adults to bring on and shape their learning. But the most important influences don't always come from the parents: many successful adults were strongly influenced as children by a teacher or family friend who encouraged their interests.

MOTIVATIONAL DEVELOPMENT

How far the child does participate, and how far it takes advantage of the educational and social learning opportunities which others can provide, depends very much on how the child is motivated. In Chapter 2, we saw how important the expectations of other people can be for children. Rosenthal and Jacobson showed how simply expecting a child to do well made an enormous difference to how well they actually did. The adults unconsciously transmitted their expectations to the children, and the children lived up to what was expected of them. There are many other aspects of teaching and learning in which interpersonal relationships and social interactions are extremely important.

▶ Achievement motivation

For example, as any teacher will tell you, some children seem to have a much stronger need for achievement than others. These children often learn well, because success is important to them and so they put a great deal of effort into studying. They aren't the only children who learn well, of course, some others do it purely because they are interested in what they are learning. But it is helpful for children to have a reasonably high level of achievement motivation, because this will see them through temporary difficulties and setbacks as they come to terms with new things.

In one early study, Rosen and D'Andrade (1959) showed that achievement motivation seems to have a great deal to do with the way that parents interact with their children. In one of their studies, they gave a child a difficult task to do, while its parents were watching. The child was blindfolded and asked to build a tower, as high as possible, out of building bricks. The researchers took note of how hard the child tried to do this – how much effort was put in to getting the tower as high as possible – on the grounds that this would give them some idea of the child's general level of achievement motivation.

Rosen and D'Andrade also observed the parents closely, while the child was trying to complete the task. They found that those children with the highest level of achievement motivation had parents who consistently gave them praise and encouragement. Their parents also had quite high expectations – they anticipated that their child would do quite well in the task, and the children often lived up to those expectations. Parents of children who had low achievement motivation, though, didn't expect their children to achieve very much, and didn't particularly encourage them either.

Key idea

Encouragement and merited praise are much more effective than material rewards in motivating children to do well. It's another example of how important social influences are in human development.

Skills and schemas

We have seen already how children's play helps them to develop skills which they will use in later life. Skills can take many different forms, but whether they are physical, mental or social, the actual way they develop is very similar – through practice and feedback. In Chapter 12 we will look at this in more detail, in terms of how sport psychologists use their knowledge of skill development to enhance sporting performance among athletes. But all human beings develop skills, whether they be in cooking, driving, arithmetic or animal care. And it is practice, as they say, that makes perfect.

We saw earlier how different types of play encourage the child to develop physical skills. For most children, their experiences are carefully graduated so that new skills build on their existing competences, and also provide the foundation for later ones. So, for example, the early years of primary school tend to have many activities emphasizing hand–eye co-ordination. As the child grows older, what is required of them in this respect becomes more subtle, as the child becomes more capable – learning to write develops an emphasis on good handwriting; artwork trains the child in representational drawing and management of colour; physical activities become structured physical sports, and so on – all part of Vygotsky's zone of proximal development, in which the child's abilities are refined and brought on by adult contact.

Key idea

Developing skills with words and logical thinking is just as important in childhood development as learning physical skills. Like all other skills, they are developed with practice and feedback, which is something that comes from families as well as schools.

SCHEMA DEVELOPMENT

Jean Piaget developed a theory of the child's cognitive development, which detailed the mental skills which children acquire at different stages in their development. Piaget believed that young children are fundamentally egocentric – that is, they are entirely driven by their own experiences, and are unable to conceptualize abstract concepts, or ideas outside of their own experience. This egocentricity reduces gradually through childhood, as the child develops cognitive schemas which it uses to make sense of the world.

Schemas are mental structures which organize the child's knowledge, and they grow and develop from each other. As we've already seen, the very first experiences of the world become gradually organized by the young infant into 'me' and 'not-me' – the beginnings of the body-schema. As the child grows, these schemas develop and become more sophisticated through the two processes of assimilation, in which new experiences are absorbed into the schema so that it can be used more widely, and of accommodation, in which the schema itself is stretched, or even divided, to fit the new experiences.

In this way, schemas grow and multiply, eventually giving the child a firm cognitive base to use when making sense of things, and also to use when performing what Piaget called operations on the environment. An operation may be a thought, a remark, or an activity, but its important characteristic is that the child is using its knowledge to do something – to answer a question, or perform a task. Piaget also believed that children only became capable of certain kinds of operations when they reach certain cognitive stages, which are listed in Table 10.4.

Table 10.4 Piagetian stages.

Stage	Age (approx)	Description
The sensorimotor stage	0–2 years	Learning to organize and interpret sensory information and to co-ordinate motor activity.
The pre-operational stage	2–7 years	Beginning to reduce egocentricity, but can only take account of one feature at a time, and is unable to decentre.
The concrete operational stage	7–11 years	Able to undertake adult-style cognitive operations, but only with real-world targets.
The formal operational stage	11+	The child is now fully decentred, and can undertake abstract reasoning and perform logical operations.

There has been a great deal of controversy about Piaget's stages – many psychologists nowadays feel that they over-simplified what children are capable of, and also ignored their social competences. As we have already seen, children are a lot more sophisticated socially than people used to think. Piaget's theory also didn't really take account of how systematic training by adults can influence how the child's mind develops. In recent years there have been many examples of how an enriched environment can help a child to develop its schemas more effectively, and how early learning programmes can bring on a child's mental development.

One of the main problems was Piaget's insistence that children are simply not capable of certain kinds of operations until certain ages. Many researchers since have shown that the tasks which Piaget used were only difficult for children because they were taken out of context and presented in an abstract way. If they are presented differently – for example, by putting them in a familiar context and making the task into a game – children can deal with even quite complex matters. The important thing is to start with what the child already knows, and make sure that any new learning serves to extend and develop the schemas that the child already has. When we do this, we find that children's mental development isn't nearly as limited as the Piagetian stages would imply.

The idea of the schema, though, is very useful. It helps us to see how the child builds up its knowledge, and also becomes more skilled at applying it in different contexts. In Chapter 3 we saw how important social scripts are for our understanding of our social worlds. These, too, are types of schema which help us to understand the world. Throughout childhood – and adulthood too for that matter – we pick up social scripts and apply them to make sense of what is around us. And we use them to work out how we 'ought' to behave in different situations. We will be coming back to this idea in Chapter 13, when we look at the influence of TV.

▶ Developing personal constructs

Other types of schema concern the way that we understand other people. As we grow older, our unique store of experience leads us to develop our own ideas about what people are like. These ideas are known as personal constructs (see Chapter 6) and are the individual theories and ideas about the world that we develop from our personal experiences, and apply to new situations. Driver (1983) showed how these can be extremely important when people are trying to understand information at school. If our own personal understanding of the world doesn't fit in with what we are supposed to learn, then we will absorb only part of what we are learning. We will adjust the information so it fits with our own personal construct system.

This, Driver argued, is the source of most of the common factual errors which schoolchildren – and adults – make. She looked at children's everyday understanding of scientific ideas, such as heat or falling (gravity), and showed that if we develop knowledge of these things purely from our own experience, then the conclusions we come to are not the same as those developed by physicists. By the time children learn about these things in school, they have had plenty of time to develop their own theories and ideas about how the world works. As the children try to understand what they are learning, these theories get in the way.

Driver showed how understanding how students develop and apply their own personal construct systems to what they are learning can help teachers to teach more effectively. Mistakes don't come from stupidity, or an unwillingness to learn, but from applying the wrong kind of ideas to what they are supposed to be learning. Understanding this helps teachers to know what kind of explanations will be needed and why some students are having difficulty.

Key idea

Children, as well as adults, are always trying to make sense of their experiences. Schemas and personal constructs are how we go about this, and many of the amusing explanations given by children arise because of the personal constructs which they have developed as part of making sense of their worlds.

SOCIAL SKILLS

The most fundamental of all human skills are social skills. As we have already seen, even a very young infant will smile, grimace and make eye contact with others. These are very basic signals in human interaction – so much so, that we often regard people who don't use them in the usual way as being 'odd' or 'difficult'. We can convey tremendous amounts of information through facial expressions, and we automatically take that into account when we are communicating with other people. On the phone, or in written language where it isn't possible to see the person we are communicating with, we have to substitute for them: we use different tones of voice on the phone, and punctuation in writing, to let the other person know what we really mean.

It isn't just facial expressions either. They way we stand, sit or move also conveys social meanings – like being bored, or being interested, or being in a hurry. All this body language is an important part of social competence, and children acquire these skills more or less automatically by interacting with others. Social play gives them an opportunity to practise their social skills, but again, as with so many other skills, they can be developed and enhanced by experience and interacting with other people.

The fact that so little teaching is required for these skills indicates that they are hard-wired into our mental frameworks – that is, we develop them as a natural part of our growth. All human societies recognize the basic expressions of emotion and affection, because these skills have been fundamental to our evolution as social animals. And many studies have shown that we attach far more importance to body language and tones of voice than we do to the actual words that people use when they are speaking to us.

Not everyone is equally good at these skills, of course. We all know people who are 'good listeners', or other people who are difficult to get on with, and often this comes down to the way that they use body language to communicate. One of the more reliable gender differences is the way that female humans tend to be more sensitive to these skills than men – as a general rule – but this is only a general rule, and doesn't apply to everybody. Some men are very sensitive to social signals, and some women are not. But generally, possibly because of the influences they experience when they are younger or possibly because of inherited potential, women and girls do tend to be more socially skilled. Some evolutionary psychologists attribute this to the fact that women are more involved in child-rearing and caring for others, while men have traditionally adopted social roles which are more concerned with hunting and defending. Whatever the reason, it is noticeable that in modern societies there are more women in jobs which involve interacting with and caring for other people. But there are also many men in such jobs, too.

Childhood, then, can be seen as a lengthy period of skill development. Most responsibilities and pressures are taken off the child, at least in Western societies, and during this time, the child develops and refines the social, mental and physical skills which will help it as it grows up and begins to take more of a part in society. Through developing competences, positive self-efficacy beliefs, effective schemas and personal constructs, children develop their understanding of their world and their ability to operate effectively within it.

Adolescence

As their body matures, the child begins to enter adolescence. Adolescence is often thought of as a turbulent period – a period of upheaval and rebellion from parental authority. This image of adolescence has been very popular with Hollywood since the 1950s, and it has passed into our everyday consciousness. But it's questionable just how realistic this impression of adolescence is. Although some people, undoubtedly, do have a turbulent time in this period of their lives, others pass through adolescence quite smoothly, and without major upheavals. Every child is different and these differences have been reflected in psychological theories, too. Cockram and Beloff (1978) identified four different models of adolescence. Each of these applies only to some people and not to everyone, but they are useful in helping us to understand something of what is going on during these years.

ADOLESCENCE AS 'STORM AND STRESS'
This view sees the adolescent as inherently rebellious, rejecting the authority of parents or other representatives of 'the establishment', and looking only to their peer group for social

influence. Adolescents in the films of the 1950s and 1960s were portrayed as moody and emotionally unstable, and as implicitly difficult for adults to interact with. Various explanations were put forward for this phenomenon, including that it was a throwback to the animal passions of an evolutionary past, that it resulted from the hormone imbalances of puberty, and the psychoanalytic notion that it was an emotional reworking of early childhood sexual conflicts.

Some anthropologists and psychologists, such as Margaret Mead (1972) and Bronfenbrenner (1974) argued that it arose as a result of the alienation of young people from adult culture in Western capitalist societies. In non-technological societies, Mead argued, adolescents were fully participating members of their communities, and so were not left to their own devices and regarded as a separate culture. Even in Soviet Russia, Bronfenbrenner argued, young people were more integrated into their society than they were in the USA, and showed fewer signs of alienation.

All of these theorists, however, were working on the assumption that a turbulent adolescence is the normal state of affairs for young people in Western societies. But gradually this view was challenged as psychologists such as Albert Bandura began to study 'normal' adolescents, rather than adolescents who were attending clinics or courts because they were disturbed or troublesome. Bandura found that most adolescents didn't particularly oppose their parents' values or show hostility or rebellion. Rather, for many people, adolescence was a period in which they developed a more trusting and positive relationship with their parents, rather than the reverse.

Research by other psychologists confirmed Bandura's arguments, and the 'storm and stress' model of adolescence became increasingly regarded as one which had only a limited usefulness – appropriate for some adolescents, but not for most. So, different models of adolescence began to emerge.

ADOLESCENCE AS ROLE TRANSITION

One of the most popular of these alternative models was the idea that adolescence can most usefully be seen as a period of role transition – a time when teenagers are changing how they interact with society in general, and with the other people around them. Moving from school to work, or from school to higher education, involves adopting different social roles, and these in turn can produce changes as different sides of the personality emerge.

There are several different aspects to the changing roles of adolescence. Sometimes, we retain the same roles, but there are changes in how we are expected to perform them. We would expect a ten-year-old older sister to act differently from a sixteen-year-old older sister, for example. But there are entirely new roles, too, which appear during adolescence, and these have to be learned. A Saturday job in a shop, for instance, involves learning a way of interacting with people which is entirely different from the styles which we adopt with family or friends.

Part of being an adolescent, then, involves balancing out the different demands of the social roles that we are called on to play. Sometimes, these result in widely differing expectations: someone might be regarded as a responsible adult in their Saturday job, as a child by members of their family, and as an irresponsible teenager by their schoolteacher. Each of these expectations will bring different 'selves', or aspects of the personality, to the fore, so balancing their different demands is something which takes a bit of learning.

ADOLESCENCE AS A DEVELOPMENTAL STAGE

A third way of looking at adolescence identified by Cockram and Beloff (1978), is to see it as a developmental stage. This idea is based on Erikson's theory of life-long development (Erikson, 1968), which identified a number of different conflicts which each individual has to resolve as they pass through life. These are listed in Table 10.5. The successful resolutions of early conflicts, Erikson argued, set the foundation for the later ones, so all the stages are important in the person's psychological development.

Table 10.5 Erikson's stages of lifespan development.

Early infancy	*Trust vs mistrust*
	The infant has to strike a balance between trusting people and risking disappointment, or being mistrustful and unable to relate to other people fully.
Later infancy	*Autonomy vs shame and doubt*
	The toddler has to develop a sense of personal agency and control over its behaviour and actions, rather than mistrusting its ability to do things.
Early childhood	*Initiative vs guilt*
	The child has to develop an increasing sense of personal responsibility and initiative, rather than simply feeling guilty and uncertain.
Middle childhood	*Industry vs inferiority*
	The child has to learn that systematic effort will overcome challenges, rather than just giving up and accepting failure.
Puberty and adolescence	*Identity vs role confusion*
	The adolescent needs to develop a consistent sense of inner self, rather than being swamped by the range of roles and choices available.
Young adulthood	*Intimacy vs isolation*
	The young adult needs to learn to develop intimate and trusting relationships with others, rather than avoiding relationships because they can become threatening and painful.
Mature adulthood	*Generativity vs stagnation*
	The adult needs to develop a productive life, recognizing their personal achievements and abilities, instead of stagnating psychologically.
Late adulthood	*Integrity vs despair*
	The older person needs to be able to look back on their life positively, rather than to feel that it has been meaningless and futile.

The particular conflict which needs to be resolved during adolescence, Erikson argued, is that of identity versus role confusion. In a sense, this relates to the perspective on adolescence that we were just looking at – the way the adolescent needs to come to terms with the many new social roles that they are expected to play. In terms of the individual's own psychological development, Erikson saw it as important that the adolescent could accept the fact that they had a single, integrated identity, despite the fact that they played so many different social roles and acted differently in each one.

It was only by maintaining or developing a coherent sense of identity, Erikson believed, that an adolescent would be able to set a firm foundation for mature and satisfying relationships. If the different role demands which they experienced were too stressful, the person would experience what Erikson called a state of identity diffusion, in which they would have difficulty forming relationships with other people and would also find it difficult to make coherent plans for the future, and work towards achieving them. Without a clear sense of who we are, such things are very difficult, and yet adolescence is often an important time of preparation for adult life, and can involve a considerable investment in work, effort and planning.

THE LIFESPAN APPROACH TO ADOLESCENCE

The fourth type of theory of adolescence described by Cockram and Beloff is the lifespan approach to adolescence. This model presents the adolescent as an active agent in their own lives – unlike the other ones, which tend to see the person as passive, merely suffering or experiencing all these different demands. But adolescents are very active in interacting with their own environment, and can shape what happens to them to quite a high degree.

Lerner (1985) argued that adolescents interact with their environment in three ways. The first of these is that they act as a stimulus to other people, and people respond differently to them. Secondly, adolescents process information mentally: they think about what they are experiencing, interpret it, and respond accordingly. And thirdly, adolescents act as active agents in their own lives, making their own choices, and deliberately influencing what is likely to happen. All these combine to mean that the adolescent is much less passive than the older psychological models implied.

Key idea

Adolescence is a time of challenge, discovery and growth. A healthy society provides plenty of legitimate opportunities for this, but adolescents without such opportunities will still look for challenges, and may end up finding them in less socially desirable areas, such as in gang or drug cultures.

CHANGES AND STAGES

So what can we conclude from all this? Essentially, it seems, there is no single way of looking at adolescence which will explain what everyone experiences. There are a lot of role changes which take place during this time, and a great many major life changes too. But each person will cope with them in their own way, and according to the awareness and understanding that they have developed as a person in their own right. Throughout this book, we have been looking at mechanisms which influence people, and which give us clues to understanding why people are like they are. They apply just as much to adolescents, too!

Adolescence has its own internal stages – a young adolescent is faced with different types of challenges and transitions than someone in later adolescence. So it isn't very helpful to think of all adolescents as going through the same kinds of experience. Some psychologists, in fact, question whether it is useful to think of development in terms of stages at all, since so much development happens within each stage, and each period of development tends to blend with the one before and the one after. People develop in complex ways, and rarely show an abrupt transition from one stage to another. So it's important to remember that stages may not really exist! They are just a shorthand way of describing that particular time in a person's life.

In the next chapter, we will look at other aspects of our development – the development which happens as we become adults, have families, grow older, and eventually retire.

Focus points

Play allows children and young animals to practise the different skills that they will need in later life.

Social development includes learning how to interact with other people. Small children are particularly good at this, especially with their siblings.

Vygotsky showed how children's learning is aided and enhanced by adult influence – for example, achievement motivation is strongly influenced by parental encouragement and support.

Developing positive self-efficacy beliefs is one of the most important aspects of childhood development.

Adolescence is often seen as a stormy period, but this is not inevitable. It depends on the child's home environment as well as the ideas and personality of the child itself.

Adolescence is a time of changing roles and responsibilities, which can often be difficult as the child makes the various transitions needed at this stage.

11

Adulthood, retirement and ageing

In this chapter you will learn:

- ▶ *why research into adulthood is generally 'culturally specific'*
- ▶ *about changes in retirement theories*
- ▶ *to differentiate between 'cross sectional' and 'longitudinal' methods of studying ageing.*

Contrary to popular belief, our development doesn't stop when we become adult. We continue developing and changing throughout our lives both mentally and physically. In recent years the study of lifespan development has become much more popular, so in this chapter we will look at development throughout the rest of the lifespan – that is, development in adulthood and during the ageing process.

Adulthood

It is only relatively recently that psychologists have begun to study adulthood in its own right. Of course, psychology is about people, and so the various aspects of how human beings function which we have looked at earlier in this book are all relevant to understanding adulthood. In that sense, psychology has always studied both adults and children. And work psychology, which we will be looking at in Chapter 13, has a long history too, and is entirely concerned with adult life. But the idea that the period of life which we know as adulthood might also be worth studying in its own right is a relatively new one. Quite a lot of this research has been concerned with looking at the various phases which people pass through in the course of their adult life: charting what happens to us – or at least to many people in Western industrial societies – as we grow older.

Key idea

Research projects follow the trends of their times, and lifespan psychology has developed as the post-war baby boom generation has matured. The current wave of research into ageing and care of the elderly, for example, can be seen as directly resulting from that generation reaching retirement age.

LIFE TRANSITIONS

Gould (1978) developed the idea that adult life consists of a series of transitions, or life changes, which occur at different times in our lives. The first of these is that of adjusting to the responsibilities of being independent and living away from parental care. Looking after ourselves without someone in the background is quite different from the kind of independence which occurs when living as part of a family group, where there is always someone to fall back on, or to look after you if you become ill.

This transition, Gould argued, takes place usually between the ages of 16 and 22. Then there is another transition, which takes place during our 20s, in which we develop our own competences and autonomy, and choose our own rules to live by, rather than simply conforming to our parents' rules and principles. A third transition, according to Gould, happens between 28 and 34, as we come to know ourselves better, and learn to come to terms with aspects of our nature which we weren't really aware of before. And the final transition involves accepting that life isn't going to last for ever – that is, developing a sense of our own mortality. This final transition, Gould argued, happens between the ages of 35 and 45.

There are some big problems with this type of approach to studying adulthood. One of them is that it is very culturally specific – it was probably fine for describing the lives of middle-class white North American men during the 1970s, but things are often different for people of other backgrounds, where the normal course of living takes different forms. Another is that it doesn't account for variations in lifestyle. Some people don't leave home until much later in life; some people don't experience a lengthy period of independence but marry from their family home; and some come across these transitions at very different ages. So it would be difficult to say how the model applied to them.

Key idea

We will all experience several life transitions, but they will be different for each of us. It is more useful to try to explore the psychological processes involved as we tackle our life transitions, than to try to predict categorically what those life transitions will be.

If there are so many problems with this type of model, why should we bother with it at all? Well, mainly because it's a start. By identifying the kinds of things that are missing from a model like this, we can move towards developing better theories. Psychology doesn't have all the answers: it is continually changing, and trying to improve its theories and ideas. When a new area is first opened up, the initial theories are often quite limited, but they provide a useful basis for further research which can help us to develop a deeper understanding.

▶ The family life cycle

Even if a theory is a little bit limited, it may still be useful. For instance, Duvall (1971) developed a model of the different stages of marriage which has been criticized in similar ways – it is culturally specific and it doesn't take account of the experiences of single parents, or of divorce, for example. But, despite its shortcomings, the model can still help us to understand how a consistent long-term marriage goes through different phases: how these phases actually involve different behaviour on the part of the couple, and different assumptions about what they are actually doing.

Duvall identified eight different stages of marriage in all. The first of these is the honeymoon period, in which the married couple are learning to live together, without children. At this time, they are getting to know each other and setting the foundations for their later life together. Statistically, a couple whose honeymoon period lasts for two years or more before children come along are much more likely to stay together in the long term than those who only have a brief interval before starting a family. This may partly be because they have the time to get to know one another as people much better.

The second period in Duvall's model is the nurturing period, when the oldest child is less than two years old, and the couple are learning to cope with being new parents. It can be a stressful time for both of them, and it isn't made easier by lack of sleep, and anxiety about how the child or children are progressing. So at this time, the couple are likely to need to give one another quite a high level of both practical and emotional support, and knowing each other well can make for fewer misunderstandings and quarrels.

The third stage is what Duvall referred to as the authority period, in which the family are bringing up pre-school children, with the oldest between two and five years old. Essentially, the parents have to train their pre-schoolers to behave in a socially acceptable way, and not like tyrannical little monsters! This, too, can be a deeply demanding phase for the parents.

Things often ease up a little when the family enters the interpretive period, in which the oldest child is between five and 13 years old, and at school. (The reason why Duvall categorizes these stages from the age of the oldest child is mainly because this signals the need for the parents to learn new behaviours. They have already learned most of the behaviours they will need for younger children – although each child is different, of course.)

The fifth period in the family life cycle is the interdependent period, which consists of families with teenagers. At this time it becomes possible for the teenagers to take more of a share in the emotional and physical aspects of the family, and the relationship between parents and child can become a two-way, interdependent one rather than a simple, one-way, dependent one.

Then there is the sixth period, which Duvall refers to as the launching period, as the young adults emerge to become independent in society. Typically, this period involves some degree of support from home – perhaps providing a home for a child who is away at college during term-time, or providing help with furnishings or a regular Sunday lunch for a young adult who is independent and working. This period lasts from the time when the first child leaves, to when the last child leaves home.

The seventh of Duvall's stages is the empty-nest period, when all the children have left and the parents are together at home. This can be quite a difficult adjustment for some couples, particularly if the children have been the exclusive focus of attention for most of their time together. Some couples, though, find it a pleasant relief, because it means they can simply enjoy one another's company again. They often begin a number of co-operative activities that they weren't doing before, such as redecorating, or travelling.

The final period in the family life cycle, described by Duvall, is the retirement period, in which the members of the partnership who were working are now retired. This, too, can be a period of re-adjustment, particularly if one of the couple has been accustomed to having the house to themselves for most of the day.

We can see, then, that each stage of the family life cycle involves different adjustments and new forms of learning.

Although, inevitably, it doesn't fit every single family, identifying the different stages in this way has proved very useful for marriage guidance counsellors and others who are either trying to help people to adjust to changes in their relationships, or who are trying to do the adjusting themselves.

Having said that, the number of modern families which fits this simple pattern is becoming increasingly few. Families break up and re-form with new members, single-parent families are increasingly common, and people with grown-up children often find themselves in new relationships which involve bringing up much younger children. Models like Duvall's can be helpful, but they are not by any means the whole pattern of our lifespan family development.

Key idea

The family life cycle model can help us understand the adaptations that parents must make. But modern families are not always so neat, with overlapping generations, stepchildren from previous relationships and other complications. So, relatively few families follow the pattern exactly the way in which the theory proposes.

▶ The mid-life crisis

Another popular idea in recent years is that of the mid-life crisis. In many societies, adults work from the time that they are grown (or in some cases before) until they become too old. But in modern Western societies, it is no longer the case that we stay doing the same job throughout our working lives. Temporary work, redundancies, adult re-training schemes and a greater emphasis on job satisfaction mean that many people hit a period in their 40s or 50s when they begin to re-evaluate their lives, and decide that they want to do something which is more personally meaningful for them.

Sometimes, this crisis simply takes the form of the person looking for a different job, either deliberately or because it has been forced on them by redundancy. But in the modern world, such decisions usually mean re-training, and some people go back into full-time education to achieve this. Universities have growing numbers of adult students, as do colleges and training schemes, and even people who left school feeling that they were too 'thick' to gain qualifications find that this is not so, and that they can learn as effectively as anyone else.

Other people may make more dramatic changes in their lives – perhaps moving to start a new life in a different country, or a different town, and taking up an entirely new occupation. Making such dramatic changes sometimes doesn't work very well, but often people report increased feelings of well-being and confidence, and more positive life experiences. As we have seen, we continue to grow and develop throughout our lives, and the mid-life crisis can be seen as a way of taking control of that growth and channelling it into new directions.

Key idea

Some researchers see the mid-life crisis as a myth, arguing that people can engage in life changes at any time in their lives. That is true, but if we look at people who have re-evaluated their lives and make dramatic changes as a result, the majority were in their 40s and 50s at the time they made those changes.

RETIREMENT

Another major transition, of course, is retirement. In earlier times, the period of retirement used to be a brief interlude before old age and death. But in modern living, it has become quite different. Changes in diet, lifestyle and general health mean that most people continue to live an active, productive life for a long period after they finish formal working – as long as 30 years or, if they have taken early retirement, even 40. This period is very nearly as long as many people's working life, so the idea of retirement as a 'restful interlude' isn't really very practical. Instead, lifespan psychologists nowadays see retirement as a way of developing in new and different ways, that weren't possible under the constraints of working life.

▶ Disengagement

The first psychological theories about retirement tended to take a rather negative position. Cummings and Henry (1961) saw retirement as a gradual process of separating off from society. Old people might be numerous, but they were less visible than younger people, and less involved in social activities. Cummings and Henry saw this as part of a natural mechanism, similar to a weakened animal withdrawing from its herd to die.

Cummings and Henry put forward a biological explanation for this. They proposed that, as people grow older, there is a kind of inherited biological mechanism which encourages them, gradually, to withdraw from society. They have fulfilled their evolutionary function by bringing up families and helping their offspring to survive and now, Cummings and Henry argued, evolution has no place for them. As a consequence, they become less and less involved in social affairs, leaving decision-making and social organization to younger people, and become increasingly withdrawn into their own lives.

This rather gloomy process is known as disengagement, based on the idea that there is an innate, biological tendency to disengage from society with age. This theory reflects a tendency of psychologists at that time to look for biological explanations for all human behaviour. But there are many problems with this model. For one thing, the relative lack of social involvement of older people isn't anything like an animal creeping away to die, because the period of being 'an old person' or a pensioner is so very long. Nowadays, it isn't uncommon for people to live for 30 years or more after they have retired, and that's quite different from a couple of days of being ill and weak before dying – the normal state of affairs among wild animals.

▶ Activity theory

That type of explanation also ignores the social factors involved in retirement. An alternative explanation for why older people don't seem to take as active a part in society as they might was put forward by Havighurst, in 1964. Havighurst attributed it to the fact that older people have relatively few opportunities to play meaningful social roles in society. When someone is active and working, they play a large number of different social roles. These include various roles at work as well as roles to do with the family. In other words, as Havighurst put it, their role-count is high. But when someone retires from work, their role-count drops dramatically, because all the social roles that they played which were relevant to work – even ones as simple as being a commuter – vanish. All that is left are social roles to do with family and home.

In other words, Havighurst argued, people become less visible when they retire simply because they don't have as many opportunities to play a part in everyday social living. And this has personal consequences, as well as social ones, because people can easily come to feel apathetic and useless as a result. The way to counteract this, Havighurst proposed, is for people to replace their lost social roles deliberately, by adding new ones such as joining clubs and societies for older people, or volunteering for organizations like Oxfam, which employ people over conventional retirement age. Keeping up one's role-count, according to Havighurst, is the way to ensure a positive experience of old age.

As the 'baby boom' generation has become older, the idea of an active old age with a substantial role-count has increasingly become part of normal everyday living. Newly retired people often comment that they are busier now than when they were working, and there is a much wider range of possibilities for people to play an active part in their society. The removal of compulsory retirement ages has also made a significant contribution to this change, as people can opt to continue to work for longer than was previously possible.

Key idea

Retirement was originally introduced to give people a couple of years' rest before death. But people died younger in those days: nowadays, we can expect a healthy 20 or 30 years of life after retirement. Using that time constructively is one of the personal challenges of modern society.

▶ Social exchange

In 1975, Dowd proposed another approach, suggesting that retirement is actually a sort of social contract that the person makes with society. They obtain increased leisure time, and an 'honourable discharge' from the idea that all responsible members of society ought to work as hard as possible – the Protestant Work Ethic – and in return, they give up their involvement in how society's affairs are run. This social exchange was seen, according to Dowd, as a fair trade, both by society and by old people.

Dyson (1980) interviewed a large number of people about their experiences of retirement, and challenged the idea that people see it as a fair exchange. Dyson's respondents saw it as fair for old people in general, but not in their own personal case. They felt that, for the most part, society had thrown them on the junk heap too early, when they were still perfectly capable of making an active and useful contribution to society. But they did think it was probably fair for other old people, and for old people in general.

Dyson's research gave some interesting hints about the emergence of a new perspective on ageing, which developed during the 1980s. This view sees the lower visibility of older people in society as a product of social labelling. We live in an ageist society, in which stereotypes of old people are very strong – even though most of us are personally acquainted with individuals who don't fit those stereotypes at all. But it is very difficult for an individual to break through the social stereotyping and be regarded as an intelligent person with something useful to contribute, because too often they are seen as someone who is old, and therefore useless. Or they think this is how they will be seen, and so they don't bother trying.

The stereotypes associated with old people are particularly unpleasant. They are often regarded as sick, stupid, or even dirty. Because a minority of old people become confused, or suffer from mental disorders such as Alzheimer's disease, it is assumed that any old person is likely to become mentally incapacitated – although, in fact, the evidence is very different. Because of this, the positive contributions which older people can make to social events and processes were often overlooked, or simply ignored. But this has begun to change.

MODERN RETIREMENT

Over the past three decades, both organizations and individuals have begun to challenge these stereotypes about ageing, and many of the attitudes about older people have changed. This is partly because older people themselves are less prepared to accept this type of social labelling. After all, we live much longer now than we did when retirement was first introduced, and we keep our health for longer, too, so it is much more practical for people to continue to take an active part in society. Among business and professional people, it is not at all uncommon for retirement to signal the beginning of a second career, and a much more independent one that allows them to use their experience, such as working as a consultant. And many communities benefit from the fact that they have a pool of active people able and willing to act on their behalf, because they have the time to do it.

For many people in Western Society, retirement is seen as an opportunity to do new things. Organizations like the University of the Third Age encourage retired people to develop new hobbies and pursue new interests, and are becoming more popular and successful all the time. Many psychologists now take the view that successful retirement is all about making sure that you acquire new social roles, to replace the ones that you have lost through work, and activities of this sort are exactly the way that people do that.

▶ Retirement and responsibility

Some people who reach retirement age, though, still hold onto the old negative ideas about retirement. Sometimes they feel that society has simply thrown them away, even though they are as fit as ever. There is also a strong tendency to interpret any aches and pains as being evidence that they are becoming old and useless, so they stop doing activities which would help them to keep fit. Anyone would grow infirm if they do nothing all day but sit in the house and watch TV – muscles need exercise to keep toned, and a healthy retirement means an active one. Also, feeling socially useless is a major source of stress and helplessness. Without another source of self-esteem, such as a hobby or voluntary work, people can become extremely depressed, and appear to give up on active living.

The people who take this view are the ones who still hold the older stereotypes about ageing. But this can become self-fulfilling: they have been shown to be much more likely to die in the first few years of retirement than people who take a more positive view. It seems that they find it much harder to find anything worth living for, because they feel so useless.

This also helps to explain why women live longer than men (although there are other factors to be considered too). Women who are past retiring age now, grew up in a culture in which the home was considered to be a woman's primary responsibility. Even after they have retired, that responsibility still remains, so they still have something in their lives to be involved with. But men of the same age were often brought up to believe that their primary responsibility was to work and be the breadwinner for the family. That responsibility vanishes with compulsory retirement and this can be emotionally devastating. Even people who have looked forward to retirement can find that, after the first few months, feeling socially useless is more than they can cope with, and they can become very depressed even, sometimes, to the point where they give up trying to live.

This is why it is so important for retired people to make sure that they have some other interest in their life, and more than just one if at all possible. Many retired people take up another responsibility where they can still feel needed, such as voluntary work. Gardening is particularly popular, because a garden needs to be looked after – it can't be neglected or it will quickly turn wild. So gardeners know that their efforts are necessary and worthwhile. Some people develop hobbies such as travelling, or learn a new sport, such as golf or bowls. All these are ways for people to develop other sources of self-esteem, to compensate for being without paid employment.

Key idea

Having responsibilities and being needed seem to be the core of successful retirement. That can take many forms: some people feel needed by their gardens, and devote much of their time to taking care of them; others take on more social responsibilities.

Ageing

As we've seen, many people live healthy, happy and productive lives for many years after the standard retirement age. But sooner or later, barring accidents, we all become old. It used to be thought that ageing was a steady decline in functioning, with people going inevitably downhill from the age of 50 or so. But now we know that is not so. The research evidence which suggested this pattern of ageing was seriously flawed in the way that it was done, and modern experiences show that ageing occurs quite differently.

The general pattern seems to be that, as long as we remain active, we only have a gradual decline in our older years, which can be slowed down by exercise and activity. Eventually we do reach a period of more rapid physical decline, but this rarely lasts for more than about five years, in that death usually comes at some point during the five-year period. It is not uncommon for that decline to be brought about by an accident – a fall or some similar event – which damages the person physically but, more importantly, shakes their confidence and makes them feel unable to cope with life as they once did.

How inevitable the decline is, once it has begun, is something nobody knows. We do know, though, that even old bodies can respond surprisingly well to exercise. In one study, 90-year-olds who began a programme of physical exercises were found to be putting on muscle mass as a result – in other words, their muscles were responding to the exercise and becoming stronger. This finding has been repeated a number of times now, and it shows that the saying 'it's never too late' may be even truer than we realize.

The real danger in ageing, as we have seen, is the person's own beliefs about it. Someone who expects to decline and become incapable as they grow older is not likely to face their body or mind with extra challenges. Without exercise, our bodies have no incentive to grow stronger or to maintain their normal levels of strength, so they become weaker. This, to the person who expects to be weak as a result of age, is 'proof' that they were right, and their belief in inevitable decline is confirmed. But really, it began as a self-fulfilling prophecy.

Key idea

The negative view that we have of old people is like other stereotypes, having a small grain of truth in some cases but with a lot of exceptions. Interestingly, although old people often share this negative stereotype, they almost always see themselves as one of the exceptions. So who is left to fit the stereotype?

INTELLIGENCE AND AGEING

The same thing seems to happen with mental abilities too. For example, intelligence is often inaccurately cited as one of the areas which declines with age. For many years, people 'knew' that various abilities, including intelligence and physical strength, reached their peak in the early 20s, and then declined steadily from then on throughout a person's life. This knowledge was based on a series of studies reported by Miles in 1931, which involved measuring various human characteristics in people of different ages. When they plotted the results of these measurements on a graph, Miles found a steady decline: the older the person was, the less strong, or intelligent (as measured by IQ tests) or able they were.

Other researchers found similar results, so for a great many years there was a strong belief in an inevitable decline with age. This belief is still held by a great many people, including some doctors and social workers, but when we look more carefully at the evidence, what we find is actually quite a different picture.

▶ Cross-sectional studies

The problem was that all of these studies were done using cross-sectional methods. That is, the researcher tested several different groups of people, of different ages. But someone who was 60 in 1930 had experienced quite a different upbringing and lifestyle from someone who was 20 at that time. Their schooling was quite different, their life experiences were quite different, and their standards of living were different too. The same thing applied to cross-sectional studies that were conducted later on in the century: they failed to take account of the very major changes in education and healthcare which had taken place.

It wasn't surprising, for example, that older people did badly on intelligence tests in the 1960s, when they had experienced an education which consisted, in the main, of learning large chunks of information off by heart. Younger people, by contrast, had experienced a form of education which stressed reasoning and mental skills, and so they naturally performed much better on IQ tests.

▶ Longitudinal studies

When psychologists actually began to look at how individual people developed, following them up through their lives, a very different picture emerged. Obviously, longitudinal research like this is quite hard to do because researchers need to follow it up over many years. So there are fewer longitudinal studies of lifespan development than there are cross-sectional ones. But there are some. For example, in 1966, Burns reported on a study of intelligence and ageing which had begun in the 1920s with a group of teachers who were just emerging from their training colleges. The researchers tested the teachers' intelligence throughout their careers and found that, contrary to what the cross-sectional research showed, their IQ scores had actually increased as they had become older. The apparently inevitable decline with ageing wasn't inevitable at all!

What was even more interesting was the particular scores which the teachers had obtained on their IQ tests. The tests assessed intelligence in two parts: verbal intelligence, which was to do with the use of words and knowledge of vocabulary, and numerical intelligence, which included the use of symbols and logical reasoning as well as arithmetical abilities. When the researchers looked at these scores, they found that the 'arts' teachers, who taught subjects such as English and history, showed an increase in their verbal intelligence scores, but a slight (though not very great) decline in numerical intelligence. The science teachers, though, showed an increase in their numerical intelligence but a slight decline in their verbal intelligence scores.

What this clearly implied was that, more than anything else, it is the amount of practice we have which is most important in whether we are likely to improve our intelligence as we get older or not. If we adopt a passive mental approach to living, just receiving information that comes to us and not bothering to learn new things unless we absolutely have to, it's likely that our intelligence will decline. Our muscles waste away if we don't use them and, in the same way, our intelligence declines if we don't use it. But if we remain active in our thinking, and ready to learn new things or to challenge our previous assumptions, then we are likely to retain our intelligence, and even increase it. The more we use a skill, the better we get at it.

This is only one example, but both psychologists and doctors are finding, more and more, that getting old has almost as much to do with lifestyle and practice as it has to do with the number of years that we actually carry. Everybody gets older, of course, but ageing doesn't mean an inevitable steady decline from age 20, as people used to think.

Key idea

Longitudinal studies of ageing are a lot more valid than cross-sectional ones. But it is almost impossible to guarantee the continuous funding and administration of a large research project for 50 years, so until recently, longitudinal studies of ageing have tended to be fairly small-scale.

MEMORY AND AGEING

The problem, though, is that we all have our own beliefs about ageing and sometimes, as we've seen, these can become self-perpetuating. For example, most people believe that memory inevitably declines as you get older. Because they believe this, they notice each time they fail to remember something, and take it as 'proof' that their memory is really getting worse. Their belief becomes a self-fulfilling prophecy, because they become convinced that there is less and less point in trying to remember things because they won't manage it anyway. And then they don't remember things, because they don't make any effort to store the information.

Harris and Sunderland, in 1981, decided to put this idea to the test. They assembled a group of people aged between 20 and 36, and compared them with a group of people aged between 69 and 80. When they tested their memories for events in everyday life, they found that the younger people in the study actually experienced more memory failures than the older people!

It was possible, of course, that the younger people forgot more simply because they had more going on in their lives. After all, the older group comprised all retired people. So Harris and Sunderland repeated the study, this time with a group of people who were still working, aged between 50 and 60. This time, they found an even stronger difference between the two groups. Again, the younger people were much more forgetful than those who were older, even with information that they were trying to remember.

So why is it that older people are so convinced that their memories are poorer now than they were when they were young? It's possible, of course, that they really did have better memories when they were young, and that for some reason the younger generation studied by Harris and Sunderland didn't have very good memories at all – after all, this was a cross-sectional study. And the educational system which was current when the over-60s were younger did involve quite a lot of memorizing. But what seems more likely is that it is much more to do with motivation and attention.

Key idea

Human beings are so powerfully driven by their beliefs and expectations that reality is sometimes irrelevant. People start worrying about memory decline from their 30s or 40s – even though real age-related decline doesn't actually begin until after 70, and later for many people. But each example of ordinary absent-mindedness is seen as evidence of decline, so the belief becomes self-fulfilling.

▶ Attention and motivation

Young people, by and large, don't worry too much about their mental abilities. Older people, though, sensitized by society's belief in an inevitable decline in mental ability with ageing, do worry about it. When a younger person forgets their key, or can't remember someone's name, or forgets what they came into the room to do, they hardly notice it because it simply doesn't matter to them. When an older person does the same thing, though, it sticks in their mind because they are always wondering if it is a sign of age.

So where the younger person simply shrugs off everyday forgetting, the older person worries about it, and notices it much more. And when older people look back on their own earlier lives, they don't remember being worried about forgetting things at all when they were younger, so they come to the conclusion that they simply had better memories. This reinforces the belief that their own mental abilities are declining, and so it becomes a circular process.

That doesn't mean, though, that there is no memory loss at all – just that it often isn't as bad as we think. We can become more forgetful as we get older, but we can also do things which will minimize that. Mohs *et al.* (1998) carried out a comprehensive memory enhancement programme with elderly people who were otherwise healthy, but had found themselves getting more forgetful. They found a significant improvement: mental exercises which stretched and strengthened their cognitive abilities made a real difference to how forgetful those people were.

A psychological decline with ageing, then, isn't nearly as inevitable as it once appeared to be. If we use our mental abilities, we are more likely to improve them than to lose them, at least until the very final years of our life. For people who lead full and active lives, and don't hesitate to make efforts or to stretch themselves a little, it seems that they can retain their abilities almost to the end of their lives, with only a relatively sudden decline in the last five years, rather than a continuous steady one.

Of course, your system responds to the demands that you make on it – which is why sports doctors and physiotherapists know how important it is to exercise injured muscles as soon as healing has begun. Resting simply means that the muscles adapt to limited demands, and become weaker. It's the same with ageing: people who believe in a continuous decline, and don't push themselves to make an effort, naturally become more and more frail and feeble, because they are never stimulating their bodies or minds to become stronger. There are limits, of course, but we haven't yet begun to discover what they are, and they certainly aren't encountered in most people's lives.

Key idea

Motivation is the most important factor in cognitive ageing, as it is in physical health. People who see age degeneration as inevitable don't bother to practise or give themselves challenges – either mentally or physically – so their decline is quicker and more noticeable than those who keep active.

DEMENTIA

For some people and their families, though, ageing brings another problem: that of dementia. Dementia is a neurocognitive disorder – that is, it is a set of cognitive problems brought about by neurological damage in the brain. Simply becoming forgetful is not necessarily a symptom of dementia: many people experience forgetfulness who are otherwise perfectly healthy in cognitive terms. Dementia is more severe: its sufferers may experience difficulties with thinking, problem-solving or language, confusion, and sometimes even hallucinations or emotional problems. It can arise from a disease, like Alzheimer's, or it can be produced by strokes or other causes of brain damage.

Dementia is generally considered to be progressive, which means that once it starts it will get gradually worse. There is no known cure at the present time, but how rapidly it progresses can be influenced by other factors. One of these, for example, is through exercise. For people with severe dementia, regular exercise can be a problem, although some care homes are beginning to find ways of introducing it. However, if it is diagnosed early, several studies have shown that regular exercise can ease the symptoms of dementia.

It's not just dementia which can be helped by exercise. Deslandes *et al.* (2009) showed how regular exercise could reduce the symptoms of Parkinson's disease (which produces uncontrollable muscle tremors) and also major depressive disorders. It's thought that part of the reason for this is because of the increased blood flow around the body, including the brain, which exercising produces. Also, the improvement in overall physical health may help the body and brain to cope with the confusion and lack of concentration involved in dementia.

One encouraging finding, though, is that dementia rates appear to be declining, at least in Western populations. In the UK there was a 22 per cent decrease in the incidence of dementia between 1990 and 2016; in the USA, the rate of dementia in the population fell from 11.6 per cent in the year 2000 to 8.8 per cent in 2012. There are a number of possible explanations for this, including a reduction of chemical contaminants in the diet and generally better population health. One of the main factors, though, seems to be what has become known as cognitive reserve (Stern, 2002).

A recurrent finding is that – in general – higher levels of education are associated with lower levels of dementia. In other words, dementia is more common among people with less education, so one explanation for the decline in rates of dementia might be the increase in educational levels in the population as a whole. It has been suggested that the effect happens because education gives people higher levels of cognitive reserve – that is, they are more likely to exercise the brain, to find new things to interest themselves, and to engage in curiosity and problem-solving. So the positive effects of cognitive reserve in dementia might be because of the increased level of exercise in the brain, or possibly because the generally higher level of neural activity helps the brain to rewire itself after damage.

Research into dementia is continuing, and it is likely that we will eventually understand more about how it happens and, more importantly, how it can be treated. But it is important to remember that dementia is by no means an inevitable part of becoming older: it has always only affected a small proportion of the population, even if that is the side of ageing we hear most about.

LIFESPAN PSYCHOLOGY

In the past two chapters we have seen how developmental psychology covers far more than just childhood. It covers the whole lifespan. Sugarman (1986) identified four central ideas in lifespan developmental psychology. The first of these is the idea that development always needs to be seen in its social context. How people develop is influenced by their society, their family, their social class and their culture, and social influence can come from many other sources as well. So we can't really study development without taking these into account.

The second idea which Sugarman identified has to do with the fact that social influence isn't just a one-way process. People influence one another, and are influenced by others – it's a two-way process, which we call reciprocal influence. This influence isn't static either – it changes all the time. We are influenced by family members and by changes happening within the family, as well as by changes among our friends and work colleagues. And we exert our own influence on these changes as they develop.

Reciprocal influence is important, but it's far from being the whole story. We are also active agents in our own lives, making our own choices and decisions. In that sense, we are all active in shaping our own development, and how we understand what is going on is an important aspect of that. For example, as we saw earlier, we know that mental abilities don't inevitably decline with age, but someone who believed firmly that they did decline would tend to 'take it easy' and avoid challenging situations as they grew older, because they wouldn't think it was worth trying. And because of this, they would decline faster than someone who understood lifespan development in a more positive way.

Another fundamental principle that Sugarman identified in lifespan psychology is that of complexity. Essentially, this is the same principle that we have encountered so often throughout this book. People are not simple beings, and no single approach is going to be enough to tell us about human beings. We have to take into account different levels of explanation, and to explore connections and issues which arise from them, if we are to get any useful awareness of what human beings are really like.

Focus points

We continue developing and changing throughout our adult lives, mentally as well as physically. Some people experience a mid-life crisis in which they make a dramatic change to their lifestyle.

Maintaining responsibilities and roles is important in retirement.

Most people remain healthy and active throughout old age, and only decline in their final five years or so. Past studies of ageing were more negative then they needed to be because they used cross-sectional methods.

Studies show that intelligence can increase as we get older if we use it. Memory does not necessarily decline with age, but older people notice memory lapses and worry more about them than young people.

Dementia affects fewer than ten per cent of the ageing population. It is progressive, but symptoms can be alleviated by exercise and other activities.

Lifespan psychology emphasizes social context, reciprocal influence, complexity and active agency.

12

Leisure

In this chapter you will learn:

▶ *to identify the positive and negative effects of watching TV*

▶ *why computer games are psychologically appealing*

▶ *how to differentiate between external and internal motivation.*

In this chapter, we will look at some of the psychology which underlies our leisure activities. The concept of leisure has become increasingly important in modern society. By comparison with pre-industrial society, or even with the industrial society of 50 years ago, we spend far less of our day-to-day lives working (even though it may not always seem like that!). And for significant chunks of the week, we have specific times when we are not actually working at all.

It is difficult, really, to define leisure activities, because many of the things that some people regard as leisure are regarded as work, or at least chores, by others. Shopping is one of those things. Some people enjoy it, and treat it as a leisure pursuit, while others detest it and treat it as an unfortunate necessity of life. It certainly happens during 'leisure' hours; but whether it is truly leisure is open to question. So we will not look at consumer psychology here, but we will look at some aspects of the decisions we make as consumers in Chapter 15. Here, we will look at activities which are more self-evidently the kinds of things that people regard as leisure.

People have varied interests and hobbies and, as we saw in Chapter 2, it's possible to see them as an expression of our basic need for self-actualization. We enjoy developing our skills and interests, but we also sometimes spend our leisure time in less active pursuits, such as watching TV – which can sometimes involve learning things, as in the large number of DIY and cookery programmes, but may equally well be nothing more than passive entertainment.

So we will begin this chapter by looking at TV watching as a leisure pursuit. Then we will go on to look at a slightly more active way of interacting with a video screen, in the case of computer games, before concluding our sampling of psychology and leisure by looking at sport psychology. Of course, for some people sport is a profession rather than a leisure activity, and many of the insights from sport psychology have been developed with professional sportspeople in mind. But equally, sport is something that many people play as a hobby or pastime.

Watching TV

In Western society, watching TV is a very large part of our relaxation activities. Over 98 per cent of homes in Britain have a TV, and most of them have more than one TV set. People spend on average about four or five hours a day watching TV, which makes it a significant cultural activity. But ever since TV became popular, people have been concerned about it. Psychologists have been studying its effects for some time.

THE EFFECTS OF TV VIEWING

One common debate, of course, is whether TV increases antisocial behaviour, and particularly aggression, or not. Most psychologists firmly believe that it can do so, although it is hard to obtain definitive evidence, since there are so many other things which also influence people's lives and can lead to increased aggression – notably the frustration which arises from constant poverty.

The earliest studies of TV's influence on aggressive behaviour were laboratory experiments. These were designed to assess an immediate change in behaviour as a result of people being exposed to aggressive images on TV. Typically, research participants would be shown a piece of film which showed distinctively violent behaviour, and then they would be observed to see whether they mimicked that behaviour, or showed heightened aggression in response to a stimulus or a questionnaire. These studies did show some modelling effects, although not as strongly as some people expected them to, but other studies failed to find the same results.

Key idea

Some media professionals claim that people aren't particularly influenced by what they see on TV. But if this were the case, TV advertising would have died out years ago. Companies which advertise on TV are well aware of how even a brief exposure can have a powerful influence.

▶ Problems with studying the effects of TV

These laboratory studies, though, were very artificial. Even if someone has been influenced by violence on TV, it's unlikely that it would show up straight away. Instead, as Bandura showed in his studies of imitative learning, we would show the aggressive behaviour when it somehow became relevant. This is one reason why laboratory studies of TV violence often produce contradictory results.

Another problem with these studies is that they tend to look for group influences, rather than for specific effects on individuals. They study a large number of people and see whether, on the whole, their behaviour seems to be influenced by the type of programmes that they watch. By studying people as a whole, they aim to cancel out individual differences and just look at general trends. But when it comes to something as important as this, it is individuals who matter. Even if only one extremely disturbed person out of six million viewers imitates a TV murderer, that is one too many.

▶ Social scripts

It is difficult, therefore, to obtain absolute proof that violence on TV directly affects people. But this doesn't mean there is no evidence at all. As we saw in the early part of this book, human beings are particularly ready to acquire social scripts and different types of social understandings, and people can learn from any kind of social contact. TV has a capacity to define a form of reality for people and this can make a great deal of difference to how we live our lives. It acts as a window into the wider world, and tells people what that world is like. So studies of the amount of TV that people actually watch can tell us quite a lot.

One thing they tell us, is that watching a lot of TV can distort how we see the world. Studies which compared heavy TV watchers and people who don't watch very much have found that heavy viewers have a very unrealistic perception of the outside world. They see it as an extremely dangerous place, sometimes even believing that they are likely to be attacked as soon as they step outside their own doors – unlikely in just about anywhere. But because TV tends to concentrate on violent action, both in reporting news and in its drama, they believe that the world is a much more dangerous place than it really is.

People who watch less TV, on the other hand, generally have a much more realistic perception of the risks of everyday living. They are aware that some dangers exist, of course, but they don't exaggerate them the way that the heavy viewers do. They can weigh up, realistically, the odds against something untoward happening, and so carry on with their lives in a positive way. These findings were first identified back in 1976, but recent replications of the studies have shown this effect to have become even stronger than it was then.

The problem isn't really the fact that violence occurs on TV. It's more to do with the proportion of violence that is shown on TV by comparison with the amount of other types of human activity. Most people go their whole lives without ever coming across a murder in real life, yet the average TV-watching child has seen something over 600 TV murders by the time it reaches ten years old. Such an unrealistic proportion can't help but distort any child's picture of what the world is like.

It's not just extreme violence like this: the social scripts in many soap operas portray people acting in extremely aggressive ways towards one another, even though they may fall short of actual physical violence. These ways of behaving can easily spill over into everyday life, so that they become seen as acceptable ways to behave in social situations. There is some evidence, for example, that verbal aggression in everyday situations like queueing has become more common, and that people – not everyone, of course, but some people – are more intolerant or impatient with someone who is slow in making their way around.

Key idea

Moral panics are generally about people copying things they see on TV. But the real danger isn't in people copying actions: it's in the social scripts these programmes use of how people deal with revenge, betrayal, anger and frustration. By suggesting that this is a normal way of behaving, they undermine more positive community values.

POSITIVE TV

Not all TV is bad, of course. Nature and science documentaries or historical programmes, for example, broaden our awareness and understanding of the world in which we live. Sports coverage allows people to participate vicariously in competitive activities, to express their loyalties and develop their understanding. For many people living in modern industrial societies, TV has replaced books as the main way that we come to know our world. It's become the major agent of socialization, showing both children and adults how the world works.

TV also contains positive messages in terms of humour and fun. Entertainment programmes like game shows may appear trivial to those who look for high-culture entertainment, but they actually show a friendly and positive approach in their dealings with people – most of the time, at any rate – which is more useful in modelling behaviour than the aggressive behaviour shown in soap operas and dramas. Sports and music programmes, too, serve positive psychological functions, stimulating people's interest and enthusiasm.

Key idea

The popularity of prosocial TV programmes indicates that the viewing public quite enjoy them. But market research is misleading and directs programme-makers towards antisocial TV, partly because of the way that dramatic events stick in people's minds, and partly because we are not often able to articulate more positive values very clearly.

▶ Teaching prosocial behaviour

There have been a great many studies on the influence of children's programmes in teaching children prosocial behaviour (prosocial is the opposite of antisocial). For example, in 1976 Rubinstein and others found that five- and six-year-olds who saw an episode of *Lassie* in which a boy helped a dog were more likely to help puppies in distress than children who hadn't seen the programme. The programme illustrated positive social scripts which the children had adopted for themselves.

There is some evidence that the early soap operas, or at least the British and Australian ones, had prosocial effects on children – and possibly adults too. The Australian soap *Neighbours*, for instance, used to contain a number of clearly positive messages in its content. It contained ideas such as: if you see your friend is in trouble, try to help them out; or if someone has upset you, try to work out the problem with them so that you can be friends again. Soap operas of this type used to portray people as belonging to a community in which people helped one another out – a very different message from the competitive aggression of so much TV drama.

Unfortunately, however, recent trends in TV drama have meant that the positive messages of soap operas have become lost, and there is much more of a focus on the negative aspect of human interaction than used to be the case – aggression, murder, jealousy, and so on. So what used to be a positive viewing experience, both for children and adults, has now become as negative as other forms of TV drama, with the result that many parents are beginning to restrict their children's exposure to these programmes too.

The real problem is that programming decisions are based heavily on market research, and market research, because of the way that it asks the questions, will always find that people identify the most dramatic episodes as the ones that had most impact on them. They are, after all, the most memorable. But that doesn't mean that such drama should drive the programme's basic content. Partly, they are most memorable when they are uncommon. And, as we've seen in other chapters, people are often less able to talk about positive experience, but it still makes an impression. And, of course, drama has more effect in a context where it is unusual, rather than when it is what happens every week. The success of programmes with more positive social scripts, such as *Countryfile*, which has one of the highest TV ratings of all in the UK, shows that the public does enjoy positive TV which is interesting and friendly.

TV AND READING
There has always been concern regarding the influence TV has on children's reading, and some of that can be justified. Gunter (1982)

showed how heavy TV viewing can seriously impair a child's learning to read, particularly during the earliest years of the child's education. The reasons for this are all tied up with the child's own perceptions – of what reading is for, and why it should make the effort to learn to read in the first place.

As we saw in Chapter 9, the experience of an expert is quite different from the experience of a novice, and this applies to reading too. Expert readers see reading as a doorway into another world of information, but children who are only just learning to read have quite a different experience. One reason why some children find it hard to learn to read is because they haven't actually realized that it will become much easier once they are good at it. Novice readers are often so concerned with the mechanics of reading that they hardly notice the story. To them, reading is very hard, and they sometimes can't see any point in doing it.

This is made even more extreme when the child watches a lot of TV, because it sees TV as similar to reading, but much easier. Reading needs a lot of practice: it takes time and effort before you recognize words at a glance, and are free to concentrate on the meaning of what you are reading. TV, on the other hand, gives you instant access to information. Moreover, it tells you stories, and lets you know about the outside world. So some children simply can't see the point in learning to read, and unless someone takes the time and trouble to show them what the point is, they will never put in the effort needed to become fluent readers. This is one reason why reading stories to children is so important – it shows them the kind of experience which they will be able to get in the long run, if they carry on making the effort to read.

And TV isn't really a substitute for reading. It's an entirely different type of cognitive experience. Researchers comparing the two have shown how reading trains children's imagination, because children need to create their own mental pictures about what they are reading. It also introduces children to abstract ideas, that can't really be portrayed in a concrete form – and that forms an important basis for later understanding and analytical thinking. TV, on the other hand, is much more concrete, and also passive: the child doesn't particularly need imagination to understand it. It isn't all bad: TV, as we have seen, can have some positive effects on children's development. But reading is an entirely different skill, which trains different mental abilities. So it is important that young children see it as such, and not as being equivalent to TV.

Digital games

Digital games of one form or another are another aspect of modern leisure life which have influenced a great many people – not quite as many as TV, but an increasing proportion of the population. They have become a major sector of the leisure market since the advent of the very first game, 'Pong', which was invented in the early 1970s. Since then, digital games have become far more sophisticated, and each year sees the launch of new developments and new ideas.

Key idea

Carl Rogers showed that people have a strong drive to develop skills and refine their abilities, which he called self-actualization (see Chapter 2). Computer games are all about learning and getting better at things, in many different ways, and this accounts for a good part of their popularity.

Computer games are tailored for several different interfaces, ranging from mobile phones to specialized games consoles. The accuracy of representation which they provide also varies, from very simple games such as 'Tetris', to highly complex games with realistic, film-like backgrounds and characters. So there is a range of possibilities available to those who enjoy playing computer games, and most people have their own favourite types. In recent decades there has been a huge increase in online gaming: the internet means that people can play games with or against one another when they are not acquainted in any way. Some games of this kind have become huge: games like 'World of Warcraft', for example, are known as MMORPGs, or Massive Multiplayer Online Role Playing Games, because they involve huge numbers of players at any one time. In 2012, 'World of Warcraft' had 9.1 million monthly subscribers.

The role playing in these games occurs through avatars – characters which the players have chosen to represent themselves as they play. These may or may not resemble the real person behind the avatar: Suler (2004) found that men playing 'World of Warcraft' often chose female avatars, either to express aspects of their personalities which didn't often come to the fore in their real lives, or because they felt that female avatars were more likely to receive help and assistance from other players. On the other hand, Coghland and Kirwan (2013) found that some women chose male avatars because they felt that it made the game more challenging. It's really a matter of personal choice. In another study, Wadell and Ivory (2015) found that generally, and regardless of gender, more attractive avatars do tend to be helped by more gifts and assistance.

Other avatar-based games are less competitive. 'Second Life', for example, is an online game in which avatars live in a world much like our own. It has businesses, professions, universities, and the players develop skills and occupations – and relationships. There has been more than one case where couples have come together through 'Second Life' and ended up getting married – and some cases where 'Second Life' infidelity has even led to divorce! The fantasy life which people experience through their avatars can also be helpful, allowing the person to compensate for real-world problems. In 2012, Sublette and Mullan analysed a number of interviews with gamers, and found that they reported positive feelings of friendship, achievement, and a sense of community from their participation.

THE PSYCHOLOGY OF COMPUTER GAMES

Whether someone enjoys a particular computer game or not will depend on a number of factors: their own personal interests, their personality, the structure of the game, the equipment they have available, and the skills which they already have in handling that equipment. Some games, for example, require more sophisticated handling than others, or more experience. But game designers are very careful to gauge the levels of difficulty within the game itself, to ensure that players can develop their skills and advance from one level to another as they get better at playing it.

Rewards and incentives

This carefully staged learning is important, because it helps to keep up players' motivation. By providing manageable goals for people to aim for and achieve, the game designers help to build a player's sense of competence and excitement. Added to this, when each new goal is reached, some kind of reward or recognition is offered. Sometimes this is an extrinsic reward within the game, such as obtaining a new type of weapon or a points bonus but, sometimes, it is an intrinsic reward that comes about as the person recognizes what they have managed to do. As we saw in Chapter 9, learning through rewards is a fundamental form of learning which has been studied in detail by psychologists, and is very effective. The popularity of video games gives us yet another example of just how effective it can be.

Self-efficacy beliefs

The idea of staged learning and the acquisition of more sophisticated skills taps into other aspects of human motivation as well. In particular, it helps to build up the person's self-efficacy beliefs – their sense of competence at being able to undertake particular challenges or perform particular tasks. We looked at self-efficacy beliefs in Chapter 6 and saw that they can be important in building up our personal self-confidence, as well as affecting our preparedness to learn. Computer games encourage success through perseverance, and so encourage children (and adults) to recognize that they can achieve things if they work hard at them – a useful message in any walk of life!

Sensation-seeking

Another aspect of human psychology which is activated by many computer games is that of sensation-seeking. Many people enjoy activities which are exciting, or which provoke a certain level of anxiety. The popularity of fairground rides is an example of this, and computer games tap into some similar types of psychological mechanisms. They don't do it in the same way as fairground rides do, of course, but the level of concentration which they require, and the skilled control, means that they can become quite thrilling and absorbing for the person playing them. The effect is increased, of course, by the background music of the game, which has been designed to heighten these emotional responses and to keep the player absorbed in what is going on. Wireless-based physical activity games also build on this psychological mechanism, as players gain the kinaesthetic feedback from the movements of their own bodies.

▶ Social interaction

A fourth aspect of human psychology which is involved in many computer games (although not all) concerns the way we respond to other people. The team-based 'Dungeon'-type strategy games involve co-operation between players, and those who play them find this type of interaction very rewarding – perhaps because it avoids the challenges and ambiguities of other types of human contact. Some people have expressed concern that teenagers with social problems may use this type of contact to avoid more direct face-to-face interactions, but the evidence seems to suggest that such teenagers have always devoted themselves to hobbies in any case, and at least these activities do bring them into contact with like-minded others. So such games may actually result in these teenagers becoming more social than they would if they had been engaging in a more isolated activity such as model-building.

More commonly, though, games tend to tap into the psychological mechanisms activated by competition. Most games offer some opportunity for comparison with other people, even if it is only on the high-score board, and many games are designed explicitly so that two or more players can compete directly with one another. Wii-based sport and music games allow players to compete directly with one another, or to co-operate, for example by taking part in a virtual band. By offering a social dimension as well as a personal one, computer game designers encourage the game to be an interactive event between people, as well as between the person and the machine.

ARE COMPUTER GAMES HARMFUL?

Just about any form of new technology raises social concerns about whether it is beneficial or harmful. When computer games became popular, many people worried about whether children would be damaged by playing them. Effectively, these concerns took three forms. Firstly, the fact that many games were based on violent concepts, such as beating up 'baddies' or shooting things, was thought to encourage a culture of violence among young people, or to make them more aggressive. Secondly, the fact that children spent so much time playing computer games raised concerns about damage to their physical health. Thirdly, the obvious enjoyment and preference which children showed for computer games was considered to be potentially harmful in terms of their future learning.

Key idea

Research indicates that computer games are more likely to be beneficial than harmful, by encouraging values such as perseverance and accuracy. But doing anything to excess isn't a good idea, and the inactivity involved in many games can result in health problems.

▶ Does gaming increase aggression?

Many games, like 'Second Life', 'Minecraft' or sporting simulations are not particularly aggressive, but others, like 'Grand Theft Auto' or 'World of Warcraft', are entirely different. Bartholow and Anderson (2002) compared a violent game ('Mortal Kombat') with a non-violent game ('PGA Tournament Golf'). They found that there was a noticeable increase in aggression in both male and female players after playing the violent game, by comparison with the other one. And in 2010, Anderson *et al.* analysed the findings of both Western and Japanese studies, and found that there was overwhelming evidence for increased aggression with the playing of violent games. Players felt more aggressive, acted more aggressively, and were also significantly less likely to help other people. Their correlations, they commented, were much stronger than the link between smoking and lung cancer, and should be taken just as seriously.

Controlling how people act in their choice of gaming, though, is not as easy as it sounds, and it is unlikely that there will be any significant changes in the near future. It's also complicated by the fact that not all games are violent, and the way that some involve fighting but not necessarily against people. Some versions of 'Minecraft', for example, involve defending what you have built by fighting off monsters – an activity which is unlikely to spill over into modern life in any literal sense.

A large proportion of computer games have nothing to do with aggression, of course. There are many sporting, driving, and hobby-based games, and also games which represent puzzles and problem-solving challenges. Some games are information-based, and there is also an increase in online learning. Strictly speaking, online courses are not games, but they are certainly a way in which some people use computers and the internet in their leisure time, and they are increasing in popularity all the time. Even major educational institutions like Harvard University offer open-access online courses, and smaller ones like the Shaw Academy, based in Ireland, have increasing numbers of people taking short online courses and learning about new topics in a manageable way.

So it's important to remember that, even though most research has focused on negative effects, most computer gaming is positive. Many computer games reward persistence and learning and so help people to build up their self-efficacy beliefs, and several studies have found that teenagers who do gaming often score more highly on school engagement, friendship networks and family closeness than those who don't. There is even evidence that some degree of online gaming contributes to positive mental health (Durkin and Barber, 2002). Many professionals are looking at the gamification of education or tests, as a way of keeping people interested and motivated. When Le and Peng (2006) reviewed nearly 30 years of studies of computer games, they found that non-violent games had been shown to improve spatial and cognitive skills, sociability and academic performance.

▶ Time spent game playing

Concerns about the amount of time that children spend playing computer games are another matter. Computer games, as we have seen, are designed to keep the person playing, and children may not realize how long they have been spending on that particular activity, without the intervention of an adult. Physical exercise is important for healthy development – and for a healthy adult life, for that matter – so it is important for a child to have a balance of activities, with some time being spent in physical play or sport, and some time being spent on more passive activities.

This doesn't mean, though, that computer games are the worst offenders in this respect. The interaction between the person and the computer is a more active and, in many ways more psychologically healthy form of engagement than the passive receptivity required by TV watching. Rather than simply watching, the child who is playing on the computer is acting and thinking, which is preferable to being passive. If it comes to a choice between watching TV and computer games, then computer games have a definite advantage – depending, of course, on the game and the TV programme. Too long staring at any kind of screen, though, can be damaging to the eyesight, because eye muscles need exercising in the same way as any other type of muscle, and too long sitting down can encourage obesity; the ideal is always that children have a balance of activities rather than doing just one type of leisure activity. Wii games took on that challenge by offering a physically active though still virtual experience, and 'Pokemon Go' aims to get people out into the real world while still interacting with the virtual one. Whether that type of strategy will challenge, say, childhood obesity, is yet to be known.

Remember this

The personal satisfaction involved in learning physical skills can be profound. Just the sensation of getting better through practice can motivate people to quite extreme efforts. And that's just as valid for beginners as it is for professionals, because it taps into our deep personal need for self-efficacy and self-actualization.

▶ Harm to learning

The third main objection to computer games is that they might be harmful to children's learning, because they encourage children to fritter away their time on the games instead of reading or doing things which are more obviously educational. This objection is more complex, because children learn in many different ways and, also, because there is relatively little research evidence. Overall, what evidence there is suggests that children who like to read still read for pleasure whether they play computer games or not – they appear to regard them as separate activities, not as substitutes for one another. Also, as we have seen, the perseverance which children devote to video games is regarded by some psychologists as a valuable form of learning in itself. And some computer games actively encourage literacy.

Many educational programmes, too, use children's enjoyment of computer games to convey educational messages. There is a range of educationally based games and activities available for children of all ages, which combine educational information with engaging activities and challenges for the child, and many other games, as we have seen, have an educational undercurrent. So some video games and other computer activities can actually enhance children's formal education rather than interfere with it. Computer-based learning of this type may be regarded as different from the classic computer game, but it can equally well be argued that the popularity of video games helps to create the climate for the children's enjoyment of educational activities, and their readiness to learn. Again, it depends on the game, and this is definitely an area which needs more psychological research.

Gaming, then, is a significant contribution to the leisure activities available to most people. There is an ever-increasing range of games, and increasingly complex control systems, ranging from sophisticated driving simulators to film-quality displays. 3D-based virtual reality devices have been less obviously successful. Home-based virtual reality equipment has not taken off in the way that its designers hoped, partly because of the personal vulnerability experienced by people cut off from their immediate surroundings. DVD-based realism, by contrast, caught on very fast. This may have been the result of clever marketing on the part of the DVD people, but few inventions which have made people feel vulnerable have been successful in the mass market. Modern Wi-Fi games have overcome these problems, and are much more popular. So computer games are likely to be with us for a very long time, and understanding their underlying psychological mechanisms is interesting in its own right.

Sport and music

Sport is another important way in which people use their leisure time. Many of us are involved in sport in one way or another, whether we do it ourselves, or whether we just watch other people doing it. Sporting activities range from everyday exercises such as walking or jogging, to team sports such as playing football, rugby or hockey, to performance sports like skating, athletics or cycling. In many ways, it is difficult to draw a hard and fast line between exercise and sport, but when the full range is taken into account most of us do something vaguely sport-like, even if it's only to go swimming now and again.

Some people, though, engage in sport much more seriously. They decide from a relatively early age, that they are going to compete seriously in their particular sporting activity, and from that point they devote tremendous amounts of time to improving their skills, learning new techniques, and ensuring that their physical and mental condition is as perfect as they can get it. Some people do this as amateurs, participating in sport as a serious hobby, but not intending to make a living from it. Others aim to take sport up as a profession, by achieving international standards of performance or, possibly, by training others. Whatever their ultimate aim, these people devote a considerable amount of their lives to perfecting their sporting performance.

▶ Music and dance

Sport isn't the only area of human activity which is like this, of course. Exactly the same thing applies to both dance and music. To become a professional dancer or musician doesn't just require a personal talent, it also requires devoting a large part of one's daily life to learning and perfecting performance techniques. This is particularly true if someone aims to take up music or dance as a profession, but it is also true if they want to acquit themselves competently as an amateur. Many of the findings of sport psychologists also apply to the psychology of music and dance.

Sport psychology is all about using psychology to help people to learn skills, keep motivated, and perform as well as possible. It draws from psychological knowledge and experience of sporting practice to try to understand how different factors can influence sportspeople in their performance, and what the best methods of training might be. One of the central aspects of sport psychology, therefore, is how we learn physical skills.

LEARNING PHYSICAL SKILLS

Learning to perform a complex physical action precisely is really quite a complicated thing. It involves hundreds, or even thousands, of different muscle groups, each contracting and relaxing at precisely the right moments. Each muscle contracts in response to a message from the brain, so the different messages which are sent from the brain to the muscles need to be highly co-ordinated if the movement is to be exactly right.

In Chapter 9, we saw how this involves automatizing our actions, so that they can be carried out without any conscious thinking, apart from the decision to perform them. This happens as the sequence of actions becomes controlled by the part of the brain that co-ordinates action, the cerebellum, instead of being controlled by the cerebrum, which is the part of the brain that we think with. And, as we saw in Chapter 5, drugs such as nicotine interfere with the messages from the brain to the muscles, which is one reason why high-performance sportspeople don't smoke. The other reason, of course, is that it also interferes with how efficiently we breathe, and with the amount of oxygen that the blood can carry.

▶ The learning curve

When we are learning something new, we generally take quite a long time to do it successfully at first. But the more we do it, the easier it becomes. Someone learning to perform a new tennis stroke may fail entirely the first time they attempt it. As they practise, though, they are likely to succeed more and more often, until eventually they can do the stroke successfully all the time – at least, while they are practising!

It's the same with any other physical skill. Someone who is learning to type will be very slow at first, but will become faster as they become more familiar with the positions of the letters on the keyboard. If we were to plot their speed of typing on a chart, measuring it against the amount of practice, we would find that it made a curve which picked up very steeply at first, and then rounded off more gently. And if we were to do the same with the practising of the tennis stroke, we'd find that it, too, made the same curve (Figure 12.1). This is known as the learning curve, and it shows how we go about learning any new skill.

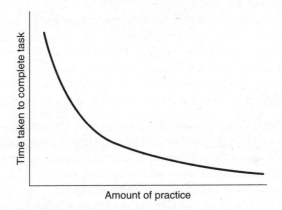

Figure 12.1 A learning curve.

Actually, though, the basic learning curve is only the beginning. In a complex sport or skill, we often experience several different curves, with a levelling out between them (Figure 12.2). With practice, we improve a great deal at first, but then we hit what is known as a plateau, where we don't seem to get any better for a while. But if we keep on working at it, then eventually we begin to improve again. Most complex skills involve plateau learning, because they actually consist of many skills combined together, and it takes time to master each one. It's also possible that the time spent apparently not getting any better is useful because we consolidate those skills we do have, and make sure that they are fully under control.

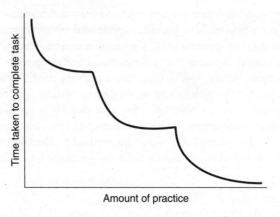

Figure 12.2 Plateau learning.

▶ The use of feedback

Feedback is another very important part of skill learning. Feedback is all about knowing what we have done – knowledge of results. If we didn't get any feedback about the outcomes of our actions, we wouldn't be able to learn anything. You couldn't get better at darts if you were blindfolded, and couldn't see where the darts had landed on the board! Instead, when playing darts, we use the outcome of our first action – throwing the first dart – to help us to aim the second one more accurately.

One of the most important tasks of a sports coach is to provide feedback. But the kind of feedback matters a lot. Den Brinker *et al.*, in 1986, investigated how important feedback is when learning to ski. They used a ski simulator, and asked people to learn how to make slalom-type movements while on the machine. The researchers varied the kind of feedback, and found that the most useful type was when people were given feedback about the amplitude of their body movements – how much they swayed with the actions. They learned much faster from this than they did when they were given feedback about how often they moved, or how smooth their movements were.

▶ Mental training

Mental training is another aspect of complex skill learning that sport psychologists have become experienced in developing. Mental training involves using the imagination, in a carefully controlled way, to improve performance. For example, Ainscoe and Hardy (1987) developed a training programme with gymnasts, in which they were asked to practise their performance not just physically, but also mentally – visualizing themselves going through each action successfully and smoothly. They found that using this method produced a noticeable improvement in how well the gymnasts learned.

Ainscoe and Hardy weren't the only psychologists to have discovered this. In 1983, Feltz and Landers reviewed 60 different studies of mental training of physical skills. They came to the conclusion that this method was a useful way of improving performance. Many athletes and other sportspeople use visualization as a regular part of their practice, and find that it doesn't just help their physical learning, it also helps their concentration.

Key idea

One of the major insights of sport psychology is the recognition of how important mental training can be. In fact, it can be so effective that techniques like visualization can sometimes make all the difference between success and failure – if they are also accompanied by appropriate physical training, of course.

▶ Practice and automatization

Any new skill requires practice – it won't become a skill until enough time and effort has been put into perfecting it for it to have become virtually automatic. Some sport psychologists have investigated whether it is better to have long, concentrated sessions of practice, or whether it is better to break them up into smaller chunks. The answer seems to be somewhere between the two. Practice sessions need to be long enough for the person to get some physical control of the skill that they are working on, but it is also important to have breaks. These don't just give the person a chance to rest: they also seem to help us to consolidate the learning, physically, so that it comes more easily the next time we try it.

Gruson (1988) looked at how skilled pianists practise, and compared it with people who were still working through the lower grades. She found that the experts go about their practising in a different way from the novices. The experts, for instance, spend much more time practising whole units. They wouldn't ever repeat single notes – if they made a mistake, they would repeat the whole section. Novices, on the other hand, would repeat single notes if they made a mistake, which didn't really help them to learn the whole piece of music at all.

The implication, then, is that practising whole units is important for the development of fluent skills. If we wish to produce a performance which is polished and continuous, then we need to practise what we are doing in a way that is also continuous. It's obvious really, when you think about it, but it's surprising how many people don't do it!

MOTIVATION

Another important aspect of sport psychology is studying how it is that successful athletes manage to maintain their motivation. Success requires continual training and striving to improve performance. Becoming a competent sportsperson involves giving up a great deal of free time, and putting oneself through a considerable amount of physical effort. For many people, such efforts would be too much. So what is it that distinguishes someone who is prepared to do this, from the rest of us?

▶ Internal and external motivation

One of the most important distinctions which sport psychologists make is between internal and external sources of motivation. An internal source of motivation is one which comes from inside ourselves – which derives from our own intentions, ambitions and personal goals. An external source of motivation, as its name suggests, comes from outside. External motivators include rewards, avoiding punishment, and living up to other people's expectations.

Interestingly, there is quite a lot of evidence which shows that giving people external rewards, such as money, for achieving success in sport, music or exams, can actually be counter-productive. It can reduce someone's motivation, not increase it. For example, Orlick and Mosher (1978) asked children to carry out a balancing task on a bar, for ten minutes. Before and after the test, the children could spend as much time as they liked practising. The amount of time that they practised was taken as showing their level of intrinsic motivation.

Orlick and Mosher found that all the children spent much the same amount of time practising before the test. When they did the test, they gave one group of children a special award, saying that it was because they had done such a good job. Another group of children didn't get any reward at all, even though they were just as good. These children didn't know about the other group, so they didn't feel disappointed. But after the test, the children who had received the award actually spent much less time practising than the children who hadn't been given anything. Receiving the award had actually decreased their level of intrinsic motivation.

Of course, this doesn't mean that all awards are a bad thing. Sometimes, they can help motivation because they encourage people to feel competent, and that they are getting somewhere. When Orlick and Mosher told children beforehand that they could earn an award by doing the balancing task, those children didn't lose motivation at all. So things which tell us that our skills are improving as a result of our efforts help us to feel competent, and don't reduce our motivation. But rewards which aren't relevant to our efforts, such as money or unexpected awards, can sometimes reduce intrinsic motivation.

The reason for this seems to be that we generally focus on just one explanation for why we are doing things. Even though, as we have seen, human beings often do things for more than one reason, we still prefer to identify just one reason at a time. So if someone receives an external reward for doing well, then they are likely to see themselves as being motivated by the reward instead of by their own interest and commitment. If the rewards don't continue, or don't seem to be as important, the person loses motivation. Someone who knows that they are doing something for their own personal pleasure and ambition, though, isn't likely to lose that motivation unless their ambitions change.

Key idea

External rewards for success have been shown to be damaging to motivation. But rewards which come through successful competition are much more effective. This may be because they are also tied to successful social recognition.

▶ Competence

This doesn't mean, though, that we could carry on putting lots of effort into mastering a sporting or musical skill if we didn't feel that we were getting anywhere. It is very important that we should be able to feel competent in our learning – that we should feel that our skills are improving, and that our own personal abilities to do things are getting better. Having good feedback is a part of that, because it shows us when we are improving. But another important part of this is the way in which we set our personal goals. We need to have something to aim at, and that something must be something we think we could manage. It needs to give us a challenge to rise to, but should not be so far ahead that we feel we could never get there. Setting manageable goals is an important part of retaining motivation, because the feeling that we have achieved another target helps us to keep going.

ACHIEVING PEAK PERFORMANCE

Sport psychology is also concerned with making sure that people can perform to the absolute limit of their ability, at the times when it matters. Training and motivation are part of that, but there are other factors, too, which are the concern of sport psychology. On the training field, for instance, many athletes reach top performance. But when it comes to actual competitive events, some people consistently win, while others just don't seem to be able to manage that last, final edge which means success.

▶ Positive thinking

Positive thinking is a crucial factor in distinguishing between people who are likely to be successful and those who aren't. Highly successful sportspeople don't allow themselves to think about failure. They don't just block it off – instead, they think positively about success. Not about winning the gold medal, but about actually doing the activity successfully. When it is being used in this way, the person imagines him/herself going through the whole activity successfully – running the race, or taking the exam, or whatever it is. By concentrating only on positive thoughts, and systematically imagining each successful stage of the activity, the person leaves no mental room for the doubts and worries which would add to their level of stress.

This sort of approach requires a high level of mental discipline on the part of the athlete or performer. There are various techniques for doing this. One of them is learning how to concentrate your mental focus, so that you are aware only of the part of your surroundings which matter. The champion tennis player Billie Jean King described how her mental focus would change from a wide range, encompassing the whole court, while the ball was over the other side of the net, to a tight, narrow focus the minute the ball was hit by her opponent. The gold medal-winning athlete Linford Christie used to limit his mental focus to the track in front of him during the few minutes before the race began, ignoring everything else except the starting pistol.

Another way that successful athletes use positive thinking is in visualizing achievement. The hurdler, David Hemery, described how one year he tried to prepare himself for disappointment, by imagining realistically how he would deal with failure. He lost. The next year, throughout his training, he allowed himself to think only about success, and didn't entertain the thought that he might not win. That was the year that he won his Olympic gold medal. Taking a more optimistic approach by thinking positively gave him an overall edge which the more pessimistic outcome didn't.

As with using visualization for training, Hemery's mental images weren't about standing on the podium. What he would visualize was completing the track without a single mistake, in the best possible time. By creating a positive mental image of what he was capable of achieving, Hemery was able to build up his feelings of competence and confidence, and to make sure that his performance on the day was the very best that he could do.

▶ Managing performance anxiety

Another aspect of making sure that you do the best you can, whether in a sporting competition or in an exam, is ensuring that your anxiety levels don't get out of hand. We saw in Chapter 4 how being anxious or upset can interfere with how well we do things, so it is important for athletes not to allow themselves to get too worried. Using positive thinking is also a good way of doing this. By filling the mind up with positive mental images, there isn't much room for thoughts about failure or mistakes.

Athletes also manage performance anxiety by making sure that their bodies are not physically stressed in the wrong way. Anxiety can be increased by eating the wrong things, or by eating at too infrequent intervals. If we haven't eaten for several hours, for instance, we automatically become more anxious and aroused, because this is an ancient biological mechanism encouraging us to go out and look for food. Many athletes drink milk, because it contains naturally calming substances which work in the brain to reduce anxiety without interfering with our physical abilities. And, of course, they regard it as very important that they are properly rested and have a good night's sleep before a key competition.

Exactly the same principles apply to any sort of demanding human experience. It's just as important when you're doing an exam to eat properly and to be rested, for instance, as it is when you are entering a sporting competition or taking a graded sports test. But it is astounding how many people ignore the physical demands of their bodies, and make their anxiety much worse by not eating properly, or by staying up late the night before to 'study'. There is a physical aspect to managing any kind of performance anxiety, even exam performance.

Key idea

Performance anxiety is a two-edged sword. It can help people to perform better, or it can damage their performance to a disastrous extent. So learning to manage levels of performance anxiety is as vital to any serious sports competitor as it is to a musician or actor.

▶ Using setbacks constructively

Another feature which seems to distinguish top performers from those who don't do as well, is how they handle failure when it actually happens. Many people respond to failing a test, or an exam, or losing a competition, by feeling upset and disappointed. But top sportspeople don't do this. Instead, they react by being angry with themselves. They know that they can do better than that, and so they resolve to make sure that it won't happen again.

This has everything to do with the process of attribution, which we looked at in Chapter 3. Attribution, you may remember, is about the reasons that we give for why things happen. And this makes all the difference to how we respond to failure. As we have seen, negative attributions tend to be global, stable and uncontrollable – that is, they are seen to apply generally to most things, to be unlikely to change, and to be something that the person can't do anything about. Making those sorts of attributions about setbacks or failures can seriously damage our chances of improvement.

If someone attributes their failure at sport (or education or anything else, for that matter) to lack of talent or ability, that is stable, global and uncontrollable, so they are unlikely to try very hard to overcome it, because they won't think there's any point. If they think it was because they hadn't practised enough, that is something that they can do something about, so it will spur them on to more effort. Alternatively, if it was just a 'bad day', that's unstable and not always going to apply in the future, so again they will continue with their normal training, and not be too bothered about it. If they think it is because they were doing something badly, which they could do better, then they will work very hard to learn better techniques to make sure that they don't make the same mistake again. It is the attributions they make for setbacks or failure which distinguish the champions and make them special.

Key idea

The thing that distinguishes first-rate athletes from others is how they deal with failure. By taking it as their own responsibility, and as something they can overcome with enough effort and training, they are taking control and using their failures to spur them on instead of discouraging them.

Sport psychology, then, like so many other aspects of psychology, brings together many different levels of human functioning. We have to perfect our physical skills, and ensure that they are fully co-ordinated. We learn by practice, accustoming ourselves to repetition and association. But we are also affected by our thoughts, beliefs and imagination – and these can make all the difference to how we learn, and how we perform, skilled actions.

Focus points

Research strongly suggests that violence on TV encourages violence in society, whereas TV with positive content can enhance prosocial behaviour.

People who watch lots of TV see the world as more violent than it really is.

TV has been shown to interfere with children's learning to read, partly because of its instant access. There is little evidence that computer games are more harmful to children than any other sedentary activity.

Computer games use well-established psychological principles such as self-efficacy and incentives to maintain interest and promote skill learning.

Sports and music both involve skill learning, motivation and performance.

Skill learning occurs through practice and feedback, and involves a high level of automatization of actions. Achieving peak performance involves positive thinking, using setbacks constructively and managing performance anxiety.

13

Social living

In this chapter you will learn:

▶ *how social networking is beneficial in everyday living*
▶ *strategies for overcoming shyness*
▶ *how teams and organizational cultures influence working life.*

In modern living, it is very easy for a single individual to become isolated. We no longer live in large family groups; we often don't use public transport but travel in cars; we can live alone if we want to; and we can even order our food and other necessities to be delivered to where we live. It's all very convenient, but it has brought to the surface something that is very deep in all of us, which is our need for social contact and belonging.

Our evolution as social animals, as we have seen, has given us all a range of social skills and an ability to communicate with other people. And it has also given us a strong tendency to affiliate with others – to see other people as important to us, to form relationships with them, and to see ourselves and them as belonging together in some way.

The most powerful of all our affiliations is family, of course. We form profound relationships with the people we grow up with, and our growing up takes place within a social network which is deeply important to us. Not to everyone, of course: some people grow up without personal family for one reason or another, and some families have relationships which are restrained or distant and not as close as other families. It's important to remember this, because although a close family is the social norm, it's an experience which isn't shared by everyone. But even people who grow up in collective environments without close relatives form affiliations with other people: friendships, surrogate 'aunties' and 'uncles', or special teachers. As we saw in Chapter 2, our heritage as social beings means that positive regard from other people is one of our basic psychological needs.

Social networking

When our lifestyles result in isolation, our social networks become more important to us. People have always developed social networks, bringing together groups of people with shared interests or common circumstances. They go back as far as recorded history. But the twenty-first century has provided more opportunities than ever before for sharing interests, ideas, and activities. Shy teenagers who in earlier years might have withdrawn from others and devoted their time to a home-based hobby can now share their interests with others, through social networking sites on the internet. Sports clubs, gyms and hobbies clubs are becoming significantly more important parts of a modern lifestyle. Computer game-players build up networks of like-minded others, competing against one another or working as team members against a common 'enemy'. And social networking sites like Facebook and Instagram offer the opportunity to share significant moments, images or ideas with friends and acquaintances in ways that would have been impossible before the advent of the internet.

Li *et al.* (2016) looked at how teenagers use the internet socially, and found three general styles of social use. Some people are friendship-oriented, and use the internet primarily as a way of interacting with their friends, through Snapchat, Instagram and similar types of social networking sites. Some people are gaming-oriented, using the internet mainly to play competitive games and linking up with other people through the networking opportunities offered by the game. And a third group tends to use the internet's creative opportunities: exploring, building or developing artistic skills. Li *et al.* found that the people who received the highest ratings for liking and socializing by the others was the creative group rather than the friendship-oriented group. It appeared that their additional skills and expertise meant that they were particularly well respected and liked by the others.

▶ Reducing isolation

The advent of social networking means that modern young people are not often truly alone: friends are only a click away. This became particularly apparent to the TV star Joey Essex, when he was taken to Patagonia as part of the TV series *Educating Joey Essex*. Although he experienced considerable physical hardship and intense cold during his visit, the worst part of his personal experience, he said, was the fact that he was cut off from the internet for more than a week – longer than he had ever been before. His first words when he was reconnected were: 'This is living; this is reality!' (*Educating Joey Essex*, ITV2, May 2015)

Although older people often worry about young people's apparently excessive use of computers, a study by Quinn and Oldmeadow (2012) found that actually, it seems to improve social relationships rather than damage them. In particular, they found that older boys who used social networking had a stronger sense of belonging with their friendship groups than those who didn't, and that the more they used social networks, the stronger that sense was. Similarly, a longitudinal study showed that people who had grown up with social networking showed a healthy balance in their social and personal networks (Miller, 2013), and the general conclusion is that, far from being damaging, social networking is a positive aspect of growing up for modern young people.

It's not just teenagers who benefit from social networking. Online interest groups like Mumsnet, for example, provide a forum for practical advice to their members, and they also take up issues of general social interest in the wider society, often challenging social figures like politicians on specific issues. Belonging to a group like this can provide a broad range of social interaction for someone who is physically isolated from other people, allowing them to express opinions or join in social campaigns in ways which were simply not available in earlier times.

Key idea

Social networking has made a profound change to modern living. It has removed the social isolation which comes from living alone or in small groups and travelling in cars rather than public transport. Now even people who are bedridden or living in distant places can be in contact with friends, family, or people with common interests on a day-to-day basis.

As our life changes, and new life-events happen, the way we use social networks changes too. Wrzus *et al.* (2013) compared the findings from 277 research projects, and found that our use of global, widespread social networking increases through our teens, reaching a peak in young adulthood, and then steadily becoming less. In particular, our use of personal and friendship networks tend to decrease throughout our adult life, although our family networks tend to remain stable in size right through from adulthood to old age. Networking with work colleagues or neighbours, on the other hand, is related to what we are doing at the time and doesn't tend to last when life moves us into different circumstances. Mumsnet, for instance, is a network for mothers, and generally becomes less relevant to people whose children have grown up and left home. So we find different uses for the internet at different stages in our lives, and it serves different purposes for us.

▶ **Other networks**

Social networking doesn't just happen through the internet, of course. There are many other types of clubs: hobbies clubs, sports clubs, and volunteer groups. Sporting venues such as ice rinks generally have adult classes for beginners as well as children's groups, and these can also provide useful opportunities to meet other people and form friendships. Some of these sporting groups have formal memberships, but some, such as park running groups where people jog or run around their local parks, have developed spontaneously as people have discovered their shared interest. Gym membership – and gym provision – has grown considerably as society recognizes the importance of physical fitness for people whose jobs involve sitting at a desk for hours on end, and these too provide opportunities for people to meet socially and share common interests.

Some clubs are humorous as well as sociable: there is a wide network of Secret Cake Clubs, for instance, where members are secretly informed of a venue and meet there, bringing cakes they have baked which are then shared by everyone who attends. The venue is communicated through the internet, but it's a real meeting with real cake! And many parents of young children appreciate the social value of meeting other parents at the school gate, and how useful those conversations can be. These are only a few examples, but they show us how networking and affiliating with others is a fundamental part of our natures. Contact with other people has been shown to help us to remain psychologically balanced, and to deal with stressful events as they happen. It's just another example of how profoundly social people are.

Shyness and loneliness

So what happens when we are just not able to be as social as we would like to be? Interacting with other people, as we've seen, is important for us as human beings. But in the modern world, it isn't always as simple as it might seem. We may feel comfortable with our friends, or with people who know us well, but modern life is full of strangers who don't know us at all. Living a full life in modern society means that we often need to interact with people that we don't know.

SHYNESS

Most of us feel shy at some points in our lives. Walking into a room full of strangers, performing on stage in front of other people, or even going on a date can make us feel socially anxious and self-conscious. Most people manage to deal with it and carry on anyway, but for some, that social anxiety, or shyness, can be so extreme that they avoid social situations altogether.

There are a number of different aspects to shyness. There is the cognitive level, which involves the negative thoughts and worrying which shy people do. There is the emotional level, with feelings of embarrassment, shame or anxiety. There is the physiological level, in which the arousal produced by the anxiety (more about that in the next chapter) gives us an increased heart rate, sweating, and sometimes even trembling. And there is the behavioural level, which means that people experiencing shyness tend to avoid eye-contact with others and show defensive or avoiding body language.

Another aspect of shyness is the way that shy people take more time to engage in social interactions with other people. Carducci (2000) found that shy people generally prefer to observe people for a while before they talk with them, and take longer than other people to warm up and relax in social interactions. Since most everyday social encounters often don't allow that sort of time, they often don't manage to get a conversation going.

Shy people often believe that other people are making judgments about them, and that is made worse by the way that they often compare themselves with the most successful and popular people rather than with other, ordinary people. Carducci found that these inappropriate comparisons can then become an excuse for being shy, because the shy person expects themselves to be perfect in every way, which is simply unrealistic.

Key idea

Many people describe one of the benefits of being in their 30s as freedom from the self-consciousness which they felt as teenagers or in their early adulthood. Recognizing that people are much more accepting than you imagine they will be can be a liberating experience!

A study by Henderson, Zimbardo and Carducci, in 2001, found that shyness was quite common – nearly half of the people they asked described themselves as shy. But most of them were able to deal with it quite well. They took longer in starting their relationships, but they usually managed it in the end. And for many in the modern world, the combination of internet social networking and also the increased use of dating and matching agencies means that meeting people has become much less of a problem than it used to be in the past.

Researchers investigating shyness have found that shy people use a variety of different strategies to deal with their shyness, ranging from using alcohol to 'loosen up', to consciously developing social skills. But the most effective strategies, Zimbardo and Carducci (2001) found, were to adopt the same social strategies as those used by highly popular people. Table 13.1 lists these strategies.

Table 13.1 Social strategies used by popular people

Scheduling their social life	Making sure they have plenty of opportunities to practise interacting with other people.
Thinking positively	Expecting people they meet to be positive, rather than expecting them to be negative and critical.
Social reconnaissance	Being interested in other people, rather than trying to be interesting.
Entering conversations gracefully	Listening to conversations and stepping in only at an appropriate time, to enhance the conversation.
Dealing with failure	Remembering that negative reactions or rebuffs usually come from external causes – like the other person having a personal problem or bad day – rather than being personal.
Managing emotions	Keeping a grip on negative emotions, and projecting a positive emotional atmosphere as much as possible.
Defusing disagreements	Suggesting compromises, apologizing, or doing other things to reduce tension.
Using humour	Telling jokes and being lighthearted as a fast track to being liked.

Source: Henderson, Zimbardo and Carducci (2001)

LONELINESS

Being shy is one thing. As we've seen, it's something people can learn to deal with. Being lonely, on the other hand, can be trickier. For some people, loneliness results from social isolation – a type of loneliness which has been called situational loneliness. But other people can feel lonely even when they are surrounded by others, and would seem to have quite a good social life. Some people have very few social contacts and look as though they must be lonely to outsiders, but actually feel perfectly OK and don't experience lonely emotions at all. So defining what we actually mean when we say that someone is lonely is more difficult than it seems.

Effectively, what is important about loneliness is how people actually feel, which means that the two types of loneliness have to be challenged in different ways. For most people, situational loneliness is a temporary experience, resulting from changes in life-experience which have seriously reduced their social interaction. Increasing opportunities to meet people, through hobbies or interest clubs or through volunteering can help them considerably. The internet, too, offers a number of ways to interact with other people, and the use of social networking or other kinds of internet-based interaction can make a considerable difference to how lonely people feel.

For chronically lonely people, the problem is more challenging. Williams and Solano (1983) showed that there are differences in how chronically lonely people interact with others. One of these is in self-disclosure: chronically lonely people reveal much less about their personal experiences or beliefs than other people. This is important, because self-disclosure is a significant element in forming relationships. If we don't know anything much about a person, our relationship with them tends to stay fairly superficial: relationships only develop as we find out more about the other person and get to know them more deeply.

There are other differences too. Jones, Hobbs and Hockenbury (1982) found that chronically lonely people tend to give other people less attention and to ask fewer questions when they are in conversation. They also tend to be less talkative generally. The researchers in this study developed a programme which involved training chronically lonely people in social skills, so that their conversations with other people involved more exchanges and participation. It took a bit of practice, but their participants reported a much lower experience of loneliness after the training programme.

Another way that chronically lonely people are different from people who don't feel lonely has to do with the attributions that they make. In Chapter 4 we saw how the reasons that we give for why things happen can show distinctive styles, and how negative attributional styles can produce depression. These negative attributional styles are also characteristic of chronically lonely people: they tend to see their problems in forming social relationships as arising from stable and dispositional causes. Stable causes are ones which are not likely to change in the future, and dispositional ones are causes which arise from the person's character and personality, rather than from the situation.

People who are not chronically lonely, on the other hand, tend to make unstable and situational attributions. So if they experience a difficulty in forming a relationship with someone, they see it as being only temporary, and as happening because of the situation they are in. This means that it doesn't bother them as much, and they don't see it as a permanent state. Many chronically lonely people have found that cognitive therapy, which challenges their attributions and shows them how to think differently about things, has made a big difference to their lives and reduced their loneliness considerably.

HUMOUR

One of the strategies which people use to help them in social situations is to use humour. We judge humorous remarks and jokes as being different from other forms of social situation: because they don't really 'count' as being serious, people say things in a humorous context which they wouldn't say if they felt they would be taken seriously. So humour can be useful in relaxing tense situations, and helping people to step back and take something less seriously. Some therapists have found that teaching lonely people to use humour effectively can be useful in helping them to learn how to engage with other people. At the same time, it can also be a shield: some comedians have described how they felt lonely as children but learned to use humour because it covered up their inner feelings and helped them to get on with others. We can see from Table 13.2 that humour serves other purposes too.

Table 13.2 Functions of humour

Coping	Humour gives people a bit of distance from difficult personal situations. So, for example, members of the emergency services may use 'black' humour to help them to cope with the emotional pressure they are under.
Reframing	Humour allows us to look at things in a fresh light, and sometimes helps us to see that things may have different implications.
Communicating	Humour allows us to say things we wouldn't be able to say otherwise. This is particularly useful in highly emotional contexts.
Expressing hostility	One of the reasons that social campaigners oppose certain types of jokes is because they are actually expressing hostile and anti-social feelings – for example, by ridiculing groups of people – but dressing them up in ways that appear acceptable on the surface.
Constructing identities	Groups often develop 'in-jokes', shared by their members, which help the group members to identify with the group.

Source: Kahn (1989)

Researchers have found, too, that humour at work can be a useful way of relaxing tensions and helping people to get through their working day. In the 1920s, a style of management emerged which has still, sadly, not quite died out. It was called 'scientific management', and was based on the modernist principles of its day. Basically, it regarded people as machines, whose task was to carry out their working functions as rigidly as possible. The idea was that this made the whole working operation more efficient. But people are not machines, and what that approach really produces is a great deal of covert rebellion.

Sometimes that rebellion is unconscious. The rates of industrial accidents, for example, increased with the introduction of scientific management. It wasn't a matter of being accident prone, or even of deliberate sabotage – rather, it was a simple consequence of expecting human beings to act in exactly the same way, day after day, hour after hour. That isn't what human beings do. Sickness and absenteeism rates also increased, as did rates of staff turnover – the number of staff who simply left. Treating people like machines just isn't a good idea.

Key idea

It is useful to look at staff turnover, sickness and absentee rates in a company. These are all indicators of the quality of the company's management, because people who are happy in their work take fewer days off and don't want to leave. That also makes them more profitable to employ.

People who find themselves in working situations like that often use humour to cope with it. For example, in one study, Kenny and Euchler (2012) found that staff in a tightly controlling organization coped with it by sending frequent humorous emails to one another. By subverting the managerial control in this way, they avoided difficult and unpleasant situations. The management didn't like it, but it actually reduced a lot of working tension, and made the whole organization work better.

Humour, then, is an important aspect of our everyday social behaviour. It can redefine situations, help us to emphasize or augment what we mean, establish common bonds with other people, and even change awkward social situations into positive ones. And we use it everywhere – in our family life, our social life, and our working life.

Work, teams and organizations

For many people, working life is an important source of social interaction, as well as a major source of self-esteem. Although we might daydream about a life of leisure, the reality is that most of us are psychologically and physically healthier if we are working. If we are prevented from working, by unemployment or redundancy, we are very likely to become depressed. If that unemployment continues for a long time, we might also fall into a kind of learned helplessness, and find it difficult to make the sustained effort that is necessary to take up other working opportunities.

UNEMPLOYMENT

Unemployment has other negative effects as well. Warr (1987) found that between 20 per cent and 30 per cent of unemployed people showed a deterioration in their physical health. Binns and Mars (1984) found that unemployment often leads to difficulties in personal relationships as well, often because of the additional strain brought on by continuing financial difficulties. And, of course, the longer we are unemployed, the more these problems are likely to become exaggerated.

Jahoda (1982) suggested the reason that long-term unemployment is so damaging is because working serves more functions for us than we realize – much more than just the obvious function of earning money to live on. Jahoda identified five latent functions of working, which are listed in Table 13.3. We don't really notice these while we are working, but they are extremely important in helping to keep our emotional and psychological life balanced.

Table 13.3 Latent functions of working.

1 Employment imposes a time structure on the waking day.
2 Employment brings about regularly shared experiences and contacts with people outside the family.
3 A job links the individual with goals and purposes beyond their own.
4 A job defines aspects of personal status and identity.
5 Paid employment enforces its own activity.

Source: Jahoda (1982)

Thinking of work in this way can be useful, because it gives us some hints as to how unemployment can be survived. For example, people who are unemployed but keep themselves busy by doing voluntary work don't usually suffer from the depression and learned helplessness that so many other unemployed people experience. This seems to be partly because they gain the same latent functions of working from their voluntary commitment. It can sometimes be like this for people who are committed to a particular hobby too.

SOCIAL ASPECTS OF WORKING LIFE

In the 1930s, a group of psychologists challenged the scientific management approach by showing that there are important social dimensions to working too. In a series of studies at the Hawthorne Electric Plant, in Chicago, Elton Mayo and his colleagues Roethlisberger and Dickson began by trying to find the best lighting levels in a particular workshop. They began by raising the lighting levels, and found that production increased. Then they lowered the lighting levels and production increased again. Finally, they put the lighting levels back to how they had been originally, and production was higher than it had ever been.

The Chicago researchers had hit on an important discovery about working life. Almost regardless of what they did, the employees in that area worked harder as a result. The one exception came when they varied the tea breaks, and had a condition with about eight short breaks throughout the day. The girls in that part of the factory complained that they didn't get time to concentrate on what they were doing. But apart from that single case, it wasn't their physical conditions of work that mattered. The fact that the researchers were taking an interest in what the employees were doing was enough to increase their motivation.

Key idea

The most important part of many people's working life is the people they work with on a day-to-day basis. So good management comes from ensuring that people can carry out high-quality work and also maintain good working relationships. This is not something that can be managed by slogans or mission statements.

▶ Group standards

The researchers also investigated a department called the bank-wiring room. This consisted of a group of people who were usually left to work without much supervision. Interestingly, the workers in this section of the factory seemed to be unaffected by the changes introduced by the psychologists. They had developed their own way of working, which produced a regular, steady rate of production. They didn't increase it much, even when paid extra, but then they didn't slow down either.

When they looked into it a bit more deeply, Mayo and the others found that this group had developed a clear code of practice about how each person should do their share, and not do anything which might get the rest of the group into trouble. The principles by which they were working are listed in Table 13.4, and all the members of that department held to them. As a result, it was one of the most reliable and dependable parts of the organization.

Table 13.4 An informal 'code of practice'.

1 You shouldn't work too hard –'rate-busting' is not acceptable behaviour.

2 You shouldn't slack over your work – do your own fair share.

3 You shouldn't tell a supervisor anything which might get a fellow worker into trouble.

4 If you hold a position of authority, you shouldn't pull rank or act officiously.

Source: Roethlisberger and Dickson (1939)

What these early studies show us is how important social interaction is at work – both between people who work together, and between managers and their workforce. More recently, researchers have found that it is possible to draw on that human tendency by encouraging and organizing positive teamworking.

TEAMWORKING

Teamworking is a way in which our natural tendency to be social can work to the benefit of an organization. By bringing people with different skills together to focus on a single task, the organization is able to tap into their various stores of knowledge, enabling better solutions than those which a single individual might have developed.

Teamworking also benefits the people in the team, although the personal benefits of belonging to a team are not always the visible ones. In Chapter 2, we looked at the process of social identification, and how people like to be able to feel proud of belonging to a particular group. Hayes (2002) argued that this is also a fundamental aspect of teamworking. Belonging to a successful, achieving group, and being recognized as contributing to it, is sometimes enough on its own to satisfy people's social needs. But teamwork can also be seen as a way of accumulating useful experience which will help in later promotion.

Key idea

Building up a team can take time and effort, especially if people are unused to that way of working. But once it has been properly developed, a working team can make a lot of difference to how a company or organization works.

▶ Team building

A team is different from a working group because it is task-focused and much more clearly structured. Organizational psychologists have developed various kinds of team-building exercises which can be used to help to train people to work together. Some of these exercises focus on helping people to get to know one another – they adopt an interpersonal approach, encouraging people to be honest with one another, and creating an open and safe climate in which people feel able to admit their weaknesses and identify their training needs.

In the 1960s and 1970s, many team-building exercises focused on sensitivity training of this type. People learned to become more sensitive to one another. They would learn, for example, about non-verbal communication and how we signal intentions or emotions by our body language or behaviour. They learned how to listen carefully to what people are really saying (something that most of us are quite bad at), and how to offer support if someone was doing something particularly challenging and needed help. In other words, they learned to respond to the interpersonal messages of other members of the group.

These techniques are still useful, but there are other approaches to team building too. Later approaches tended to emphasize the roles and tasks which the team had to do. Adair (1968) argued that any effective team has to take account of three sets of needs: task needs – the practical things which have to be done in order to do the job at hand; group needs – to do with overcoming interpersonal quarrels or disputes, and making sure that people can act together effectively; and individual needs – to do with what the individual members of the team want to get out of it.

The job of the team leader, in Adair's model, is to pay attention to all three types of need and to make sure that they are all at least partly satisfied. It isn't enough just to concentrate on the demands of the job at hand and to ignore the group's needs, because this could mean that tensions between members of the group become so strong that afterwards, those people couldn't work together again. And it isn't really a good idea to concentrate only on the task and the group's needs and to ignore individual ones. It might get the job done, but in the long term people work much better when they benefit personally from being involved, too.

Key idea

Working teams are an effective way of harnessing both people's social motivation and their individual abilities. If they are given sufficient autonomy and responsibility, teams can be powerful contributors to the success of an organization.

One other significant factor in effective team building is the attitude that management has towards teamwork. Imai (1988) discussed how Japanese management systems involved all of the workers, at any level in the company, in a continuous drive for improvement. People were encouraged to feel proud of, and committed to, their company, and were treated as intelligent and responsible, no matter what job they were doing. So if they were asked to join a specific team to solve a problem, they were often pleased to be involved, and to be recognized as someone who could make a worthwhile contribution.

In too many organizations in the Western world, however, the potential contributions which can be made by their workforce is ignored or unrecognized by the management, so joining working teams can easily be seen as just an additional chore for the individual. A skilled team leader might be able to get around this, by ensuring that their team, at least, pays attention to people's individual needs. But the organization can make their job a great deal harder or a great deal easier through its attitude and policies on teamworking. With a positive managerial attitude that brings people truly on-side, however, work teams can be invaluable in helping an organization to cope with change and develop responses to challenges.

ORGANIZATIONAL CULTURES

Any organization contains a whole host of in-groups and out-groups: there are friendship groups, departmental groups, working teams and many others. People often feel more loyalty to some of these groups than to others. Some organizational change doesn't happen, for instance, because it is resisted by 'canteen cultures' that keep certain beliefs and ideas going among the workforce even when management are trying to change them.

The classic example of how a canteen culture can work against official policy and organizational change is in equal opportunities. An organization may adopt an official equal opportunities policy, but groups of employees may still perpetuate racist beliefs, meaning that anyone from an ethnic minority background has a very hard time indeed. In the 1990s, for example, several studies showed how canteen cultures in the police service perpetuated a high level of racism, which wasn't really affected by official policy. And it was the canteen culture, of course, which new recruits would encounter when they were learning practical policing, not the official culture of the higher management. Fortunately, matters have improved significantly in policing as social attitudes in general have changed, although there are still remnants of the old 'canteen culture' to be found.

Hayes (1998) discussed how an understanding of the social identity processes which we looked at in Chapter 2 could help us to understand how canteen cultures work, and why they are so influential. Knowing about social representations, too (see Chapter 3) helps us to understand how shared beliefs develop. People tend to take more notice of people who they think are like themselves, or who belong to the same in-group. So it's particularly easy for a group in an organization to develop shared beliefs about their work, and about life in general. Applying these two social psychology theories, therefore, can help us to understand how to tackle this sort of problem.

Key idea

A positive organizational culture makes people feel valued and able to do good work, so they are proud of belonging to that organization. A dictatorial culture, or one where cost-cutting means that people have to do inferior work they are not proud of, produces high staff turnover and dissatisfied workers.

Organizational cultures can work positively as well as negatively. Some organizations perpetuate a culture of loyalty, enthusiasm and flexibility which helps to keep them successful and competitive in the modern world. Organizational culture is all about the general assumptions, beliefs and practices in an organization – its distinctive style of working. Sometimes, you can find two organizations in exactly the same line of work, but which go about doing that work in entirely different ways. The people working in those organizations have quite different approaches to what they are doing; they deal with problems differently, and they expect different attitudes from management. Effectively, they are participating in different organizational cultures.

► Levels of culture

Some organizational researchers have spent their time trying to classify different types of organizational culture, but organizational psychologists tend to be more interested in how cultures work, and why they influence the people working in them the way that they do. Lundberg (1990) observed that organizational cultures seem to have three different levels, listed in Table 13.5. Psychologists have studied culture at each of these levels, but we tend to be particularly interested in the deepest level of shared assumptions and beliefs.

Table 13.5 Levels of organizational culture.

The manifest level	Symbols, language, stories, rituals, etc.
The strategic level	Beliefs about the company's direction, planning and expectations, internal management strategies.
The core level	Ideologies, values and assumptions about human nature and what people and the world are like.

Source: Lundberg (1990)

Organizational cultures aren't really just single phenomena, with everyone in the organization thinking the same way. Instead, different groups within the organization have their own ways of thinking. In a strong organizational culture, these different groups overlap, so they all have something in common. But in other types of organization, different groups may have entirely different assumptions and beliefs. In these cases, the organizational culture is weaker.

Key idea

Organizational cultures develop their own symbols and legends. But it is important to realize that these are only powerful because they reflect deeper beliefs in the culture. Trying to change the culture simply by changing the symbols and slogans can't work.

Being social can, of course, have its drawbacks. In Chapter 3 we saw how people are particularly inclined to conform to the immediate social demands on them – even if they think differently – and in a working group or committee, this can be disastrous. In Chapter 7, too, we saw how groupthink can lead to really bad decisions. But overall, our tendency to be sociable and to get on with other people is one of the things that enrich our day-to-day lives – both at work and outside it. It is very much what makes us human, and it keeps us both psychologically and physically healthy.

Focus points

The affiliations people make in their lives are both necessary and important, promoting psychological health as well as comfort.

Social networking has been shown to have many benefits, including helping teenagers and others to engage in more social interaction. We use physical social networks as well as virtual ones, through clubs, sports, hobbies, and other groups.

Shyness is a common experience for many people. Situational loneliness is often temporary, but people suffering from chronic loneliness may need help to overcome it.

We can tell how important work is to people by looking at the negative effects of unemployment, which include depression, ill-health, and learned helplessness.

Organizations consist of many groups and social networks. Successful organizational cultures build positive social identifications for their staff.

Teamworking has been shown to be a positive asset, both for organizational life and for managing organizational change.

14

Mental and physical health

In this chapter you will learn:

▶ *about three types of psychological therapy*

▶ *how health psychologists have improved medical communication*

▶ *how to cope with stress by changing thinking habits*

In this chapter we will be looking at how psychology is involved in health – both mental and physical. It has been a concern of psychologists from psychology's very earliest years, but over the past century or so, psychological ideas and knowledge have changed a great deal.

During the first part of the twentieth century, for instance, this area of psychology was strongly influenced by the ideas of the psychoanalyst, Sigmund Freud, who believed that people were largely acting out the demands of unconscious parts of their personality. Freud believed that unconscious infantile conflicts could lead to both mental and physical disturbances, even in adults.

Modern psychology, though, is entirely different from psychoanalysis. Although some ideas have been useful to clinical psychologists – in particular the idea of defence mechanisms, which we looked at in Chapter 6 – psychoanalysis adopts a different style of reasoning, and takes a different view of scientific evidence, than modern psychology. So the two forms of knowledge rarely come into contact in the modern world.

Key idea

Many of the books which claim to interpret dream symbols or personality from your choice of favourite flower are based on psychoanalytic ideas – some more firmly than others. They have very little to do with modern psychology.

In this chapter, we will look at some of the main ways in which psychologists working in health fields can help us to understand people. Psychologists help people who are suffering from problems in living; they help ordinary people who just have temporary problems; and psychological research can show how we can improve our physical health too. There are three branches of modern psychology which are particularly active in this area: clinical psychology, health psychology and counselling psychology.

Clinical psychology is concerned with people who are suffering from some kind of mental or behavioural problem.

That includes people who we might call mentally ill, although, thinking of them as 'ill' often isn't the best way to understand what is going on. Clinical psychologists often work alongside psychiatrists (doctors who specialize in mental illness) in psychiatric hospitals or clinics, but their approach to dealing with the patients is very different. Where a psychiatrist draws on a knowledge of physiology, which means adopting treatments such as chemotherapy (drugs) or physical treatments such as electro-convulsive therapy, clinical psychologists use their knowledge of human psychology to tackle these problems in a different way.

Health psychologists, on the other hand, are concerned with general health. That includes helping people to adopt healthier lifestyles, or to manage chronic illnesses such as diabetes so that they have a good quality of life despite their problem. Health psychologists are also active in developing public education programmes, and with helping medical personnel to communicate effectively with their clients. They also often work with schools to develop strategies to overcome common problems like childhood obesity. Their concern, as the job title suggests, isn't with illness, but with health and well-being, so their work applies to all of us, not just to people with problems.

Counselling psychologists work with people who are suffering from problems in living – that is, problems which are not mental illness, but which make life difficult for them. They might, for example, provide therapy for people who have been through traumatic experiences, and we will be looking at the problem known as PTSD, or post-traumatic stress disorder, in the next chapter. Counselling psychologists may help people who have developed anxiety disorders, which make it hard for them to get out of the house, or to overcome chronic shyness. They also help people who have been through abusive experiences – both adults and children – and need professional help to recover from them. They help people in many other ways, too, such as developing stress alleviation programmes in organizations, or by providing family therapy or relationship counselling.

Key idea

Too many people feel that getting therapy is a sign that they are sick or disturbed. In fact, therapists also help quite normal people to deal with everyday problems, like overcoming emotionally difficult childhoods or learning to manage bad tempers.

Clinical psychology

Clinical psychology is one of the oldest areas of applied psychology. Ever since psychology began, its insights have been used to help people who are mentally ill, or who have severe problems in living which make it difficult for them to cope with a normal life. As we have seen, clinical psychologists often work with psychiatrists in the mental health field, and their insights can contribute to the diagnosis and treatment of people suffering from severe mental illnesses such as schizophrenia or other psychotic disorders.

THE SCOPE OF CLINICAL PSYCHOLOGY

Clinical psychologists, as their name suggests, are trained to work with clinical problems; that is, psychological problems which have become so acute that they interfere with people conducting their day-to-day lives. Some clinical psychologists work in psychiatric hospitals, working closely with psychiatrists to help people who are suffering from a 'mental illness', or some other kind of severe problem in living. Some clinical psychologists work with other medical practitioners. It is becoming increasingly common, for example, for a clinical psychologist to work in a general medical practice, dealing with the type of problems which people bring to their doctor, but which are psychological in origin and better dealt with by a specialist in psychological matters.

Key idea

Psychologists and psychiatrists are sometimes confused, but really they are quite different. A psychologist specializes in understanding the human mind, in both normal and abnormal conditions. A psychiatrist is a medical doctor who specializes in illnesses and disorders, and often uses drugs or other kinds of medical treatments to deal with them.

Other clinical psychologists work with specialist treatment units of one kind or another. Paediatric (children's) clinics, for example, have clinical psychologists among their team members, who are able to provide psychological evaluations, guidance for parents, and therapy for children who need it. Some clinical psychologists work in community contexts, contributing their skills to teams which deal with a wide range of issues such as the problems of homelessness and street drinkers, or the challenges created by lack of institutional care for acute schizophrenics.

In addition to this, clinical psychologists often contribute their skills to emergency relief. They work closely with counselling psychologists and other professionals to help to relieve the psychological consequences of disasters or traumas. This often involves dealing with the common problem of post-traumatic stress disorder – a series of psychological problems that people experience after they have been involved in some particularly disturbing or traumatic situation.

THE SKILLS OF CLINICAL PSYCHOLOGY

Clinical psychologists bring a number of skills to these contexts. Because of the intensive training they have undergone (it takes at least eight years to become a fully qualified clinical psychologist), a clinical psychologist is trained in evaluating and diagnosing psychological problems, in techniques for ameliorating them – making them more bearable or less severe – and also in a number of different approaches to therapy. Although most clinical psychologists tend to develop preferred ways of working, their training is deliberately eclectic; that is, it covers different approaches and frameworks, and explores how they can each be used in practice. It is their depth of knowledge of so many different approaches that makes professional clinical psychologists so effective.

Key idea

One of the hardest challenges for clinical psychology is defining what we actually mean as 'normal', since what counts as 'normal' can vary so much from one culture, group, or even family to another.

▶ Evaluating psychological problems

When a clinical psychologist is dealing with a new client, for instance, they don't adopt just one single approach. Instead, their evaluation of the problem will draw on elements from a number of different approaches. If it is someone with a recurrent anxiety problem, for example, they might gather information about their childhood experience and family relationships, in the way that a psychoanalyst might. But they would also be likely to gather information about that person's daily habits, and the environmental stimuli which provoke anxiety attacks, as a behaviourist would. And they will learn about the person's way of seeing and understanding their own problem, and the kinds of styles of thinking that they commonly adopt, so that they can bring in insights from cognitive therapies. By combining these, and many other different sources of information, they can make use of the best insights from a wide range of approaches, which will help them to see what is best for that particular person.

All this means that one of the most important tools of the clinical psychologist is the clinical interview. Clinical psychologists need to be able to interview people in such a way that they can listen carefully to, and learn from, what that person is saying. This means that they need to be trained in listening skills, and in ways of encouraging the person to feel able to talk freely without imposing their own views and ideas on the conversation. That might seem easy, but actually it's a very difficult skill to learn. Counselling psychologists need to learn it too, in order to work effectively, and many professional clinical psychologists become involved in teaching counsellors and nurses these types of skills.

Key idea

Because clinical psychologists understand 'normal' people as well as disturbed ones, they are more able to help in situations where people are attempting to cope with difficult conditions, and becoming disturbed as a result.

▶ Diagnosis

Another aspect of the work of a clinical psychologist might be in helping diagnosis. For example, some specific cognitive disorders, such as problems brought about by head injury, or a specific neural deficit, mean that the person is unable to process certain kinds of information – like being unable to recognize faces even though they can remember names and people. One of the tools clinical psychologists can use for this work is a type of highly specialized psychometric test, which can detect abnormal functioning or areas of cognitive deficits. These tests are not available to unqualified people, but they can be very useful in a clinical context.

Using specialized psychometric tests, then, is another part of the training of clinical psychologists. Psychometric tests are sets of carefully developed questions or tasks, which give an insight into particular psychological issues. Some psychometric tests look just like questionnaires on the surface, but actually they are very different. Each item on a psychometric test has been through a rigorous process of development, being tested, re-tested, standardized on different populations, and carefully balanced with all the other test items to produce an exact result.

Psychometric tests are useful in a variety of contexts. Some tests are diagnostic – that is, they are able to alert the professional administering the test to particular types of problem. The diagnostic tests which can identify specific forms of brain damage, such as the exact consequences of a stroke, are a good example of this. Other tests don't diagnose problems as such, but they are used to assess how skilled someone is, or how severe a particular problem is. Some tests, by contrast, are used to give a general picture of what that particular person is like, such as personality or general intelligence tests.

Clinical psychologists have to know how to use all of these types of test, and many of the more powerful diagnostic tests can only be used by people who have had the appropriate clinical training. This is because they can give very misleading results if they are administered in the wrong way, or if someone who doesn't really know what they are doing is trying to interpret the test outcomes.

But testing is only one small part of the clinical psychologist's repertoire. As we saw earlier, they are also required to have a detailed knowledge of a range of different types of psychological therapy. In a book like this, of course, there really isn't enough space to deal with these to any detailed extent, but in the next part of this section we will look at how psychology has contributed to dealing with behavioural problems.

BEHAVIOURAL THERAPIES

Clinical psychologists often deal with the types of mental disorders that we know as neuroses – fears or anxieties which have become so extreme that the person has difficulty living a normal life. In the 1950s, psychologists who were interested in learning theory took the view that many of these problems could be understood as problems of behaviour. What had happened, they argued, was that these people had learned inappropriate ways of dealing with their environments, and this inappropriate learning was causing them problems. So the way to tackle those problems was for them to learn appropriate ways of dealing with their environments instead.

This led to the development of a number of different, behavioural, methods for dealing with neurotic problems. Psychologists began to use conditioning techniques for dealing with the irrational fears known as phobias. By treating the feared object as the stimulus, and substituting new, learned associations such as relaxation for the fear reaction, people could learn to deal with their phobias, and overcome them. In Chapter 9 we saw how the treatments for phobias known as systematic desensitization and implosion therapy work on these principles.

Other clinical psychologists used approaches which derived from social learning. For example, Bandura (1977) showed how modelling could also be useful in teaching people to overcome everyday fears. Seeing someone handling a snake harmlessly often gave those who were frightened of snakes a role model to imitate, and they found that their own level of fear lessened as a result.

▶ Behaviour shaping

Some clinical psychologists working with disturbed people adopted the idea of behaviour shaping, which is based on operant conditioning. Using this, a person becomes able to carry out an entirely new type of behaviour by learning it a little at a time. This principle has been very successful, for instance, in helping people with agoraphobia – a fear of open spaces. Rather than forcing them into dealing with the whole problem all at once, a psychologist will gradually help the person to build up their abilities, a little at a time. They might begin, for instance, by getting used to standing in the open doorway of their own home. Once they can do this easily, then they might venture out for just one or two steps; each time a little more is added until eventually they can manage to deal with the outside world easily.

Another use of behaviour shaping was in token economy systems, introduced to help long-stay psychiatric patients to take more responsibility for their own lives. In the 1960s and 1970s, some patients had been in psychiatric hospitals for decades, and they had become thoroughly institutionalized – dependent and unable to look after themselves. Psychologists developed training systems which would allow them gradually to learn how to do basic things, like sweeping a floor or taking care of their own clothes.

Since it is important for operant conditioning that the reward or reinforcement should happen immediately after the person performs the behaviour which is to be rewarded, the patient would be given a token when they did something right. In very severe cases, this might at first be for something as simple as holding a broom and making vague sweeping movements. Once they had learned this, behaviour-shaping techniques would be used, so they would only be rewarded for sweeping a bit more thoroughly. At the end of the day or week, they could exchange their tokens for privileges of one kind or another. In this way, long-stay patients were gradually taught the kinds of behaviour which they would need if they were ever to leave the institution and live in a hostel.

Key idea

There is a constant debate about which types of therapy are 'better' than others. But everyone is different, and as long as a therapy suits both the client and the therapist, then it will probably work. Different methods suit different people's understanding.

Modern clinical psychologists are able to use any or all of these approaches, but whether they choose to use them or not will depend on the type of work they are doing, the needs of the person they are dealing with, and the issues they are faced with at the time. Clinical psychologists are also often involved with psychiatric nurse training, sensitizing them to symptoms or obscure forms of communication, helping them to develop alternative ways of interacting with their patients, and showing how different approaches may produce different outcomes.

Health psychology

Psychologists are also involved in working to enhance physical health. Health psychology is a very broad area because it is concerned with the psychological aspects of our physical health, and there are a great many of these. Maintaining physical health isn't just about avoiding illness: it's also about making sure that we stay well, so lifestyles and beliefs are very important in health psychology.

DOCTOR–PATIENT COMMUNICATION

Some health psychologists are interested in doctor–patient communication. For example, people often don't give their doctors all the information they need to make an accurate diagnosis because they feel intimidated by the doctor's manner, and by the formal setting of the surgery. Health psychologists use their knowledge of non-verbal communication and social appraisal to help doctors to communicate more effectively, so that they can overcome these problems.

Another aspect of doctor–patient communication concerns the issue of following medical instructions. Surveys show that as many as 60 per cent of people don't actually use medical treatments in the ways that they have been told – and this is important, because it can make all the difference to whether or not the treatment is effective. A drug which has to be taken with food will not do its job properly if it is taken on an empty stomach, because it needs to interact with the chemicals involved in digestion to have its effect.

So health psychologists look at the various reasons why people do or don't follow medical instructions. They explore issues such as lifestyle – given the person's everyday life, is it actually difficult for them to do what they have been told to do? They also look at people's beliefs about medicines and how they work, and at how instructions can be misunderstood. And they conduct training sessions with medical personnel to teach them how to explain what they mean in simple language. Their research and professional work has produced a number of recommendations for medical practice which have been shown to improve how accurately people use their treatments.

Key idea

Power and status imbalances mean that patients often feel unable to speak freely to their doctor. So it is important that doctors are aware of this, and can check whether the patient is actually in a position to follow the treatment regime they are prescribing for them.

BEHAVIOURAL TREATMENTS

Another aspect of health psychology is concerned with behaviourally based treatments. In some physical illnesses, such as diabetes, there is no known cure. All that patients who have diabetes can do is to manage their disorder by behavioural control of some kind. Health psychologists help people to do this, by looking at aspects of behaviour such as diet control, lifestyle and how people monitor their own health.

If you have read through this book as far as here, it should come as no surprise to discover that one of the most important factors in managing diabetes, as well as other behaviourally based disorders, is that people should have a sense of control over their own health. People who see their illness as not under their own control are likely to suffer more, and to do things which will make the situation worse, than people who see what happens to them as the outcome of their own actions. A passive approach to an illness such as diabetes has demonstrably worse outcomes than an active management of the problem. So health psychologists are also involved in training people in techniques for managing their own lifestyle, stress levels, and so on.

HEALTH EDUCATION

Health psychologists are also involved in health education programmes: public campaigns which are designed to encourage people to take up healthy behaviours and minimize risks. Anti-smoking campaigns, AIDS avoidance campaigns and, more controversially, advice about what constitutes a healthy diet are the kinds of area in which psychologists have been involved.

Persuading people to take up healthy lifestyles is not as easy as it may sound. Simply giving people information doesn't really work, because there is often quite a difference between what we know and what we do. We may be aware that something is risky, and yet do it anyway. And there are also social factors involved, which can influence what we actually end up doing. For example, there is a big discrepancy between the number of people who are aware that they should use a condom when they are having sex, and the number who actually do. Even though the risk of AIDS is high, and the consequences of contracting HIV can be tragic, many people still engage in extremely risky behaviours.

Psychologists studying this area have identified a number of factors which maintain this risky behaviour, such as the belief that sticking to only one partner will minimize the risk – even though the person may have had earlier relationships – or the idea that it detracts from the spontaneity of the experience, and makes it seem too 'planned'. There are questions of habit: many older people are reluctant to adopt condom use because they have established sexual habits without them. And there is also, of course, the question of a power imbalance between men and women, since some men oppose the use of condoms and many women do not feel confident enough to insist on their use.

It is these kinds of factors that show how complex the problem of risk avoidance really is. It goes much deeper than simply providing people with information, and an awareness of human psychology is necessary to tackle these complex issues. As we have found so often, healthcare and the promotion of healthy behaviour involves understanding the human being on a number of different levels. It is far from being simple and obvious.

Key idea

Psychologists have found that people stay motivated if they have manageable goals. So healthy lifestyle programmes tend to encourage making very small changes at first, so that we can do them successfully. Big changes are harder to keep up with, so we can easily get discouraged and give up.

Counselling psychology

Another form of clinical psychology first emerged in the 1950s, with the work of the psychologist Carl Rogers. As we saw in Chapter 2, Rogers believed that human beings have two basic needs: the need for positive regard from others, and the need for self-actualization. From his experience with his own patients, he came to the conclusion that providing an environment in which people would experience unconditional positive regard would allow them the security to be able to explore their own potential and to make their own choices. Rogers' work became the foundation of what was later to become counselling psychology.

Client-centred therapy

Rogers developed an approach which he called client-centred therapy, to emphasize that it was the client who held the responsibility and made the decisions, rather than the professional who was supposed to be helping them. In client-centred therapy, the therapist provides a supportive, warm environment in which the person explores their own options and makes their own decisions. Following on from this, Rogers concluded that it was equally possible for other people to provide a supportive and warm environment. He developed the idea of encounter groups – groups in which people would share their problems, and encounter one another openly, as individual human beings. It was this which started off the self-help groups which have become such an important part of Western societies.

Rogers' ideas became extremely influential in many areas, and were taken up by many people, both psychologists and otherwise. Counselling as a profession was developed on the basis of Rogerian principles, although it has since developed other approaches as well. Although many counsellors are not psychologists, the area of applied psychology known as counselling psychology has been growing considerably in recent years, and it consists of qualified psychologists who apply their professional skills and training in counselling work.

COGNITIVE THERAPY

In the late 1970s and early 1980s, as psychology changed its emphasis, clinical psychologists began to develop new approaches, which drew on other areas of psychological knowledge. A new form of therapy, known as cognitive therapy, emerged. Psychologists began to work on the self-defeating beliefs of many of their clients, showing them how to recognize negative attributional styles and how to develop realistic and positive self-efficacy beliefs. Research into stress management showed how important it is for people to have a sense of control over their own lives, and many clinical psychologists adopted these principles in their work.

Later on, clinical psychologists integrated the best of the insights and techniques of the behaviourist approach with the cognitive approach, to produce the general approach known as cognitive behaviour therapy, or CBT. Psychologists using this approach work with their clients to develop more positive cognitive styles, but they also show them how to use behavioural techniques to change ingrained self-destructive habits. By combining the two, they can develop interventions which work at more than one level of analysis, and so are more likely to be successful overall.

Cognitive behaviour therapy is concerned with three aspects of the client's experience: their thoughts, their feelings, and their behaviour. A psychologist adopting this approach will build strategies into their therapy which will tackle all three of these. That might involve behavioural desensitization exercises, activities which can help the person to deal with their emotional reactions, and attributional exercises to help their thinking styles. Approaching therapy in this way has been shown to be far more effective than counselling methods which only tackle a single aspect of the problem. There are other approaches adopted by counselling psychologists, but most of them have CBT as a core, and develop it further in one direction or another.

BEREAVEMENT COUNSELLING

Counselling psychologists often find themselves helping people to deal with the kind of stressful life-events which all of us have to face at some point or other in our lives. One of the most common of these is helping people to deal with bereavement. When someone who is close to us dies, the psychological effects are profound. To people who have not encountered this type of experience before, the depth of the emotional reaction can be quite bewildering, and a lot of people benefit from the help that counselling psychologists can provide.

In order to provide the best type of help for their clients, though, counselling psychologists need to have a good understanding of how bereavement usually affects people. Everyone finds their own ways of coming to terms with what has happened – indeed, that is what the whole counselling process is about. But an understanding that, say, anger is often a common part of grieving can help both the psychologist and the client to find constructive ways of coping.

Grief is a complicated emotion. It isn't just a single thing, but a mixture of all sorts of different feelings. Sometimes they happen at the same time, sometimes separately, and it can be very disconcerting for people who consider themselves balanced and rational to find their emotions shifting from minute to minute, and through such a range of different sensations. So a significant part of the job of the counselling psychologist in that situation can be in reassuring people that what is happening to them is (a) understandable, (b) to be expected, and (c) not permanent.

Key idea

Bereavement almost always involves strong feelings of anger, and one of the functions of all societies is to ensure that such feelings don't just lead to savage reprisals or acts of revenge. The purpose of laws and judicial structures is to punish people who have committed crimes in a balanced and considered way. Social policies should not be dictated by strong emotions, even if those emotions are understandable.

There are at least nine different components of grief, and for some people even more. I have listed these briefly in Table 14.1, but it is worth looking at them in more detail here. One of the components is a feeling of shock or numbness – a kind of sense that it can't really be true. Another is that the person often becomes disorganized, both physically and mentally, finding it hard to get even simple tasks done. People who are grieving often have times of simple denial, in which they refuse to acknowledge that the death has really happened. It may seem irrational, but even the most sensible people can slip into it from time to time.

Table 14.1 Components of grief

1 Shock or numbness
2 Disorganization
3 Denial
4 Guilt
5 Anger
6 Depression
7 Despair
8 Anxiety or panic
9 Resolution and reintegration

Almost all grieving includes some sense of guilt. People blame themselves for what has happened, or for failing to do something or other relating to the dead person, even when it is obvious to an outsider that their guilty feelings are completely unreasonable. And that guilt can often be mixed in with periods of intense hostility and anger. Sometimes, that anger is directed inwards, adding to the feelings of guilt and leading the person into self-punishment of one kind or another. Sometimes, though, it is directed outwards, at other people such as medical staff or relatives.

Grieving also includes feelings of depression and despair – periods in which someone simply pines for the person they have lost. These can be acutely painful, or mixed up with apathy to produce periods of mental and physical inactivity. But people also often have periods of anxiety or panic attacks combined with these periods of depression, which may happen because of the fear of being left alone and uncertainty as to how they will cope. The whole complex of feelings is so strong and so unlike how that person is normally, that they may wonder if they are going mad and panic as a result.

As the worst of the grieving dies down – which can take some time – the bereaved person begins to experience episodes of resolution, in which they begin to feel a little more capable and able to deal with things. At first, these periods tend to be short and temporary, as other feelings come up again, but they gradually become stronger and more common. Similarly, as the grieving process proceeds, it includes a sense of reintegration as the person begins to reorganize their new life, and to come to terms with living without the person who has died. Many people find it quite hard to do this straight away, because it seems disloyal or callous, but it is common for the reintegration process to begin after a couple of weeks or so.

We can see, then, that grieving is a complicated process, and one in which it can be very helpful to talk things over with a qualified counselling psychologist who understands this complex of emotions and is able to offer constructive help where that seems appropriate. Grief is one of those intense experiences which often takes people by surprise, and which shows us just how deep our social bonds are.

Some of the most intense grieving often comes from people who had very disturbed relationships with the person who has died. When that happens, it generally surprises everyone, including the person experiencing the grief – but it is partly because the person is grieving for the relationship which might have been, as well as for the relationship which actually was. Again, this is an area where counselling psychologists can help a great deal, and in which they are often involved.

Counselling psychologists don't just help people to come to terms with interrupted relationships. Many counselling psychologists also work to strengthen relationships, dealing with couples or families where the relationships between people have become strained or difficult. Organizations such as Relate employ a great many counsellors and counselling psychologists, and many others are employed in local medical practices, or in family guidance centres.

Stress and coping

There is one aspect of human experience which just about all applied psychologists have to deal with in one way or another, and that is the question of stress. Managing stress has become an important issue in modern life, partly because modern living does involve a great deal of stressful activity, but also because we are increasingly recognizing that managing stress is a vital part of a healthy lifestyle. Ongoing stress is harmful to the body, and can cause long-term physical, as well as psychological problems. To understand that, we need to look at how stress affects us.

In Chapter 4 we saw how emotional reactions affect us physiologically. But if we have a fright, or if we become angry with someone, the emotion often passes. We calm down and get over it and, as we do, the physical symptoms of arousal disappear as well. Sometimes, though, we experience emotional arousal which doesn't go away. Being anxious about whether there will be enough money to pay the bills, for instance, is a continual worry, not a passing thing. This means that it is constantly producing physiological arousal, which stays with us, and doesn't wear off.

Selye (1956) showed that this type of long-term arousal can have many harmful effects, including interfering with our physical health. We call it stress, and it is one of the most studied areas of psychology – mainly because it is such a big problem for modern society. Long-term stress suppresses the action of the body's immune system, making us much more vulnerable to colds, infections and more serious illnesses. In the long term it can make us more liable to contract heart disease. Long-term stress also makes us very jumpy and alert to potential threats – which means that we may see something as a threat when it is really quite harmless. Because we overreact to what people say or do, we become more likely to quarrel with the people around us, and that damages our social and emotional lives which contributes even more to the stress we are feeling. And stress interferes with judgement, so that we are less likely to make sensible decisions or to appraise what is going on realistically.

Obviously, this is not a psychologically healthy condition to be in. However, understanding how stress works has allowed us to find ways of coping with long-term stress so that we do not suffer these effects. Psychologists have identified many ways of minimizing or cancelling out the effects of long-term stress and making sure that we deal with it in a positive way. As we saw in Chapter 4, not all stress is bad, and we need to understand how it can be helpful as well as damaging if we are to use it positively.

COPING STRATEGIES

Athletes, and other people who take part in highly stressful activities, need to make sure that their levels of arousal will be enough to produce the best possible performance. So they often use coping strategies, which allow them to control the amount of arousal that they experience. Some of these strategies are physical ones which involve using the adrenaline constructively, to give additional energy when exercising. People who do a lot of sport often do better in exams than people of the same intellectual level who don't take regular exercise, and one possible reason for this is that they simply don't experience as much physical stress.

Many coping strategies though, are cognitive – they involve the person's thinking in some way. They include mental exercises, deliberate thinking strategies, and ways of using the imagination positively. By doing this, we can make sure that the thoughts we have are useful, and won't simply add to the amount of stress which we feel.

▶ Attributional styles

In everyday life, people often add to the stress they feel by thinking negatively: worrying about how dreadful things are, or might become. Since even a single worrying thought adds to our level of arousal, all thinking of this kind adds to the total arousal and stress which the person experiences. Sometimes, people even develop ways of thinking which are totally self-defeating. Abramson, Seligman and Teasdale (1985) found that chronically depressed people often have what they called a depressive attributional style, which makes their depression much worse. It produces behavioural effects very like the learned helplessness which we looked at in Chapter 6.

Attributions are the reasons that we give for why things happen, and a depressive attributional style means that we habitually give the worst reasons for events or circumstances. Depressive attributional styles are global, stable and uncontrollable. Global means that the reason is taken to apply to almost everything; stable means that it isn't temporary but likely to continue for the foreseeable future; and uncontrollable means that the person can't do anything about it. So when something unpleasant happens to someone with a depressive attributional style, they believe that it is just like everything else and will only turn out for the worse, that it is always going to be that way, and that it can't be changed. These thoughts keep their depression going, partly by increasing the stress that they are under, and partly by making them feel that there isn't any point in trying to do anything anyway. In other words, they feel helpless, and unable to control what happens in their lives.

Key idea

Look out for depressive attributions in everyday conversation. They are usually the ones which say 'there's no point because ...' or 'I tried that and it didn't work ...'.

Cognitive therapists challenge these attributional styles by teaching people to see things more realistically. Life is always a mixture of positive and negative events, and by learning to notice positive things as well, people can see how an unpleasant event is specific rather than global. Therapists also encourage their clients to see how things can change, and become temporary rather than stable, and they teach them how they can influence events and gain control over them. In doing so, the person gains a more optimistic outlook which in itself reduces the amount of stress they experience.

▶ Locus of control

People with positive attributional styles, who see themselves as able to control events by hard work and effort, and who don't give up, tend to experience stress very differently. They are much less likely to become depressed, and much more likely to be able to actually do something about their situation, because they keep looking for ways to change it. These people have what is known as an internal locus of control. They believe that what happens to them is largely controlled by their own efforts. People with a depressive attributional style have an external locus of control, believing that they cannot influence what happens to them.

There is a great deal of psychological research which shows that having an internal locus of control is much healthier for a human being – both physically and mentally. Long-term stress can lower the body's resistance to disease and make us vulnerable to illness. But people with an internal locus of control experience less stress, even though their physical situation may be just as bad. This is because they channel their energies into looking for positive things to do, instead of just worrying. And because they are likely to gain at least a small success through trying so hard, they experience positive emotions such as a sense of achievement, which people who are more passive don't feel.

We acquire an internal locus of control in infancy – indeed, we can see much of infant development as acquiring control over the body and the immediate environment. But we often lose it as a result of bad experiences and traumas that we feel unable to do anything about. Childhood experiences can be an important part of that, but even as adults, experiences can shift our thought habits and behaviour, so that we move from an internal to an external locus of control.

Cognitive therapy helps to show people how to take control of their own lives, and how to avoid the self-defeating beliefs and attributions which have stopped them from doing so in the past. Almost anything which increases someone's self-confidence has the effect of giving them more of an internal locus of control over their own life. Problems may be real, and not likely to go away, but we can make their effects worse or better, depending on how we go about dealing with them.

▶ Awfulization

Challenging 'awfulization' is another problem for cognitive therapists teaching people how to deal with stress. Awfulization is a habit of thinking in which the person refuses to look at unwanted consequences, because they would be just too dreadful to contemplate. So every action or activity related to the thing which is being awfulized becomes doom-laden with a cloud of awful consequences. Exams are a good example: some students, even when they are well prepared for their exams, feel that failing them would be so awful that – well, they don't know what, because it is so terrible they haven't even let themselves think about it. People who are given to awfulizing tend to do it about even quite small, unimportant things, as well as really important ones. It's part of having a negative cognitive style.

But all this does is add to the stress that they experience. It doesn't help them to deal with things in the slightest: it just makes their anxiety even worse. Many therapists find it helpful to get their clients to face up to their fears, and make them real. They look, together, at the worst thing that can happen, and plan how the person might go about dealing with it. This exercise helps people to bring their fears into perspective, and see that there would be ways of coping after all. Just knowing that the world wouldn't come to an end if the worst happened can help a lot.

We can see, then, that psychologists are active in a great many different aspects of mental and physical health. As with all aspects of what human beings do, we can look at it from a number of levels, and each of them contributes to our overall understanding. Psychologists also carry out research as part of their work, and this means that they are often involved in developing new forms of therapy, or new ways of approaching an issue. We saw in Chapter 4, for example, how recent developments have improved our understanding of happiness and mental well-being, and many clinical and counselling psychologists are using these insights too. As our understanding of health and psychological well-being improves, so does our ability to help people to deal with their psychological or behavioural problems.

Focus points

A significant area of modern psychology is concerned with mental and physical health. This involves the work of clinical, health and counselling psychologists.

Clinical psychologists may develop treatments for psychological problems or or be involved in diagnosis, such as identifying specific cognitive disorders like those brought about by head injury.

Health psychologists apply psychological knowledge to health matters such as doctor–patient communication or the behavioural management of illness.

Cognitive behaviour therapy looks at thoughts, feelings and behaviour, and has influenced most modern approaches to counselling.

Counselling psychologists may also do bereavement therapy, helping people to come to terms with grief and personal loss.

One way of coping with stress is to change the type of attributions people make about what is happening to them. An internal locus of control can minimize stress, while 'awfulization' can increase it.

15

Decisions, disasters and forensics

In this chapter you will learn:

▶ *about some common errors in decision-making*

▶ *how psychology can help people to recover from disasters*

▶ *to identify four psychological aspects of environmental stress.*

In this chapter we will look at some of the ways that we make decisions in everyday living. That investigation will then lead us into looking at how we can sometimes make errors which can, at times, have disastrous consequences. From there, we will look at other ways in which our interactions with our environment can affect us, including how environmental stressors can increase crime, and this leads us on to explore the work of forensic psychologists. We will begin by looking at some of the pitfalls and challenges of making good decisions.

Decision-making

We make decisions all the time. Sometimes, they are major decisions such as what career to choose, or whether or not to have a family; sometimes, they are less important. In the modern world there is a large industry devoted to trying to influence the decisions that we make as consumers. So psychologists have also devoted considerable attention to looking at how we go about it.

When we make a decision, we don't always do it in the most logical way. Human beings aren't computers, and we use shortcuts in our thinking which a computer wouldn't use. For example, if I were to tell a computer 'If it is raining on Sunday I shall go to the cinema', then the computer would take that as a logical statement. However, if I said that to a human being, they would listen to the meaning of what I had said, which wouldn't necessarily be the same thing. The computer and the human being would draw different conclusions if they found me at the cinema on Sunday. The human being would conclude that I was there because it was raining outside. But the computer wouldn't. As far as the computer was concerned, it could just as well be sunshine outside because all I actually said was that I would go if it was raining. I didn't actually say anything at all about what I would do if it wasn't raining.

Key idea

Studies of human thinking often imply that humans are illogical. And we are, as far as computer logic is concerned. But when we look more closely, we find that human reasoning is almost always rational, in terms of social awareness and probabilities – even if the consumer decisions which we make are less so.

HEURISTICS

The computer works from strict logic, and what I said, logically, meant that it was possible to draw that conclusion. But a human being uses human logic, and they would know what I really meant – that I would go to the cinema only if it was raining. We apply a lot of this type of social knowledge in understanding each other, and it is why human thinking doesn't fit very easily into computer models. But sometimes, the cognitive shortcuts or heuristics that we use can actually distort our decisions, so that we don't make the most sensible ones.

Kahnemann (2011) identified a number of heuristics which have been identified by psychologists as strategies that influence our decision-making. There are many of them, but six significant ones are availability, entrapment, framing, anchoring, representativeness and confirmation bias.

Availability is the way that we are most likely to choose from options which come immediately to mind, or which we have recently been exposed to, rather than actually thinking through the full range of options that we have. We have seen how strongly we are influenced by expectations, and our most recent experiences go a long way to shaping what those expectations actually are. Vivid examples come readily to mind, as advertisers know very well, and so do the social scripts that we have recently encountered. As a result, we can often end up ignoring important information, and only bringing it to mind too late, once the decision has already been made.

Remember this

We are more influenced by availability than we realize. One of the reasons why advertisers repeat their adverts so often is because they want to keep their particular product at the forefront of our minds, so it is the first thing we think of when we are trying to choose one of them.

Entrapment is another heuristic which can influence our decision-making. This happens when we have already invested quite a lot in one course of action, so that we find it difficult to change direction because it will mean that what we have already done is worthless. One common example of this is when you have an old car which keeps developing different problems. The more money you put in, the more difficult it is to decide to scrap it, because it means all that money has been wasted. As a result, some people put off making the decision and end up spending far more than they would have done if they'd made the decision earlier.

A third factor that we are influenced by is how decisions have been framed. For example, in one study research participants were asked to choose between two options for tackling a serious disease. The participants made different decisions depending on whether one of the options was presented as meaning almost a third of the sufferers would probably be saved, or whether it was presented as meaning that two-thirds of the sufferers would probably die. Although the information was the same in both cases, 72 per cent of the participants chose that option in the 'save' condition, but only 22 per cent chose that one in the 'die' condition. That's quite a big difference, and it shows us just how much the way that a problem has been framed can influence the choices that we make.

Our decisions are often affected by a quantity or value which has just been mentioned. This is known as anchoring. For example: if you wanted to buy a particular scarf which cost £20, and you were told that it was available in another shop at £35, you would regard the £20 figure as reasonably cheap. But if you had previously been looking at scarves which cost around £10, you would see it as expensive. The figure you already know serves as an anchor point for making decisions about a new one – something which estate agents know very well when they are describing the value of their properties!

Representativeness is our tendency to judge things, or people, in terms of the stereotypes that we hold. In one study, Kahnemann described a study in which people were given a description of a man as being shy, retiring and helpful, but not particularly interested in people. Then they were asked to judge whether he was more likely to be a librarian or a farmer. In fact, since he was male he would be more likely to be a farmer, because most librarians are female and most farmers are male. But people tended to ignore this, and said that he was more likely to be a librarian, because the description was representative of their stereotypes of librarians.

Confirmation bias is all about the way that we tend to make quick judgements, and then look for evidence which will confirm them, rather than looking for information which will challenge them. It's a powerful tendency, and one which can mean that we easily overlook information that we should have taken seriously. For example, if you were buying a new shirt for a special occasion, and found one which you really liked, you might focus on the fact that it would look good and suit you, but overlook the fact that actually, it didn't go with anything else you had to wear.

Errors and accidents

Most of the time, the decisions that we make don't affect anyone but ourselves. We might make a stupid purchasing decision, for example, or find that we have made a career decision which we regret. But, sometimes, the decisions which people make, and the errors which they fall into, are much more significant.

From time to time, events happen which have massive implications, both for the people who are involved in them but also for the smooth and safe running of society as a whole. Sometimes, they are unavoidable, like large-scale earthquakes. But other disasters may arise from human factors of one kind or another. The nuclear explosion at Chernobyl, the Hillsborough football stadium disaster, the Zeebrugge ferry disaster, the Kings Cross fire, the Hatfield train crash and many others were traumatic events of such magnitude that they affected the lives of thousands of people: not only those who were directly involved, but many others as well.

SYSTEMS AND ERRORS

Psychologists studying how these disasters have happened find, repeatedly, that they show a similar pattern. In each case, a large number of minor problems have occurred fairly regularly, but these are overlooked or tolerated because they are part of a much more complex system, because they would be awkward or expensive to correct, and because the chances of them escalating into a serious problem are considered to be low. However, eventually, these ignored minor problems combined to produce tragic and disastrous consequences.

These problems are often a direct result of ignoring psychological factors in the situation. As we've seen in this book, psychological factors are many and varied, and so are the ways in which they manifest themselves in complex systems. The *Herald of Free Enterprise* was a case where a front-loading car ferry set off from its dock at Zeebrugge with the bow doors still wide open. As a result, the car deck flooded and the ferry overturned, causing huge loss of life.

There were a number of factors which contributed to this disaster. The shift work practices in the ferry company, for example, meant that the staff who were operating the *Herald of Free Enterprise* were unlikely to be functioning at their most alert, which became a major factor in causing the error. As we saw in Chapter 4, people work better with some shift systems than with others, and this needs to be taken into account in any complex system.

Key idea

Errors and mistakes are bound to happen sometimes. No system can be designed to be completely foolproof, but if we recognize that people are human, we can design our systems so that small slips don't turn into major disasters.

Similarly, there are some designs which are likely to reduce errors, and some which make errors more likely to happen. Ergonomic psychologists investigate the best possible locations for warning and alert signals, and also which types of signals are most needed. The lack of alert signals on the bridge to indicate that the bow doors were still open was another factor which contributed to the *Herald of Free Enterprise* disaster. It might seem trivial in itself, but combined with the other factors involved, it made all the difference.

The important thing about these kinds of factors is that they make the whole system more vulnerable. People don't act like robots: sometimes they make mistakes. So any type of complex system has to be capable of allowing for the occasional mistake on the part of its human operator, and it has to be designed in such a way as to ensure that these mistakes are less likely to happen. Having a shift work system where people on duty are overtired and less alert makes mistakes more likely; having a ship control system which doesn't flag up vital information such as whether the bow doors are closed or not also makes mistakes more likely.

The kinds of mistakes which people make aren't random: they are ones which can be taken into account when complex systems are being put together. The psychologist James Reason performed a number of studies of everyday errors and mistakes and found that they tend to fall into three categories: those to do with skills, those to do with knowledge, and those to do with the rules that people are working by.

▶ Skill-based errors

Skill-based errors are concerned with the way that highly practised actions can become so automatic that we don't need to pay conscious attention to them (see Chapter 9). This means that sometimes we fall back on habitual routines when really we intended to be doing something else. Unless we keep our minds firmly on what we are doing, and the choices that we are making, it is easy to slip into a familiar routine without really thinking about it. But if we are managing complex systems, the result of that can be disastrous.

Key idea

You've probably committed skill-based errors yourself, such as turning down your usual route to work or school when you were meant to be going somewhere else, because you weren't thinking about it.

Since this is quite a common type of human error, Reason (1990) argued that it needs to be taken into account when a complex system is being designed. If a mistake of this sort would be serious, then it is important to avoid it by ensuring that the kinds of routines that people are asked to follow in different circumstances are sufficiently different from one another, so that they don't just slip into automatic routines and habits. If two systems involve similar patterns of activity, then this sort of mistake is much more likely to happen.

▶ Knowledge-based errors

Most kinds of knowledge-based mistakes come from the fact that people simply don't have the knowledge that they need in order to take effective action. An operator who has been trained only in one particular job, and who hasn't had special training for what to do in an emergency, can easily make a mistake simply because they don't know what the best thing to do is. So if the failure of effective action could result in a disaster – no matter how unlikely – it is important that people should be aware of how to deal with it.

The way that this is overcome in ordinary working life is through training. It is training, whether through explicit courses or through simulations, which gives people the knowledge that they need to deal with problems so that they don't develop into disasters. Any organization which is involved in potentially risky processes needs to ensure that all of their staff – not just those who are nominally responsible – receive appropriate training, because it can happen that the 'responsible' person may not actually be present at the time. They might, for example, have gone to the toilet when an emergency happened. Even though they were only away for a couple of minutes, if their junior or assistant didn't know what to do, a slight problem could have escalated into an emergency by the time

336

they came back. So industrial psychologists emphasize the importance of all staff being informed and trained about appropriate actions in the event of unusual situations.

▶ Rule-based errors

Rule-based mistakes are often associated with tackling problems that haven't arisen before. Usually, people will try to deal with these by applying rules or principles which they have used in other contexts. As we saw in Chapter 7, we use our existing mental schemas to direct what we should do in new situations. Sometimes, though, the rule the person tries to use is inappropriate, and this can have serious consequences.

One kind of rule-based mistake happens when we are simply applying an inappropriate rule. To return to the Zeebrugge ferry disaster, Reason showed how the way in which the directors of the company saw their job was an example of people working within an inappropriate rule. They defined their primary task as being to keep their shareholders happy, rather than to ensure that the ferries ran safely on a day-to-day basis. This led to the adoption of practices which were cheap, but not safe.

This point may need a little explanation, because it is not saying that the company's finances don't matter. Ultimately, of course, a company which doesn't make a profit won't be able to run. But most similar companies would regard running the ferries safely as their primary objective, on the grounds that it will ensure confident passengers and more profitability in the long run. The directors of the ferry company, though, aimed for profitability at the expense of safety and efficiency. As the outcome of the disaster showed, it was an ineffective policy in the end. But it is a clear example of applying inappropriate rules for the situation.

POST-TRAUMATIC STRESS DISORDER

Whenever we are involved in any kind of sudden loss or bereavement, we experience grief. As we saw in the last chapter, grief is an extremely disabling emotion, which can last for a very long time and has a number of complex elements. As anyone who has experienced the loss of someone they love knows, the complexity and intensity of the experience can be overwhelming at times.

For people who are involved in major disasters, the experience is even more severe. In addition to the grief which they experience as a result of the death and loss involved in the event, there is also the shock of the experience itself. This is often deeply traumatic and can have lasting effects. Clinical psychologists working in this area have identified a syndrome known as post-traumatic stress disorder, or PTSD for short. Although it has been known about for some considerable time, it is only recently that PTSD has become acknowledged as a clinical problem in its own right.

Post-traumatic stress disorder happens in people who have experienced severe emotional traumas. It occurs in people who are engaged in prolonged and dangerous fighting, in people who have experienced torture, and in those who are involved in major disasters. Some people are more resilient to it than others, but if the stress is serious and continuous enough, it seems that most people will be affected in the end. Swank (1949) in a study of 4,000 survivors of the Normandy campaign, found that soldiers always experienced what was then known as shell shock (now recognized as PTSD) if three-quarters of their companions had been killed, no matter how resilient they seemed to be.

Emergency workers who have to deal with major disasters can also experience PTSD. Taylor and Frazer (1982) studied the people who helped out in 1979, when a DC10 on a tourist flight crashed into a mountain in Antarctica. All 257 passengers and crew were killed, and it took ten weeks to recover and identify the bodies. Several of the workers who helped to recover the bodies experienced persistent images of the disfigured corpses or suffered nightmares of air crashes. Those involved in recovering bodies from the World Trade Center in New York in 2001 were provided with special counselling, to help to minimize the effects of the trauma – an example of how widely recognized this syndrome has become.

▶ Symptoms of PTSD

There are three main groups of symptoms in post-traumatic stress disorder. The first involves re-experiencing what happened. People suffering from PTSD often have recurrent nightmares of the event, and may also experience vivid memories of it during the waking day, which are extremely distracting as well as distressing. The second group of symptoms occur as the mind attempts to cope with the trauma. These are known as avoidance or numbing reactions: people often feel detached or estranged from others, and distant from everyday life. The third group are to do with the increased arousal level of the body, so they include the inability to sleep or to stay asleep for very long, irritability, and a tendency to outbursts of anger.

These symptoms are similar to those which people would be likely to experience after any disturbing event, but what makes them distinctive in PTSD is how strong they are, and how long they last. Although in some cases the symptoms don't appear until some time after the event, they can go on for several months, or even years. They can also disappear for a while, and then reappear again. Archibald (1963) found that 15 years after a traumatic event had taken place, two-thirds of survivors still showed symptoms of PTSD.

People often don't recognize that what they are experiencing is actually post-traumatic stress disorder. Mitchell (1992) described how doctors were trying to treat the residents of the Scottish village of Lockerbie for some time after an American airliner exploded above the village, causing deep trauma and shock among the residents. But the doctors were not aware of PTSD, and so were at a loss as to how to proceed. When residents received insurance leaflets describing the symptoms, the local doctors realized that what they were treating was actually a specific and recognizable syndrome, rather than just a collection of individual reactions.

It matters whether the disorder is recognized, because then it is possible to organize therapy which helps people to get over it – but only if people know what is happening. Some clinical psychologists specialize in this type of therapy, working with the victims of disasters to help them to overcome the problem and return to normal living. Although the symptoms may not disappear altogether, having therapy does help people to get over the most severe problems more quickly, and to cope with them better.

Key idea

The most important thing to know about PTSD is that it is possible to recover from it, but this does require professional help: traumatic experiences have to be brought to the surface, talked out, and the person shown how to deal with them. Bottling them up inside means that the mind can't learn how to deal with them properly.

▶ Post-traumatic growth

The experience of surviving traumatic events is not always negative in the long term. Sometimes, these experiences help people to re-evaluate their lives and to live in a different, and more positive way. Having their worlds turned upside down can make people more aware of what really matters to them and, as they recover, they find that they are able to develop a much more positive outlook on life.

Linley and Joseph (2003) reported four aspects of the psychological growth which can occur as a result of traumatic events. People may change their philosophy of life, learning to appreciate every day as it comes and value what really matters. They may develop a greater sense of personal resilience and strength, with more of an acceptance of their own limitations. Such people may also change their activities, working for positive social change, whether that be through political activities or social ones. And many report changes for the better in their relationships with friends and family.

Linley and Joseph also found that people who experience such psychological growth after trauma tend to show better long-term adjustment, and fewer symptoms of post-traumatic disorder. Because of this, they argued that the therapy provided for post-traumatic clients should include a focus on positive psychological growth, so that people can be helped to gain from the experience rather than remain as victims. Some 43 per cent of the victims from one disaster reported positive life outcomes of this type, and the researchers believe that with therapeutic help, this figure could be higher.

We can see, then, that psychology can be usefully applied, not only in understanding how disasters and accidents take place, but also in helping people to recover from the worst of their effects. The most important message, though, is the one which becomes apparent when we look at how these disasters happen in the first place: that if we take full account of psychological factors in the design and management of complex systems in the first place, they are much less likely to happen. This doesn't mean that they absolutely wouldn't happen, of course – nobody could guarantee that – but it would minimize the risks. And when the consequences of failure are so very extreme, anything which minimizes the risk of a disaster is worthwhile.

Environmental stress

Another thing that makes us more likely to commit errors is when we are under prolonged stress. Our surroundings can exert a strong influence on us psychologically. Most of us, for example, have had the experience of being in an environment which calms or soothes us. For many people, being out in the country is a particularly restful and relaxing experience. For others, being in a bustling, busy market can be an experience which lifts their spirits and makes them feel happy. But environments can have the opposite effect too. Our surroundings can make us feel tense, or anxious, or can simply represent an increased strain as we go about our day-to-day lives. In 1982, Herzog and others surveyed a large number of people about which features of cities they found most pleasant. Trees, grass and water were popular, as was distinctive architecture which was in harmony with its surroundings. Old, untidy settings such as factories and alleyways were considered to be the least pleasant of all.

Noise

Noise can be a significant source of stress, even though we may not notice it. Whether we are aware of it or not, we are taking in information from the world around us all the time. If a stimulus is continuous, we become habituated to it, so that we are no longer aware it is happening. You will probably have noticed this if you have a fridge that hums.

You don't consciously hear the humming, but when it stops you become aware that it was there in the background before. This realization tells you that, even though you weren't hearing it, the noise was still being registered by your nervous system.

Background stimulation of this kind can be much more intense than we realize. People who live in small towns or in the country often find it difficult to sleep when they visit a large city for the first time, because they find the continual traffic activity too noisy. People who live in the city don't notice it as much, but their senses are still registering it. The continual background noise of traffic, machinery and household equipment is a source of minor, but continual, stress.

Sudden loud noises are even more stressful. People who live close to airports often have to have special sound insulation installed to protect them from the noise of the aircraft taking off and landing, and those who live close to motorways often need a sound screen, such as a dense row of trees, to baffle the noise. Loud and prolonged noise at work can cause deafness, which is why the operators of noisy machinery are expected to wear ear defenders, and this sort of noise is a source of stress as well as a physical health hazard.

A high level of noise at work also affects our level of arousal (see Chapter 4) so that we feel 'keyed up', and often irritable. It also makes it difficult for us to communicate with other people, which is stressful too. This affects some kinds of work more than others: in an investigation of the effects of work noise, Poulton (1976) found that it was skilled jobs, which require concentration or rapid action which are most affected by work noise.

Not all noise is stressful, though. The noise level at a music concert can be extremely loud, but doesn't produce serious effects – although it might, if we were trying to carry out a skilled task which required concentration. For the most part, though, the fact that we have chosen to listen to it, and also the fact that it is musical rather than simply noise, makes a lot of difference to our reactions. And the fact that it is temporary, lasting only for a few hours, rather than being part of our daily experience, makes a difference too.

Key idea

Some people are so accustomed to the background noise of the city that if they holiday in the countryside, they find it hard to sleep at first because of the silence. But that doesn't last long: the relief from the unconscious stress of noise and pollution soon relaxes them.

▶ Locus of control

As we have seen earlier in this book, when we feel we have some control over the stimuli around us we don't find them nearly as stressful. This can apply to loud, unpleasant noises too. Glass and Singer (1972) asked people to solve a set of problems while a loud, harsh noise occurred from time to time. Half of the people in the study were able to press a button which would stop the noise, at least temporarily, but they were asked not to use it unless they really had to. The others didn't have any way of stopping the noise. The group who could have stopped the noise if they wanted to, actually didn't stop it at all, but they performed much better on the problem-solving task than the others. It seemed that just knowing that they could control it if they wanted to was enough to remove the stressful influence.

There are other studies which show how important a sense of control can be in reducing stress. Lundberg (1976) investigated the levels of stress experienced by male passengers on a commuter train. The more people there were on the train, the more stress the passengers experienced, even though there were always enough seats for everyone. Lundberg also found that people who were first on the train, or who joined it at an early stage in its journey didn't experience as much stress as those who joined the train later, even though they had a much longer journey.

What seemed to be important in the passengers' experience of stress was whether they could choose their own seats or not. People who joined the train early had more choice in where they sat, and were more likely to be able to choose a favourite seat. It seems that feeling that they had some kind of control over their commuting experience made a considerable difference to the amount of stress people felt.

Key idea

Studies show that commuters feel less stress if they are on a delayed train which keeps moving slowly than on a train which stands still, even if the total journey takes longer. The perception that some progress is being made seems to reduce the stress by a significant amount.

▶ Temperature and pollution

Temperature can be a source of environmental stress, too. People working in an atmosphere which is too cold or too hot find it difficult to concentrate on their work, which can be a source of frustration. However, we have to be a bit careful when we are looking at temperature as a source of stress, because there is quite a big difference between external high temperatures – warm weather – and an indoor hot stuffy environment.

Baron and Ransberger (1978) looked at weather reports and civil disturbances in the USA, and found that riots were most likely to happen when the temperature was hot – although not when it was unusually or extremely so. This doesn't mean, though, that rioting is caused by hot weather. Many other researchers have shown that riots are sparked off by perceived social injustice, not simply because people feel like rioting. But in hot weather, more people are out on the streets, and so unfair or unjust events are more easily noticed and more easily communicated to others.

We also respond more strongly than we realize to levels of pollution in the environment. Pollution represents a source of physical stress for our bodies, because they have to cope with semi-toxic substances, such as lead or nitrous oxides, as well as trace amounts of real toxins, such as those in commercially grown vegetables. It can also produce mental effects as well. Rotton and others, in 1978, showed that when people were experiencing high levels of air pollution they felt less happy, were more likely to dislike other people, and to see the negative side of things that happened to them. On a more specific level, too, Bleda and Sandman (1977) showed that cigarette smoke could produce depression and anxiety in non-smokers.

▶ Meeting strangers

A different facet of stress is concerned with how we respond to the people around us. In modern industrial society, crowds are an ordinary part of everyday living. Yet this is a relatively recent development. For most of our history, human beings have tended to live in small village or nomadic communities, consisting of 100 to 200 people, so everyone would be known individually. In a situation such as this, encountering a stranger is a rarity, so anyone new would automatically be an object of interest.

The problem is that we still have many of our biological adaptations to meeting strangers, which evolved during the millions of years when meeting strangers was rare. We respond differently to strangers than we do to people who are familiar, and our response is more aroused and tense. Yet in city or town life in modern societies, we meet strangers all the time – in fact, we are more likely to encounter strangers than friends. So the mechanisms which evolved to adapt us for a life in which most people are known and familiar become overloaded, because they are continually being activated.

This is one of several reasons why many people find crowds stressful. In a crowd, we are unable to maintain our usual personal space, which is a source of tension. People sometimes even bump into us, which we find even more stressful, and we often perform quite complicated dodging manoeuvres when walking down a crowded pavement, in order to avoid bodily contact with strangers. We can also make accidental eye-contact with strangers, and eye-contact is one of the most powerful signals of all.

Key idea

Being surrounded by strangers is one of the unavoidable aspects of city living, and an unconscious source of environmental stress. As a result, it makes defensible space at home even more important, and adds to the already high pressures which homeless people experience.

Eye-contact – looking directly into someone's eyes while they are also looking at you – isn't a signal that we take lightly.

Prolonged eye-contact is a sign of intense interest in the other person. At its extremes, it can signal love – or its opposite, hostility and threat (there is no chance of confusing the two, because the muscles around the eyes are arranged quite differently). We look at someone who is speaking to us, which is a signal that they have all of our attention. We look away from someone if we don't want to disturb them, or make them feel self-conscious.

So even fleeting eye-contact, of the sort we have with strangers, is stressful when it happens often enough. In situations where prolonged eye-contact might happen because the same strangers have to remain close by, such as in a lift or a tube train, we tend to look upward or out of the window in order to avoid it, which is why advertisements tend to be placed high up. City-dwellers learn to cope with this type of stress, of course, but it is present in the background nonetheless.

Forensic psychology

Crowding can produce aggression as well as stress, and is also strongly linked with crime. In a well-known study back in the 1960s, Calhoun showed that laboratory rats which were allowed to breed freely and become overcrowded became much more aggressive, even killing one another as part of the competition for living space and food. Since this behaviour would normally be totally alien to these animals, it showed how much stress the crowding had created.

There are indications that human beings, too, become much more aggressive if they are crowded. Loo (1979) studied young children in a day nursery, and found a strong link between bad temper and crowding. The more children there were, the more quarrelsome the youngsters became. Similarly, McCain *et al.* (1980) showed that prison riots and also suicides were much more common when prisons were overcrowded than when they held their intended number of prisoners.

In another study, Kelley (1982) showed that there was a strong link between the density of the population in 175 American cities and the amount of crime. Even the types of area which were relatively low in crime showed more crimes as the population increased – and that included all sorts of crimes, ranging from car theft to murders. Kelley drew the implication that population density, in and of itself, is one source of environmental stress which shows itself in increased crime rates – although there are, of course, other factors which influence crime as well.

Crime, and its various psychological connections, is one of the major concerns of forensic psychology. There has been a growing interest in this aspect of psychology in recent years, partly because of the influence of TV shows which highlight their work, but also because of the many ways in which psychological research is able to enhance our understanding of legal and criminological issues.

Forensic psychology is all about putting psychological insights to work in issues of justice. So forensic psychologists might be involved with the psychological aspects of legal processes in courts; applying psychological insights to criminal investigation; understanding psychological problems associated with criminal behaviour; and ensuring appropriate treatment for people who have committed offences. Table 15.1 shows the types of work that forensic psychologists do.

Table 15.1 The work of forensic psychologists

1. **In the legal system**	e.g. contributing psychological understanding to the training and selection of police and magistrates, to interviewing processes, and to jury selection.
2. **In criminal detection**	e.g. helping police officers to identify offending patterns and to develop possible offender profiles.
3. **In the prison system**	e.g. developing treatment programmes for offenders and contributing to staff training and offender assessments.
4. **In the political system**	e.g. giving advice on the treatment of criminals, and also of their victims.

INTERVIEWING

Forensic psychologists draw on many areas of psychology in their work, and one of the most important of these is applying psychological insights to the question of interviewing. In many court cases, eyewitness testimony is the main source of evidence, and it is mainly obtained by interviewing people. But interviewing is not a simple process. As we saw in Chapter 7, just asking people questions can affect, and even change, what they remember. We saw how much a simple change in wording influenced people's memories of a car crash, and we also saw how people can believe they are remembering accurately, but still be wrong in a number of details.

Not only that, but people being interviewed pick up all sorts of non-verbal signals without really realizing what they are doing. We all check, unconsciously, to see whether the person we are talking to seems to agree with us, and we use information such as their body language, or the tone of voice that they use, to give us the cues we need. Put that together with our human tendency to agree with other people (Chapter 3) and we can see how easy it is for witnesses to be influenced by the opinions of the person who is interviewing them.

So some of the work of forensic psychologists involves training police interviewers, alerting them to the need for very careful phrasing of questions, and teaching them ways of avoiding giving away their opinions or their knowledge while at the same time being friendly and helpful so that interviewees will feel free to talk to them openly. It's a challenging balance, and one where psychological training is very important.

Key idea

An important part of police interview training is in not taking signs of anxiety too seriously. Most people, even if they haven't done anything wrong, are nervous when they are being interviewed officially. This can often look as though they are covering something up, when they are not. Trained police officers recognize this, and don't jump to conclusions.

Some interviews, too, deal with very sensitive topics. Interviewing victims of rape can be is a particularly difficult business, partly because people who have been through this type of trauma tend to rehearse it mentally over and over again, and this means that details can become distorted. In one case, for example, a woman was raped in her living room and later identified the face of her attacker as that of a famous interviewer who had been on her TV at the time. Her personal distress had caused the two memories to become fused together. Fortunately, the broadcast had been live, so the interviewer had a good alibi and the real perpetrator was eventually caught and identified. But this was an unusual case: psychological evidence shows us that, for the most part, the memories of victims of rape are clear and accurate.

The problem with individual cases of this kind is that it can sometimes mean that other people are disbelieved when their accounts are correct. This is particularly a problem in cases of historic child sexual abuse, where the victims, particularly if they are teenage and believed to be delinquent, are often disbelieved at the time the offence happened. Younger children, too, often do not reveal what has happened to them at the time, sometimes even repressing the memories and only recalling them when they are adult. In some prosecutions for this type of abuse in the USA, the lawyers argued that these memories were not true, but had been constructed through suggestions from the therapists concerned.

However, a professional investigation into the area conducted by the British Psychological Society in 1995 looked at the evidence, and concluded that while this was obviously possible, most recovered memories of this kind are likely to be genuine. There are clinical signals which accompany abuse which would be difficult to fake, and a professionally trained clinical psychologist or therapist is able to put these together with the recovered memory evidence in evaluating the evidence, in much the same way as a forensic psychologist combines the interview information with other evidence.

INTERVIEWING CHILDREN
Some child abuse cases are identified earlier, but often the child concerned is the only witness for the crime. This raises specific challenges because of the way that children who do 'tell' are often intimidated by the adults around them – their perpetrator, but also other adults who refuse to believe that the person concerned (often another family member) would have done such a thing. It is not uncommon for children who have made such an allegation to feel so intimidated by the reaction that

they retract their accusation (even though it is true), and deny that anything ever happened. Which means, of course, that the courts become powerless to act.

Key idea

One of the biggest fears that stops children from telling others about abuse is that it will cause such huge problems that their whole world will be torn apart. The problem is, of course, that in the case of family abuse this is true. Whether the child is believed or not, their world does change, and nothing is quite the same again. Convincing the child that the change will be for the better is a real challenge.

Interviewing child witnesses is a difficult challenge and requires some very special skills. The normal 'rules' of interviewing don't work in the same way when it comes to children, either. For example, psychologists have shown that when a child is asked the same question twice, it often changes its answer the second time because it assumes that the first answer must have been wrong, or not what the interviewer wanted to hear. In adult interviewing, changing the answer is seen as evidence that the first response was a lie. But in child interviewing, it is much more likely that the first answer was true, and that later changes come from the child looking for something to say which will satisfy the interviewer, since (they think) the first answer wasn't good enough. Psychological research, though, shows that children's testimony for events is just as reliable and accurate as that of adults, even though some adults believe it is not (Leippe *et al*. 1992).

In recent years, there have been a number of attempts to improve legal procedures when it comes to child witnesses. One of the most important of these allows children to record their evidence before the court case, on videotape. When it was first proposed, it was hoped that this would mean that the child would not need to attend court, but unfortunately the way it has been implemented means that this is still required, because the child must undergo cross-examination. It is possible, though, for that cross-examination to take place via a live video link if the court considers that it would be too traumatic for the child to face the person they are accusing in court.

Forensic and developmental psychologists have been involved in drawing up codes of good practice to ensure that child witnesses are able to give their evidence as freely and as fully as possible. This includes establishing a good rapport between the child and the interviewer, so that the child feels safe to talk openly; allowing a period of free recall in the same way as is done in interviews with adults; making sure that the questions that are asked are open-ended and not suggestive; and making sure that the interview ends in a way which is reassuring for the child. Similar guidelines are in place with regard to the obtaining of video evidence, where this is considered to be appropriate.

There is, of course, much more than this to the work of forensic psychologists. They administer psychometric tests, develop training procedures, identify and analyse problems, and help to develop good policy and treatments. Psychological knowledge has relevance in just about all aspects of their work, as it has in so many other areas of everyday life.

Focus points

Human decision-making involves a number of shortcuts called heuristics, which mean that we don't always make logical or sensible decisions.

Errors may be skill-based, knowledge-based or role-based. Many disasters originate with small errors which result in major systems failures.

Survivors of major disasters often experience post-traumatic stress disorder (PTSD) which can continue for life if they are not treated. PTSD can be reduced with therapy, and may sometimes even lead to psychological growth.

Environmental stress can result from factors like noise, temperature and pollution. Contact with strangers is stressful, and crowding may increase aggression and crime.

Forensic psychologists are concerned with how psychology can contribute to our understanding of legal and criminological matters.

Witness interviewing is an area of forensic psychology which covers a wide range of different areas in various contexts.

16

Teaching, learning and assessment

In this chapter you will learn:

- ▶ *what is involved in skilled teaching*
- ▶ *about two controversial aspects of dyslexia*
- ▶ *five principles for effective revision.*

Psychologists have been involved with education ever since psychology began. But over time, psychological ideas have changed considerably, as our understanding of the human being has developed. As psychological ideas have developed, so too have many of the social practices which emerged from them.

For example, in the middle of the twentieth century, a number of politically influential psychologists, particularly Sir Cyril Burt, believed that intelligence was a fixed, inherited quality. Since Burt was directly involved in giving advice to the Ministry of Education, this ultimately led to the introduction of a school system in which children were sent to different schools, offering different types of education, depending on their performance in an examination and intelligence test which they took at the age of 11 years old.

Nowadays, we don't see intelligence in quite the same way. We see it as being much more of an interaction between someone's own personal temperament and their experiences and environment. The experiences of mature students who are unsuccessful at school but who take exams, degrees and even higher degrees later in their adult lives, show that intelligence can change dramatically with experience. And as we saw in Chapter 11, as long as we use it, our intelligence can increase as we get older, not decrease. So the old idea that a person has a fixed intelligence, which doesn't change through their lifespan, is pretty well discredited.

In this chapter we will look at three different aspects of psychology as it relates to education. We will begin by looking at the psychology of teaching and learning, before looking at some aspects of educational disadvantage, and then going on to explore some of the psychological dimensions to assessment.

Psychology of teaching and learning

All of us have experienced teaching and learning in some way, and almost all of us have done some of it through formal education – classrooms, teachers, and assessments of one form or another. Some people continue engaging in formal education all their lives, through evening classes or online courses; some return to education as adults having had unsuccessful experiences at school; and some leave school and don't have anything more to do with formal education. In the modern world, though, we often find ourselves attending courses of one sort or another: workplace courses such as first aid or sales awareness training, CPD courses to ensure that professional skills are kept up to date, or training sessions associated with our hobbies or interests. It's rare to find anyone who hasn't done any kind of training at all since leaving school. For most of us, though, our main experiences of learning are of being taught in formal educational settings.

MOTIVATION AND MINDSET

As we've already seen, being interested in something can make all the difference to whether we remember it or not. And, as we've also seen, becoming skilled at anything, whether it is an intellectual skill like reading or a physical skill like ice skating, takes practice. So a vital part of the psychology of teaching and learning consists of understanding how students come to be interested in what they are learning, so that they have the motivation to keep working.

Key idea

Motivating people to learn is at the heart of good teaching. Some teachers use very strict and structured approaches, while others use flexible, consultative methods equally successfully. But all good teachers give their pupils a sense of self-efficacy and progress, which is why the pupils enjoy learning and achieve success.

In Chapter 6, we looked at the importance of self-efficacy and social expectations in human motivation. These are fundamental to the educational process, because unless children are motivated to learn, then simply exposing them to information will have very little effect. The act of teaching isn't just about presenting information – it's about presenting it in such a way that children (or adults) are engaged and can find interest in what they are doing.

If we believe we are capable of learning – that is, if we have positive self-efficacy beliefs – then we will make the effort to do it. Learning can sometimes be difficult, if we are trying to come to grips with new ideas or with new ways of presenting ideas, so believing that we can do it if we try is the way that we stay motivated to keep working and overcome difficulties. If we have negative self-efficacy beliefs, on the other hand, it is easy to become demoralized and think it is too hard for us.

Key idea

The idea of a rigidly fixed intelligence has been discredited, but everybody is different. We each have our own aptitudes, our own interests and our own talents. But even if we have an aptitude for something, if we don't see it as worthwhile we are unlikely to put any effort into mastering it.

▶ Mindsets

Dweck (2006) used research into self-efficacy as the basis of 'mindset' theory. Dweck argued that we all have our own, implicit ideas about what makes people capable or competent. At the heart of these ideas is whether we believe that intelligence or capability is a fixed thing, which we inherit or which can't be changed for other reasons, or whether we believe that intelligence or ability is something that we can work on and improve through training, learning, and persistence. Most people, Dweck argued, hold beliefs which are somewhere in between, but some people have a 'fixed' mindset, while others are closer to the other end of the continuum, which she called a 'growth' mindset.

People with a fixed mindset often have a difficult time with learning, for a number of reasons. One of them is that they are more likely to give up when they encounter difficulties, because they don't really think they will be able to get over them. There are lots of people, for instance, who believe that they are 'no good at maths', and no matter what they do they will always be bad at it. This is an example of a fixed mindset – and it isn't particularly realistic, because those same people have no problem dealing with money, and quite often they can do other complicated types of maths too, like understanding betting odds or comparing interest rates on savings or loans. So they clearly can do maths really, but their fixed mindset tells them they can't, and means that if they are faced with a maths problem, they don't even try to solve it.

Another reason people with a fixed mindset have a hard time with learning is because they react very badly to failure. When they fail at something, they think it is because of some kind of inadequacy in themselves, personally, so they worry about failing and think it is much more significant than it is. People with a growth mindset, on the other hand, don't mind failure nearly as much, because they don't attribute it to a personal failure. Instead, they see it as indicating that they have to put a bit more work into the question, or try to tackle it in a different way in order to be successful.

We saw in Chapter 6 how stressful it is for people to feel out of control. People with fixed mindsets tend to feel that their learning is not something they can control: either they can do it or they can't. So learning is stressful for them for that reason too, and failures hurt much more. People with a growth mindset, though, see things as very much more under their control, so they are usually happier about learning in general, and ready to take on challenges. Dweck argued that a growth mindset is something everyone could benefit from achieving, because it leads to a much less stressful life.

It would be a very gloomy picture if a fixed mindset was really fixed. But that is far from being the case. Dweck and many other psychologists have shown that a fixed mindset can be changed. It isn't a fixed personality trait – it is a set, or state of cognitive preparedness, and people can learn to adopt a different mindset, and to realize that their learning is much more under their control than they thought it was.

▶ Manageable goals

This is again where good teaching can make a lot of difference. Teaching is all about enabling students to learn, and guiding their learning so that they can demonstrate it effectively in assessments. One of the things which good teachers do is to ensure that their students have manageable goals – that is, goals which they can readily achieve, and which will help them to develop their skills and competences. They do this by working through the learning process that the students have to go through, breaking it down into smaller units which they can learn to deal with effectively, and giving their students the guidance that they need to make sure they go about their learning appropriately.

All this helps their students to build up growth mindsets – to feel that they are capable of the learning they are faced with, and that their success is merely a matter of putting the right sort of work into tackling it. Sometimes, this might involve a lot of time and effort learning large chunks of information, as it might for people taking a medical degree, for example. At other times, the emphasis might be more on understanding procedures and techniques and when to apply them, as in a physics or maths degree. The teacher, knowing the subject, knows what needs to be achieved, so the way that they construct their course, and the learning tasks within it, can make a considerable difference to the ways in which the students go about following it – and the self-efficacy beliefs they acquire along the way.

Manageable goals are not simply restricted to the classroom. In many walks of life, people are faced with large problems which seem to be too big to tackle. But breaking them down into manageable goals, and dealing with things one step at a time, can make all the difference. The important thing is that the goals really are ones we can manage, rather than being unrealistic or overly ambitious. The superstar Madonna, for example, had a personal ambition to be famous from an early age, but she tackled it not by dreaming, but by concentrating on acquiring the skills she knew she would need. She put in years of work learning and perfecting her dancing, singing and performance skills, all of which paid off when she became successful. Her use of manageable goals and hard work meant that in the end, she achieved a level of stardom which went far beyond just having a few successful hit records.

▶ **Positive emotions**

Another aspect of psychological knowledge which is important in understanding teaching and learning is how emotional states affect learning. In Chapter 2, we saw how people need a warm interpersonal climate if they are to be open to learning new things and developing their ideas. Nobody learns well in a climate of hostility or sarcasm, but if they feel approved of and safe, people often surprise us with what they can achieve.

Key idea

Some teachers are able to be successful even in the most difficult schools. They use supportive non-verbal cues and manage their learning environments so that even difficult pupils don't feel threatened or defensive, and can relax and enjoy learning during their time in the classroom.

So, one of the things which a skilled teacher learns is how to create an atmosphere of interpersonal warmth in the classroom, which will encourage their students to become confident and to learn positively. Although many non-psychologists, including, unfortunately, a few teachers, believe that we can learn when we are tense or anxious, all the psychological evidence points the other way. We are far less open to new ideas when we are tense and anxious. Just about all we learn in those situations is how to avoid pain, which is a very basic and primitive form of learning. But there is plenty of psychological evidence for the opposite: in education as well as in everyday hobbies and interests, people learn best when they feel safe, confident and approved of. And they can often surprise themselves, and others around them, with unexpectedly high achievement in such circumstances.

▶ The learning environment

Our behaviour is sometimes energized and directed by how we think about things, sometimes by the situation itself, and sometimes by social and cultural factors. All of these are relevant to education too. For example, if we look at learning using one of the more basic levels of explanation in psychology, we are all influenced by the environment around us. A formal classroom layout produces different behaviour from the people in it than an informal setting does.

Partly, this stems from our social understanding of what a formal layout is intended to convey: it is a kind of non-verbal communication. But partly, also, it is a learned association between stimulus and response. Our past experiences have formed that link, and so we act in the same way when we find ourselves in the same situation. If we look at the way that a 'classic' classroom is laid out, the teacher has about one-quarter of the space at the front of the room, and the teacher's desk is much larger than the students' desks. The students sit facing the teacher, which means that the teacher can see and communicate with them easily, but it is less easy for them to see each other. In other words, the room is arranged to give the teacher maximum control over the interaction.

When teachers undertake group work with their students, it is usual for them to rearrange the seating, so that students are sitting in small groups facing one another, and the teacher moves between the groups. This arrangement facilitates the students talking to one another, and reduces the emphasis on information coming from the teacher's desk. In a co-operative educational task, this type of arrangement is much more efficient, and it also conveys a different type of message to the students.

This might seem trivial, but it is one of the things that we need to take into account when we are considering the psychology of teaching and learning. For instance, many people who take qualifications in further education colleges are returning to study as mature students. Although they do want to study, often their first experience of being in a classroom again brings back unpleasant associations of school and feelings of inadequacy and failure. A teacher who is aware of this process is able to make sure that these feelings can be replaced quickly by ones which will help the student to learn, by providing more positive learning experiences in that setting. But someone who is unaware of what is going on might easily dismiss these people as not having the necessary motivation or ability to learn.

PROCESSING INFORMATION

Sometimes, effective teaching is all about finding ways of getting students to process the information they are exploring. In Chapter 7, we saw how we remember things far better if we have processed the information deeply. Being interested in something means that we do process the information because we think about what it means, and what effects it might have. So we don't usually have any trouble remembering things that we are interested in.

Knowing about levels of processing in memory can also help us with other aspects of educational experiences too. For example, taking examinations generally means learning a great deal of information, not all of which is scintillatingly interesting. But it is possible to use the idea of levels of processing to remember the information, even though we may not be totally thrilled by it. By changing the form of the information – drawing up charts, or diagrams, or making summaries – we force our minds to process the information and think about what it actually means. And once we are aware of what it means, it is much harder to forget it. We will look at the psychology of exams later in this chapter.

SOCIAL ASPECTS OF LEARNING

There are many social dimensions to the psychology of teaching and learning. We can't really separate personal and social aspects of learning, because we are all personally influenced by social factors. In psychology's earlier years, the human and social aspect of teaching was often unrecognized. Stimulus-response psychologists focused almost entirely on the information that was being conveyed, and developed systems which were intended to maximize the learning through conditioning processes. The behaviourist, B. F. Skinner, developed a system known as programmed learning, which used the principle of learning through positive reinforcement. Skinner, as we saw in Chapter 9, believed that it is better to reward appropriate behaviour than to punish inappropriate acts. So the learning system which he developed was based on the idea that the more people could get right, the more they would learn.

In a programmed learning system, information which needs to be learned is divided into very small chunks, each of which leads on to the next. By dividing it up like this, it is relatively easy for a student to get each answer right. If they don't, they go back and relearn the section until they do. Skinner believed that maximizing the chances of getting the answer right would provide the motivation for learning – unlike the conventional educational programmes of his time, which tended to emphasize failure and wrong answers rather than rewarding right ones.

A number of programmed learning systems were developed following Skinner's ideas, and many of the self-tests in modern textbooks use much the same principles. But Skinner envisaged a system in which the teacher was largely replaced by a computer, presenting the information in bite-sized chunks, and this has never really materialized. The social contact between teacher and student is much more important than those early psychologists recognized – a good relationship with a teacher can make all the difference in a child's learning, and a negative relationship can often mean that the child (or adult) feels they are completely incapable of learning that subject.

▶ Social identification

A knowledge of social identification is also useful for a teacher because it shows how inter-group conflicts can develop. If students feel that their group identity is being disparaged or threatened, they may respond by reacting against classwork, or even against being in school at all. But people can have many different social identifications, which don't have to be in conflict. A student may be a member of a teenage group, yet still work hard when he/she is in the classroom – as long as that working hard isn't seen as a threat to his/her group identity. Many extremely effective teachers have worked successfully with students who, on the surface, appear to be directly opposed to what they are trying to do. They have been able to do this because they have made it clear that there is no conflict between their out-of-school identity and their in-school work.

A vital part of managing social identification involves knowing how important social identity is to our self-esteem. This helps a teacher to see why the student's social group is so important, and why it matters that the student should see that working for the future – which is what school or college work really is – is not a threat to their social identity in the present. Without such an understanding, teachers can be dismissive of their students' social groups, or see them as inevitably in conflict with educational values. And the result is that these students, on their part, often feel misjudged and unfairly stereotyped.

Key idea

Psychology shows how important social identification is to all of us. It can be a powerful tool for knitting together a good learning group in the classroom. But dismissing or belittling a pupil's most important identifications can make them resistant and hostile to the education process.

We can see, then, that the psychology of teaching and learning spans a number of different levels of explanation. It ranges from the personal and emotional aspects of human psychology, to the cognitive, social, and even cultural levels of explanation. As with so many other aspects of human behaviour, we can gain insights from each of these levels of explanation; but if we are to get a fully rounded picture of how human beings are, we need to take them all into account.

Educational disadvantage

Some professional psychologists are also involved in helping children and adults who are experiencing some kind of educational disadvantage. They are known as educational psychologists in Britain, although they are called school psychologists in the United States, where educational psychologists are more concerned with the applied psychology of teaching and learning. In Britain, educational psychologists are responsible for assessing children who are thought to need a special type of education, and recommending what sort of education that should be.

SPECIFIC LEARNING DIFFICULTIES

There are several different kinds of educational disadvantage. Sometimes children have specific learning difficulties, which means that they find certain kinds of information very hard to learn. If they experience a special school environment, in which the teacher pays particular attention to training them to handle the things which they find difficult, they can often learn a great deal more than they would do in an ordinary school. Other children who also have specific learning difficulties, though, might benefit more from being in an ordinary school and mixing with the children there. The educational psychologist's judgement as to which type of schooling will be best for that particular child will take into account as many different facets of the child's experience as possible.

For example, we have already seen how strongly social expectations can influence us. They can affect our self-image, our interactions with other people, and how well we learn. If a child attends a special school, it is possible that people won't expect as much from them as they would do if they went to an ordinary school. So in some cases, if a child's problem isn't very extreme, then it may be better for them to go to an ordinary school and perhaps have some additional tuition which will help to overcome their difficulties, rather than to go to a special school. The decision about whether to send a child to a special school depends very much on the child itself, and on how severe their problems are.

Key idea

There is a danger that social disadvantage can become such a label that teachers don't even try very hard to teach pupils from disadvantaged backgrounds. But a positive school experience can actually help pupils to overcome their disadvantages, by providing an alternative experience where they feel competent and valued.

Educational psychologists undergo rigorous training in diagnosing learning difficulties. Some problems have a physical source: certain kinds of brain damage, for example, can produce very specific effects on how a child learns. Sometimes, it is possible to overcome these effects with the right kind of training. Most children recover very well from accidental brain injury, for instance, and often if they have the right kind of therapy, the effects disappear completely.

Sometimes, though, the problem isn't the kind you can get over. In such a case, the psychologist might decide that amelioration is the best approach, so the child will be taught how to cope with, and get around, the problem. By developing training which is relevant to the kinds of situations that the child is likely to meet, the child can learn how to live a relatively normal life, even though they may have some difficulties.

▷ Dyslexia

One of the specific learning difficulties which educational psychologists often need to diagnose is the problem known as dyslexia. Dyslexia used to be known as 'word-blindness', and people who experience dyslexia often have difficulty in identifying letters, or recognizing how they should be written. For example, a dyslexic person might write a letter like 'y' or 'r' back to front, but not realize that they had done it. They seem to be 'blind' to the image of the letter. Other dyslexics have difficulties recognizing words.

Sometimes dyslexia comes about as a result of some kind of accident which causes an injury to the person's brain. This is known as acquired dyslexia. Shallice and Warrington (1980) described two kinds of acquired dyslexia. One of them, which is known as surface dyslexia, is when someone has problems with the forms of words, such as difficulty recognizing letters, as above, or problems with spelling – like writing 'lurn' instead of 'learn'.

The second kind of dyslexia isn't about the forms of words, but about understanding them. People with this type of dyslexia have difficulty with words that are hard to visualize: they can understand words like 'tree' easily enough, but have problems with words like 'and'. Shallice and Warrington called this deep dyslexia, because it relates to a deeper understanding of words.

Acquired dyslexia isn't particularly controversial in psychology. It is a recognized outcome of some forms of brain damage, and there is a great deal of evidence which shows how people who previously had these abilities intact experience problems after their accident. But there is a second type of dyslexia – the kind that an educational psychologist would encounter – which is more controversial. This is known as developmental dyslexia.

Developmental dyslexia is a problem which becomes apparent as a child develops and goes through school. A few children seem to be virtually unable to identify words and letters properly, and so have problems with spelling. Some psychologists believe that this problem occurs because of an inherent deficit in the brain, and some have even gone as far as to suggest that it is a genetic disorder, although as yet the evidence for this is a little sketchy.

Key idea

Some experts believe that dyslexia is accepted too passively in schools, resulting in pupils under-achieving because they feel that making an effort to overcome the problem is pointless. Diagnosis should be a signal for special training and programmes to deal with the problem, rather than just used as a label.

▶ Problems with dyslexia

So far, so good. There are certainly cases in which children have difficulties of this kind, which really do result from some kind of inherent problem. The controversy comes, though, with the question of whether all children who are considered dyslexic really have these problems. Many psychologists (for example, Whittaker, 1982) have argued that the word 'dyslexic' became a convenient label which was used in many entirely inappropriate cases. Whittaker and others believe that children are often labelled dyslexic when all they really have are problems with spelling.

The problem is compounded by the fact that the concept of dyslexia became popular in Britain soon after a nationwide experiment on reading, which tried to teach reading using a special phonetic alphabet, known as i.t.a., or initial teaching alphabet. This was based on the principle that children learned to read by 'hearing' the words – a principle which we now know to be not quite right. But as a result of the use of i.t.a., a great many children became confused about the need to spell accurately, and many schools almost gave up on teaching spelling formally.

In view of this social context, and the fact that spelling is something that doesn't come naturally to anyone – it always has to be learned by heart, and that takes effort – there is anxiety that some children (and adults) may have been labelled as dyslexic when really they could have overcome their problem with a different kind of teaching at school. This problem is exaggerated by a tendency to see a diagnosis of 'dyslexic' as a message that there is no point trying to teach this child words or spelling. As with many other educational disorders, special training programmes which recognize the difficulty, and address it directly, can often overcome the problem, at least if it is in a mild form.

So there are two aspects to the controversy about dyslexia. It isn't really about whether dyslexia exists: it's clear that it does. The first aspect is about whether all the children who have been labelled dyslexic really are, or whether the label has been given to them simply because they are finding words or spelling hard. The second part is about whether an accurate diagnosis of dyslexia means that the problem is permanent or fixed. Special training programmes suggest that it isn't, and that it can be overcome, but many people seem to see such a diagnosis as if it were a life sentence.

CHILDHOOD AUTISM

Sometimes, the problems that educational psychologists encounter are broader than straightforward learning disorders. For example, the problem known as childhood autism seems to be a broadly-based emotional and personal disorder, which results in such children being unable to relate effectively to the people in their lives.

Autism was first identified as a general syndrome by Kanner (1943), who pinpointed four characteristics which autistic children possess. The first, and probably the most important, is that they have difficulty in forming relationships with other people. Although they may interact, they seem to be aware only of the way that another body impinges on them, not of the person as a human being.

The second characteristic is that autistic children rarely play spontaneously and, in particular, they don't engage in play which involves pretending. Ordinary children, though, begin pretend play from quite an early age, and don't need to be taught it at all.

Autistic children also show differences in how they learn to speak. Some of them never actually learn to talk at all. Others will talk quite a lot, but when they do, they don't speak in the same way as ordinary children. For instance, they may not quite get the hang of reversing the pronouns which we do automatically in conversation. Although ordinary children learn this quite easily, autistic children say what they have heard other people saying, so they tend to refer to themselves as 'you', and to the other person as 'I'.

The fourth distinctive characteristic of childhood autism is that these children often have an almost obsessive insistence on certain routines or repeated activities. They seem to enjoy repetition and routine, and can become very upset if their routines are interrupted for some reason.

Harris (1988) discussed how a range of psychological evidence all points to the idea that autistic children don't have a theory of mind (see Chapter 3). In other words, they are not aware that other people have a mind of their own, and may see things differently. Baron-Cohen (1992) described an autistic girl, Jane, who had no problem remembering people or information, but who had absolutely no awareness of the fact that other people were independent, thinking and feeling human beings. Her inability to empathize, or to understand someone else's point of view, resulted in a great many of her autistic symptoms.

Key idea

Most children are self-centred to some degree, and it can sometimes be difficult to distinguish between ordinary development, in which the child gradually learns to be less self-centred, and autistic disorders. That's why psychological assessment is so important.

BULLYING

Bullying is another major source of educational disadvantage. Children who are being bullied generally find it difficult to work in school, and may even become so frightened of the bullies that they find ways of avoiding school altogether. School bullying is a social (or rather, anti-social) activity, in that the bullies aim to attract attention and respect from other children by their behaviour. Educational psychologists often work with schools to find ways of changing the school's culture, so that the bullies are not admired but seen as pathetic or infantile, while at the same time providing the bullied child with the counselling and support they need to cope with the experience.

In the modern world, bullying has moved into another area. Some children experience school bullying through the internet, which is more difficult for other people to recognize because it happens privately. For many, the bullying is from people they know, through social media. But there is also a wider form of bullying, known as 'trolling', which happens to adults as well and comes from strangers who take advantage of the way that social media like Twitter allows them to remain anonymous. The TV programme *Catfish* is about tracking down people who are abusing others through the internet in this way, and making them fully aware of how they are harming other people. For some bullies this comes as a revelation, because they hadn't really seen their victims as real people. Others, though, are less concerned.

School counsellors, parents and other people can help with the personal kind of internet bullying that children experience. School awareness programmes help to educate children in how to recognize it, and many parents keep an eye on their children's social media accounts so that they can see if things are getting unpleasant. Dealing with trolls, though, is more difficult. The best way to cope with bullies, it seems, is to find ways of building up people's self-esteem so that they can ignore or disregard what the bully is doing or saying. But the first step is to identify what is going on, and to show the victim that what they are experience really is bullying, not just personal comments.

There are many types of learning difficulties, and part of the work of educational psychologists involves assessing children who are believed to be suffering from them. They use their specialized knowledge and special diagnostic tests to identify the problem, and then develop strategies which will help to give the child the right kind of educational intervention. That might include working with the school in general, with a special educational department within the school, or directly with the child's teacher or the child themselves. Educational psychologists (who are qualified teachers as well as qualified psychologists) help a great many children in this way every year.

Exams, assessment and testing

Learning is one thing, but at some time or another most of us have to face an assessment of that learning. It might take the form of a presentation or a project, or of a series of assignments, but for most people, learning is assessed by some kind of exam. Exams are important, because they are often the gateway to important aspects of our future. So we need to make sure that we can do them as well as possible.

Perhaps the first thing to realize about exams is that they have nothing to do with luck! Exams are about assessing what you know: if you know the stuff, and can show the examiner that you know it, you will pass. There are lots of urban myths about exams – for example, that they will be full of trick questions, or that your result will depend on whether the examiner has had a good dinner– but they are, really, myths. They are just not true. Modern exams are designed to ensure that you get credit for what you know. It's as simple as that.

EFFECTIVE REVISION

So how can psychology help people to deal with exams? One way is to use the insights offered from the psychology of memory, which has been studied by psychologists for nearly 150 years. Applying those insights can help your revision a lot. Table 16.1 lists five principles of revision which I have developed from well-established research into the psychology of memory. It's worth exploring each of these a little more.

Table 16.1 Principles of revision

1. The strongest memories are those which link up with other ones.
2. Things that make sense are easier to remember than things that don't.
3. Pictures and diagrams are easier to remember than text, as long as you understand them.
4. Processing information means you remember it better.
5. The more often you remember something, the easier remembering it becomes.

Principle 1 states that our strongest memories are the ones which link up with other memories. This means that one thing leads to another, so one piece of information can act as a 'cue', or hint for another one. There are two implications for this: one is that you should try to use revision methods which will give you as many links as possible. Using key words and developing mnemonic reminders are a good way of doing this. The other is: if you're in the exam and you can't remember something, don't give up. Instead, think around the topic – think of anything you can which connects with it, or that you learned around the same time. Often, you will think of something which leads on to something else which cues you into the information you need to remember.

Principle 2 is something which we have all experienced. Things that make sense are always much easier to remember than things that don't. So using revision techniques which force you to understand the material you are trying to learn is much more useful than just trying to learn it by heart. Summarizing is a good one: it means that you have to get to the heart of what you are learning, working out what is important and what can be left out. So it helps you to make sure that you understand.

The third principle is that pictures and diagrams are easier to remember than text. That's because they use visual memory as well as our memory for meaning, and you get the benefit of both. But that only works as long as you understand the information. Drawing up tree diagrams is a good way of applying this principle: remembering what the tree diagram looks like gives you a way to start, and each branch gives you a cue which will lead on to the next bit.

The fourth principle is that processing information means that you will remember it better. By processing, I mean changing its form: converting it to a picture, or summarizing it. But the best way of all is teaching someone else about it. If you can, work with a friend or family member and explain the bit you are learning to them. We remember conversations better than reading anyway, so you get a double benefit. If there are two or more of you doing the same exam, use this as a way of revising together. Each of you take turns at explaining a bit, while the other listens to see whether you are making sense, or if you have missed something important out.

And the final principle, of course, is all about practice. Things that you have learned and remembered often come to mind very easily. You don't have a problem remembering the days of the week, do you? (I don't mean remembering what day it is today. That's quite a different thing!) But listing the days of the week is a piece of information which is well-learned because you have remembered it so often in the past. So practising remembering is really helpful when you are preparing for exams, and the best way of all to do this is by answering exam-type questions. Get hold of some past papers or some sample questions, and test yourself to see how much you can remember about each of the topics. The more often you can remember things, the stronger your memories will become.

These five principles distil many of the insights into effective learning that psychologists studying memory have developed over the years. But the other aspect of effective exam performance is being able to manage our own personal anxiety about them.

▶ Exam stress

In Chapter 14 we looked at stress and coping, and what we saw there applies just as much to exam stress as to any other form of stress. Most people worry about their exams, which is not surprising given how important they can be. A bit of anxiety, as we have seen, isn't necessarily a bad thing: it can help us to do better. But some people worry too much – and it's the wrong kind of worry. What they do is to fill their minds with negative thoughts, so they have a constant 'I'm going to fail, I'm going to fail' running through their minds. That doesn't help anybody.

Key idea

Taking care of the little details before an exam can help to reduce your general stress level. Get everything you will need ready the night before – including what you will wear – and plan to arrive early, so that you won't be stressed by traffic delays.

We need to manage our exam stress in the same way that we manage our revision. But, in general, there are two ways to go about managing exam stress: mentally and physically. Managing stress mentally, as we have seen, involves making positive attributions and focusing on manageable goals. Don't aim to do more than you can really manage: that will only give you a constant sense of failure. Make a realistic revision timetable which you can achieve easily, with active revision tasks and practice questions, and remember to give yourself time off. Your brain needs to be able to relax sometimes too. Use movies, games or sports to distract yourself at least once a day.

On the physical side, we saw in Chapter 14 how demanding stress is for the body. All that extra adrenaline, and nothing to do with it! So managing your stress also involves giving your body ways to use that adrenaline through physical activity. Going to the gym, swimming, going for a jog round the park, taking the dog for a walk or going for a walk with friends: all of these activities will allow your body to use the extra energy generated by exam anxiety, so they will help you to calm down, and keep your stress to manageable levels. You want it to work for you, not against you! I have given more advice about this, and about preparing for exams in general, in my two ebooks: *How to Do Exams* (iBooks) and *How to Pass Exams* (Kindle), so if you need more detail about it, look at one of those.

PSYCHOMETRICS

Quite often in working life, we come across forms of assessment which are entirely different from educational ones. For one thing, there are no right or wrong answers: these forms of assessment are aiming to find out what you are like, not what you know. These forms of assessment are known as psychometrics. There are a number of different kinds of psychometric assessment, and some of the main ones are listed in Table 16.2. But proper assessments of this kind have one thing in common: they have all been carefully constructed and checked to make sure they conform fully to accepted psychometric principles.

Table 16.2 Types of psychometric assessment

Vocational assessment	Tests which are designed to find out what jobs someone is most suited to do.
Educational assessment	Tests which aim to identify problems which might be interfering with someone's education, such as dyslexia.
Clinical assessment	Tests which are checking for subtle forms of brain damage or other types of problem.
Personality tests	Tests which identify characteristic personality traits.
Intelligence tests	Tests which aim to assess the nature and level of someone's intellectual abilities.
Aptitude tests	Tests which are designed to see whether someone would be suitable for, and able to learn, a particular kind of work or skill.

Key idea

The Psychological Testing Centre of the British Psychological Society commissioned an investigation into the validity of graphology – handwriting analysis – as a personality test. The report, available on their website (www.ptc.bps.org.uk), concludes that there is no evidence at all for handwriting as a sign of personality. In fact, all that the research evidence shows is that people often have their own handwriting style!

The word 'psychometrics' means the measurement of psychological characteristics, and this is what this type of assessment is all about. Psychometric tests might be exploring aspects of personality or character; they might be investigating psychological problems or disorders; or they might be assessing aspects of development or ordinary day-to-day functioning. Sometimes, the test will be comparing your own scores with those of other people, to identify particularly strong characteristics or areas where you have particular difficulty. Those tests are known as nomothetic tests. But sometimes, a tester isn't interested in making comparisons: they want to know about you, personally, and at those times, the person administering the test will choose an idiographic test, which simply helps them to understand your own characteristics, ideas or problems.

While we're on the subject, it's worth pointing out that proper psychometric tests can't be administered by just anyone. In the UK and many other countries, there are special qualifications for people who use psychometric tests, and a professional register, which helps the public to know who is qualified and helps its members to keep up to date. The register and qualifications are administered by the British Psychological Society, but they are open to people who aren't psychologists and still need to use psychometric tests, like human resource managers or recruitment officers.

Some tests, particularly the idiographic ones, are administered verbally – for example, the tester might show an image or object to the person taking the test, ask them questions about it, and record their answers. Other tests don't need the individual presentation, and could even be administered to a group of people at a time. The traditional versions of these tests were paper and pencil – that is, the person taking the test would sit at a desk and fill in a specialized questionnaire. But most modern tests have converted to computer-administered ones. More recently, too, test developers have been producing gamified tests: tests which have been converted into games which people can do on a stand-alone computer or online. This can take a lot of the anxiety out of the test-taking procedure – people often have unpleasant memories of school exams – so it can give a more realistic result.

Key idea

Psychometric tests which are produced as games have to go through the same rigorous validation procedures as paper and pencil tests. But they are more enjoyable to take, and may help to give a more realistic picture of the person than formal tests, which can be quite demanding.

▶ Test validation

Whatever its form, though, a real psychometric test will have gone through a rigorous process to make sure that it has been properly developed, and that it is truly fit for its purpose. These validation procedures assess a number of different aspects of the test, including the scientific evidence it is based on, how it has been developed, a rigorous evaluation of the results it produces, and who it should be used for. There are three major criteria for a psychometric test: reliability, validity and population norms.

Reliability refers to how consistent the test is. Will it give similar results if it is applied to the same individual on more than one occasion, for example? Or will its results be similar if it is testing similar people? There are various strategies that test developers use for testing reliability. One of them, for example, is known as the alternate-forms method, where the test developer produces two precisely equivalent versions of the same test. The versions are then administered to a group of people, so that everyone does both tests, but at different times. Then the test developer compares the outcomes. If the test is really reliable, it should give comparable results when it is given to the same person on two occasions. There are other ways of testing reliability too, and test publishers must be able to provide reliability coefficients for their tests.

Validity is possibly the most essential criterion of all. Effectively, the validity of a test is whether it really measures what it is supposed to measure. But that isn't a simple thing: it's not enough just to believe that it looks about right. Test developers use many forms of validity, and four of the main ones are construct validity, criterion validity, predictive validity and ecological validity. Construct validity is all about how closely the test assesses the psychological theory, or construct, which it has been designed to measure. Criterion validity, on the other hand, is how far it measures up to some other standard – for example, how well a measure of creativity correlates with creative activities in the person's everyday life. Predictive validity is all about whether the results show a reasonable correlation with some future measurement of the same thing – for example, how well a job aptitude test predicts how easily the person really learns to do that job. And ecological validity is all about whether the measure being assessed really relates to its real-world equivalent.

A third important characteristic for psychometric tests is their ability to compare results with what would normally be expected from other people of, say, that age group and educational background. Test publishers produce population norms, which provide the standards, or expected scores, for their test in particular sectors of their population. For example, if we were administering a test of reading skill in school-age children, we would need to make different comparisons for a thirteen-year-old than for a nine-year-old. The test would reasonably be expected to give different results for those two age groups. So the test publisher needs to provide norms for each age group, allowing the test administrator to see whether one particular person's scores are in the normal range, or whether they indicate that the person might need some special help. Population norms change over time, so test publishers also need to make sure they keep their population norms up to date.

We can see, then, that a real psychometric test is very different from the questionnaires or internet games which pretend to be able to identify your personality from your choice of pet, or to tell you what kind of home you should live in. Anybody can produce those, and while they may be good for a bit of fun, they shouldn't be confused with the real thing. And they definitely shouldn't be used for anything serious, like selecting someone for a job!

Focus points

Effective learning is strongly influenced by self-efficacy beliefs and mindset. Growth mindsets can be encouraged by manageable goals.

Student motivation is affected by the learning environment, opportunities for success and the relationship with the teacher. Skilled teachers foster emotional warmth in the classroom while still maintaining high expectations.

Educational psychologists help people with specific learning difficulties or poor self-images.

Bullying can produce educational disadvantage. Strategies to deal with school bullying include changing how bullies are perceived by their peers.

Learning for exams is easier if revision follows basic psychological principles. Levels of exam stress can be managed to ensure optimal performance.

Psychometric tests are validated using the criteria of reliability, validity and representativeness.

17

Developing psychological understanding

In this chapter you will learn:

▶ *how to describe the different activities psychologists engage in*

▶ *why it is necessary to study human beings from several different angles*

▶ *about the main methods of collecting psychological evidence.*

If you've read this far, you'll have gathered that psychology is a pretty wide-ranging subject, covering a great many different aspects of human functioning. But psychology is also a profession, and professional psychologists put psychological knowledge to work in all sorts of ways. This mixture of academic and professional psychology means that psychology itself is very wide ranging. It is also changing all the time, as psychologists learn new things and develop new methods of working, so there's always something new to discover.

Key idea

Whether you study psychology formally or just have a casual interest, it's always helpful to know a bit more about people. But it won't ever give you all the answers about a single person, because psychology is about processes and how things happen, rather than about the end result.

What do psychologists do?

That doesn't mean, though, that every psychologist has to know everything there is about psychology – that would be pretty impossible. Speaking personally, I've been studying it for over 40 years now, and I'm always conscious of how much I don't know! But psychologists always specialize in one way or another. Academic psychologists, for example, generally work within a very small area of psychology. Their task is to conduct research into that area, identifying the fundamental mechanisms and processes which are taking place, and exploring how they can contribute to our understanding of people.

Professional psychologists also tend to specialize, but in a different way. They draw insights from across psychology, but apply them to just one area of life or work. They also conduct research of their own, and put that knowledge to use in helping people in one way or another. Research from applied psychology also feeds back into academic psychology – in fact, most areas of academic psychology have been influenced at one time or another by theories and evidence obtained from professional psychologists.

THE PSYCHOLOGICAL PROFESSION

Professional psychologists can be found at work in almost any area which involves dealing with people. Forensic psychologists, for example, work with police and prison staff in tackling many different aspects of crime. Sport psychologists work with coaches and competitors, developing ways of maximizing competitive performance. Consumer psychologists are at work in advertising and market research, working out how to reach new markets. Table 17.1 lists 18 different areas of applied psychology.

Table 17.1 Areas of applied psychology

Applied Cognitive Psychology	Applied Psychology of Teaching
Applied Social Psychology	Occupational Psychology
Applied Bio-psychology	Organizational Psychology
Applied Developmental Psychology	Engineering and Design Psychology
Clinical Psychology	Space Psychology
Counselling Psychology	Sport Psychology
Health Psychology	Consumer Psychology
Forensic Psychology	Environmental Psychology
Educational Psychology	Political Psychology

Key idea

Professional psychologists, like other professionals, are obliged to keep their knowledge current by continuous professional development (CPD). So being a professional means that you keep learning for all of your working life – you can't just sit back and think your initial training will give you everything you'll ever need.

Training for professional psychologists takes many years. It begins with a three-year first degree in psychology, which is then often followed by a year or more working in a related area – for example, someone who wants to become a clinical psychologist might work first as a psychological assistant for one or two years, which would help them get on to the advanced course. That would take them another three years, learning the specialist work knowledge and skills for their area, and then it would be followed by a couple more years in supervised practice. It's a lot of work, but worth it in the end.

There are other types of work that psychologists do too, and the 18 areas in Table 17.1 are only a sample. As a rule, though, people who begin to study psychology don't usually know what area of work they want to go into when they have finished. What they do know is that they are interested in people and want to learn more about them.

Key idea

Professional psychologists, like clinical or educational psychologists, spend as long in training as doctors or lawyers – sometimes even longer. They need that time to develop enough knowledge and expertise to be able to take responsibility for tackling psychological problems without making serious mistakes.

Some people just study psychology for interest and no other reason. Others become interested in a particular topic and aim for an academic career which will allow them to do research. Some people decide that they want to go on to further training so that they can become a professional psychologist. And sometimes people feel that having a first degree or an A Level in psychology is enough, and they go into careers as policemen, social workers, doctors, nurses, personnel officers or one of any number of occupations which involve dealing with people.

Whatever decision they make, most people find that having a good knowledge of psychology is helpful to them. Knowing about psychology may not give you all the answers, but it does help you to ask the right questions and to go about seeking solutions in an intelligent way. In an article I published in 1996, I listed a number of different skills which psychology graduates have, and which are useful in all sorts of working contexts. Those skills are listed in Table 17.2. As you can see, there are a lot of them; and they come about because psychology is such a complex subject to study and has so many different areas.

Table 17.2 The skills acquired in psychology degrees

Literacy	Writing research reports, discussion papers and essays.
Numeracy	Statistical analysis and understanding.
Computer literacy	Using information technology of one sort or another.
Information-finding skills	Using databases, journals, libraries, etc.
Research skills	Obtaining systematic scientific evidence.
Measurement skills	Operationalizing and designing complex measures.
Environmental awareness	Understanding how environments influence people.
Interpersonal awareness	Social communication and social skills.
Problem-solving skills	Sizing up situations and applying different strategies and approaches.
Critical evaluation	Appraising how adequate explanations of evidence are.
Perspectives	Exploring issues from several different angles.
Higher-order analysis	Spotting recurrent patterns and systems.
Pragmatism	Learning how to get on and make the best of things.

Source: Hayes (1996)

DEVELOPING PSYCHOLOGICAL KNOWLEDGE

So, how do psychologists gain their knowledge? People, as we have seen, are extremely complex, and understanding the ways that our minds work is never going to be a matter of one simple explanation. Everything we do is influenced by a diverse range of experiences, from our biochemical state to the culture we were brought up in and the situation we are in right now. It's the psychologist's task to bring all these together and try to make sense of them.

Psychologists are scientists, and most psychological knowledge is developed as a result of some kind of scientific research. As researchers, psychologists tend only to work in one small area at a time. It isn't possible to conduct research into the whole of human nature – we have to concentrate on just one bit at a time, or everything would be too complicated. So quite a lot of psychological knowledge consists of small bits of research, each of which can throw a little light onto a situation, but isn't enough to explain it on its own.

▶ Developing theories

This means that it is very important for psychology to have ways of linking together those pieces of research, so that they can form coherent explanations for what is going on. Scientific explanations are known as theories, and they are just as important in psychological knowledge as empirical research. Without theories to bring together research findings and make sense of them, there wouldn't be much point in doing research in the first place, because it wouldn't really tell us anything – it would just be a collection of 'ooh-look-ain't-it-interesting' facts. We can get those just as well from quiz shows or everyday reading.

Most psychological research is driven by theory in the first place. People conduct research in order to investigate whether a particular theory is true; and their findings are obtained in such a way that they can test the theory, to see how well it holds up in reality. It's all very well having a plausible idea, but lots of plausible ideas really don't work very well when we actually look closely at human beings. Part of the definition of a scientific theory is that it can be tested against empirical evidence, and challenged or refuted if it doesn't seem to work. There are other kinds of theories which don't exactly work in the same way, but we don't usually count these as scientific ones.

Even theories, though, can generally deal only with one aspect of human functioning at a time. If we really want to get to grips with what human beings do, we need to look at it using several different levels of analysis at the same time. Levels of analysis, which are also sometimes known as levels of explanation, are all about the way that we choose to study something.

If we wanted to look into the human activity known as reading, for example, we might decide to study it by investigating what happens to the nerve cells in the brain as we read. This would be the neurological level of analysis, because we would be studying the neurones which are involved in that activity. Another psychologist, though, might choose to look at reading in terms of how we process the information that we receive, mentally. This would be the cognitive level of analysis, because it is concerned with our cognitions – how we perceive, remember and apply information that we come across in everyday life. A third psychologist might choose to study reading in terms of its functions in society – what children and adults learn from books and other publications, and how this influences social living. This would be the socio-cultural level of analysis.

All these levels of analysis, and quite a few others, are involved in understanding reading. Although we might conduct research into only one level at a time, getting the whole picture of what is going on when people read needs all of them. So if they are really about explaining human behaviour, the theories that we develop need to be able to bring together, or at least connect with, several different levels of explanation. We looked at the main levels of explanation in Chapter 1, so we will conclude this book by looking at some of the different types of research methods that psychologists use to collect their evidence.

Key idea

It is sometimes claimed that knowing how the brain works will tell us all about psychology. But even if we could map the firing of every single neurone, we still wouldn't know what someone was thinking about, or why they were thinking it. No single level of analysis can tell us everything.

Conducting psychological research

Psychological research is about gathering evidence. That evidence might be used to support or refute a theory which has been developed to explain what is going on, or it might be used to identify how interventions may be more effective. Gathering psychological evidence is a bit like detective work. It is always easy to jump to conclusions about an answer. If a crime has been committed, you can always find someone who is certain who is responsible – but sometimes they are completely wrong. In the same way, when we are studying something in psychology, it is easy to jump to conclusions about it. After all, we all think we know about human beings. But sometimes, as with the crime, our conclusions are simply wrong.

So the psychologist, like the detective, has to put in hours of painstaking work collecting evidence to find out what is really going on. Sometimes all that evidence will lead to the same conclusion we might have obtained by guessing, or from 'common sense'. But even though our conclusions might not be earth-shattering, at least we know that they are based on a solid foundation. Quite often, though, what we discover is totally unpredictable. Without collecting the evidence in the first place, we would never have known.

Key idea

The reason why psychological research is so important is because when we are talking about people, we can't take anything for granted. Things which seem like 'common sense' may be completely wrong or completely right. Unless we research it carefully, we can't find out which is which.

Psychologists collect evidence in many different ways. Psychology as an academic discipline has been around for nearly 150 years, and during that time it has passed through several phases. Each of these phases has left us different methods of research. As a general rule, these phases happened because a particular group of psychologists believed that they had the best starting point for studying human beings. So the methods that they used can be helpful in giving us an insight into that particular level of explanation.

▶ Introspection

Psychology began life as a special branch of philosophy, so in its early days the approaches it used were very similar to those used by the philosophers of the time. For the most part, this involved introspection – trying to understand the mind by analysing your own thoughts, feelings and experiences. Although this method fell out of favour for a time, because it didn't seem to be scientific enough, in a more systematic form it is used in psychology again today. Cognitive psychologists, for instance, sometimes use a method called protocol analysis to give them some ideas as to how people solve problems. This involves asking people to talk aloud about what they are thinking as they do a task, and analysing what they say. Some psychologists have found it a helpful way of gathering evidence about problem-solving, or even quite complex tasks such as musical composition.

The early introspectionist psychologists, however, were eventually overtaken by a different approach to psychology which developed round about the beginning of the twentieth century. This approach was known as behaviourism, and those who supported it argued that psychology needed to become more objective and scientific. Scientific, in their view, meant sticking to things which could be observed directly by other people, and that meant, effectively, restricting psychology to the study of behaviour.

EXPERIMENTS

The behaviourists brought with them a rigorous approach to scientific method, which they tried to use to look at the 'pure' elements of behaviour. This meant that they were very concerned to cut out what they saw as 'contaminating' influences, and to design research which only dealt with the important things causing the behaviour, and nothing else. They believed that conducting tightly controlled laboratory experiments were the best way to do this.

An experiment involves manipulating a situation to bring about an effect. The behaviourists, in particular, tried to control their experiments very carefully. They would try to rule out all other possible influences, and then see what happened if the one factor that was left was altered.

This method of study has remained very important in psychology. Some research into attention, for example, has involved asking people to identify a single message or concentrate on identifying a signal on a screen, while different factors in the message have been adjusted. These experiments are carefully carried out under laboratory conditions, so that the researchers can be sure that their results really were caused by the factor they were studying.

▶ Action research and field experiments

There are other kinds of experiments though, which are much more loosely controlled. In real life, people will always be interested in what is going on around them, developing their own ideas and acting in the ways that these imply. So it is a bit naïve for psychologists, or any other researchers for that matter, to expect their participants to be passive and just do or think exactly what the experimenter wants them to do. People are not that easily controlled.

As a result, psychologists have also developed ways of carrying out research which takes more account of the real lives of the people concerned. Research in organizational psychology, for example, often consists of action research, in which working conditions or communication systems are changed, and researchers observe how the change affects the people working in that particular place. The Hawthorne experiments that we looked at in Chapter 12 are a classic example. In these types of studies, the active involvement of the people concerned is built into both the method and the analysis, and the result is a much more realistic picture – even if it is more complicated to analyse. Although field experiments like this can't be controlled as carefully as formal laboratory experiments, they tell us much more about people at work than tightly controlled lab studies could ever do.

▶ **Animal experiments**

Unlike a modern psychologist, many of the early behaviourists believed that one single level of explanation could provide the key to understanding all human behaviour. This level of explanation was to do with learning. They believed that all human behaviour was really just chains of learned associations combined together, in the same way that atoms combine to form animals, plants, or minerals.

This led them to look for the 'atom' of psychology, or the simplest unit of learning which they could find. So they spent a great deal of time studying animal learning, because they believed that it was a 'pure' form of learning. They believed that animal learning, unlike human learning, was 'uncontaminated' by memories, ideas or imagination, so studying it would help them to identify how basic units of learning combined to produce complex behaviour.

Other psychologists, too, used animals to study basic units of human experience. In the 1960s, for instance, many animal experiments were conducted to investigate visual perception, and animal studies are still used to investigate some aspects of brain functioning. But they are much less common than they used to be in psychology. Nowadays, we are much more concerned with the ethics of animal research, which fortunately has meant that only studies which are serious scientific research and are likely to be of real value in adding to knowledge, are permitted.

OBSERVATIONS

The behaviourists, as we have seen, emphasized rigorous experimentation as the main research method for psychology. Gradually, however, psychologists with wider interests began to have more influence, and non-experimental methods for studying human behaviour became more popular. They had always been around, of course, but had formerly been just a minor part of psychological research.

There was good reason for this. For example, it's not really a good idea to do experiments on children, but there was a lot of interest in the psychological aspects of child development throughout the twentieth century. So psychologists who were interested in this subject had to do their research by observing children, not by experimenting with them.

There are lots of different ways of performing scientific observations, but just looking at what is in front of you isn't one of them. Researchers need to know what they are looking for, and what it will tell them if they do actually observe it. Psychologists conducting observational research also need to make sure that their own unconscious biases don't affect how they make sense out of what they see. So observational studies are conducted in a very systematic way, and sometimes under quite controlled conditions – such as watching children play in a specially equipped playroom which has video cameras or observation windows, so that they can be observed without interfering with their play.

Alternatively, psychologists sometimes conduct observational studies of behaviour in the natural environment. This approach is known as ethology and, nowadays, it has become one of the main methods of studying animal behaviour. But it doesn't just apply to animals – ethological studies are very useful when we are looking at families, for example. We have learned a lot about how parents interact with their babies by carrying out ethological observations.

▶ Surveys

Sometimes, psychologists want to make large-scale observations of what people do or think, and they do this by conducting surveys. A survey involves a special questionnaire, which is given to a large number of people. By analysing their answers, the psychologist can observe general tendencies, or trends, in what people are doing or thinking. Surveys about AIDS, for instance, have helped psychologists to understand more about people's attitudes towards it – although they still don't tell us very much about what people actually do. They tell us what people think they might do, which isn't always the same thing.

▶ Psychometrics

Another very special type of observation that psychologists use is known as psychometrics. Psychometric tests, as we saw in Chapter 16, are tests which are designed to tell us something about the person's mind. They usually take the form of special questionnaires, which have been carefully constructed and tested, and which can sometimes give us useful clues about someone's personality, skills or abilities. Intelligence tests and personality tests are examples of this approach to research. But it is important to remember that they only give us clues – psychometric tests don't have all the answers, and they don't give the whole picture. They can be useful in supplementing other information, but they are not complete research methods in themselves.

CASE STUDIES

Experiments and observational studies, for the most part, tend to deal with information from large numbers of people. This approach dates back to the first half of the twentieth century, when it was assumed that people, on the whole, were pretty similar. The general approach to society at that time involved understanding 'the masses', and the masses were not really seen as individuals. During the second half of the twentieth century, though, attention became much more focused on the individual person, and this in turn affected psychological research methods.

One outcome was that psychologists began to ask much more detailed questions about individuals and their experiences. To do this, they began to concentrate on just a few individuals, or single cases. Case studies weren't new to psychology: many famous case studies had taken place in the past, including important ones which told us about brain functioning. But they were regarded by the behaviourists as somehow being less scientific than large-scale studies. More recently, though, psychology has begun to accept the case study as a regular research method which can give us useful information.

We have learned a lot about how the mind works through case studies of people with cognitive problems. One case study, for example, was of a respected academic who was completely unable to recognize people's faces. She was above average intellectually and, in all other respects, her mental functions were normal. Studying this single person in detail gave the psychologists undertaking the case study some useful evidence about how the mental skill of face recognition is organized in the brain.

ACCOUNT ANALYSIS

As we have seen, psychology in the twentieth century was deeply influenced by the behaviourist's insistence that studying behaviour was the only truly scientific approach. In the later part of the twentieth century, though, it became increasingly apparent that this simply wasn't good enough. Two people can be in a similar situation, but each of them can interpret what is going on quite differently. Their interpretation will influence how they react, and that will influence what happens in the end. So if we really want to understand people, we also need to study how they make sense out of the world that they live in.

So social psychology, in particular, became increasingly concerned with social and personal meanings. Obviously, it is difficult to get at this kind of information using laboratory experiments or observations, and a different research method became popular. This became known as account analysis, because it is all about analysing the accounts which people give of their own experiences.

Key idea

One of the most useful trends in modern psychological research is that we are now much better able to analyse what people say and believe than we used to be, and we also realize how important it is. During the behaviourist period, that sort of thing was almost completely ignored.

▶ Interviewing

Psychologists often collect accounts by conducting interviews. Interviewing is a skilled affair, because the person doing the interview needs to make sure that the other person feels relaxed and confident. After all, if you don't feel able to trust someone, you wouldn't be prepared to tell them much about your feelings or thoughts, would you? So an interviewer has to be good at encouraging people to speak, and at striking up a good rapport with the person they are interviewing.

There are lots of ways of analysing accounts. Some psychologists look at the ways in which people express their ideas, and the metaphors and assumptions which they use. This is known as discourse analysis. Other psychologists look at the types of reasons, or attributions, which people give to explain why things happen. And some concentrate on identifying the main themes which emerge from what people are saying. Each of these methods is a type of qualitative analysis – a way of looking at the meaning of the information, rather than just collecting information about the numbers of people who reacted in particular ways.

I have presented these research methods as if they were developed only at certain times during the century. This isn't really true. If we look back, we find that individual psychologists have used almost all of these methods at some time or other. But different methods are seen as important at different times, by psychology as a whole, and this is the process which I have been describing. It's important, because it affects how much influence a particular piece of research can have – both in psychology, and in society as a whole.

INTERNET RESEARCH

There is one form of psychological research, though, which is very much a product of modern times, and that is internet research. The prevalence of social networking and everyday digital interactions has opened up a whole new area of psychological experience and, as we saw in Chapter 13, it can be a really important part of people's everyday lives.

The internet also offers psychologists the opportunity to conduct research on a much larger scale than before. It has opened up the possibility of obtaining huge samples in terms of asking for respondents to surveys and questionnaires, allowing researchers to reach groups of people that they would have had difficulty contacting in other ways. It is now relatively common to find studies which include thousands of respondents, where previously studies of this size would have been very expensive and difficult to carry out. The internet also, through cloud computing, lets researchers handle more data and conduct more complex forms of analysis than an everyday computer could cope with.

There are new forms of social behaviour, too, which have emerged as a result of internet use. These can be positive, like the financial support offered through crowd funding or charitable appeals, or negative, like trolling; but they are all topics for psychological research. Psychologists also look at how the internet offers opportunities for existing behaviours. For example, Griffiths (2000) showed how what is called 'internet addiction' is generally only addictive behaviour which the person already engaged in (like gambling or game-playing), but done through the internet instead of in real-world settings.

We can see, then, that psychologists have a wide range of tools to help in their detective work. Most large research projects will combine two or more of these methods, to help give a clearer picture of what is going on. They will often combine quantitative approaches, which are to do with numbers and statistical probabilities, with qualitative approaches, which are to do with meanings and social or personal implications. As with everything else in psychology, the more ways we look at it, the better the picture we obtain.

This book has only really been able to give you a very superficial 'taste' of modern psychology. But I hope that you have found it an interesting one. Psychology is an intriguing area of study and one which can give us many insights into why we are the way we are. As long as we resist the temptation to go for simplistic answers, and bear in mind that there can be a lot of different influences on how we act at any one time, we can learn a great deal – and we already have! Psychological research has been used to help people in all sorts of different ways.

It is my firm belief that understanding more about human psychology will also mean that we come to understand one another much better – and that is why I have devoted such a large part of my life to learning about it, writing about it and carrying out psychological research of my own. I personally have always enjoyed the study of psychology. I hope that you have enjoyed this sample of it, too.

Nicky Hayes

Focus points

To be a professional psychologist involves many years of advanced professional training. A psychology degree provides a broad range of skills suitable for many different jobs.

Laboratory experiments in psychology involve rigorous control of variables to identify specific causes.

Action researchers work in the real world and use principles of ecological validity rather than experimental control.

Animal experiments are now quite rare in psychology, and very carefully controlled so that the animals do not suffer distress.

Observational studies including psychometrics and surveys are often used by psychologists. Qualitative research methods such as interviewing and account analysis are also favoured for their real-world relevance.

Internet research has opened up new areas of understanding, because it allows much larger-scale investigations than were previously possible.

Index